Lecture Notes in Computer Science 13851

The series Lecture Notes in Computer Science (LNCS), including its subseries Lecture Notes in Artificial Intelligence (LNAI) and Lecture Notes in Bioinformatics (LNBI), has established itself as a medium for the publication of new developments in computer science and information technology research, teaching, and education.

LNCS enjoys close cooperation with the computer science R & D community, the series counts many renowned academics among its volume editors and paper authors, and collaborates with prestigious societies. Its mission is to serve this international community by providing an invaluable service, mainly focused on the publication of conference and workshop proceedings and postproceedings. LNCS commenced publication in 1973.

John Gustafson · Siew Hoon Leong ·
Marek Michalewicz

Editors

Next Generation Arithmetic

4th International Conference, CoNGA 2023
Singapore, March 1–2, 2023
Proceedings

Editors
John Gustafson (iD)
Arizona State University
Tempe, AZ, USA

Siew Hoon Leong (iD)
Swiss National Supercomputing Centre
ETH Zurich
Lugano, Switzerland

Marek Michalewicz (iD)
National Supercomputing Centre
Singapore, Singapore

ISSN 0302-9743   ISSN 1611-3349 (electronic)
Lecture Notes in Computer Science
ISBN 978-3-031-32179-5   ISBN 978-3-031-32180-1 (eBook)
https://doi.org/10.1007/978-3-031-32180-1

This Springer imprint is published by the registered company Springer Nature Switzerland AG
The registered company address is: Gewerbestrasse 11, 6330 Cham, Switzerland

Preface

Computer arithmetic is once again a controversial topic. Before the establishment of IEEE Std 754™ for floating-point arithmetic in 1985, no one expected similar answers from different makes of computers, because the vendors all used different ways to represent real numbers. IEEE 754 compliance made it possible to get similar, albeit not *identical* answers on different systems. It also led to the casual use of double precision (64-bit) floating-point everywhere as an easy substitute for having to think carefully about rounding errors.

Adherence to that Standard began to wane in the early 2000s as system designers began to abandon hardware support for the many complicated and expensive provisions of IEEE 754, such as gradual underflow. Different vendors made different shortcut choices, resulting again in the situation that no one expects similar answers from different computers. As computing became increasingly bandwidth-limited, pressure mounted to try 32-bit and even 16-bit representations without incurring unacceptable accuracy loss. Lower precisions made more obvious the inefficiency of the outdated 754 Standard, and the Machine Learning community in particular is experimenting with new real number formats. While some cling to the idea that the IEEE 754 Standard will last forever, an increasing part of the computing community recognizes the need for fresh designs more suited to present-day priorities. The controversy is not unlike the transition from sequential computing to parallel computing in the 1990s.

As part of SCAsia 2023, the *Conference on Next-Generation Arithmetic* (CoNGA 2023) is the premier forum for the presentation of the impact of novel number formats on

- Application Speed and Accuracy
- Hardware Costs
- Software-Hardware Codevelopment
- Algorithm Choices
- Tools and Programming Environments

This is the fourth CoNGA conference, and the largest to date. The 16 submitted papers for the technical papers program went through a rigorous peer review process by an international program committee, with an average of three reviews per submission. Eleven papers were selected for inclusion in the Proceedings. Accepted papers cover topics ranging from better ways to build arithmetic units to the application consequences of the new formats, many using the *posit* format standardized in 2022.

We thank all authors for their submissions to CoNGA. Our sincere thanks go to all Program Committee members for doing high-quality and in-depth submission reviews.

We also thank the organizers for giving us the opportunity to hold CoNGA 2023 as a sub-conference of SCAsia 2023.

February 2023   John L. Gustafson
                                                               Marek Michalewicz
                                                                  Cerlane Leong

Organization

Co-chairs

John L. Gustafson   Arizona State University, USA
Marek Michalewicz   National Supercomputing Centre (NSCC),
      Singapore

Program Chair

Cerlane Leong   CSCS, Switzerland

Program Committee

Shin Yee Chung   NSCC, Singapore
Marco Cococcioni   University of Pisa, Italy
Himeshi De Silva   A*STAR, Singapore
Vassil Dimitrov   Lemurian Labs, Canada
Roman Iakymchuk   Umeå University, Sweden
Peter Lindstrom   Lawrence Livermore National Laboratory, USA
Andrew Shewmaker   OpenEye Scientific, USA

Contents

Lossless FFTs Using Posit Arithmetic

Siew Hoon Leong[1]([✉]) [iD] and John L. Gustafson[2] [iD]

[1] Swiss National Supercomputing Centre, ETH Zurich, Zurich, Switzerland
cerlane.leong@cscs.ch
[2] Arizona State University, Tempe, USA
jlgusta6@asu.edu

Abstract. The Fast Fourier Transform (FFT) is required for chemistry, weather, defense, and signal processing for seismic exploration and radio astronomy. It is communication-bound, making supercomputers thousands of times slower at FFTs then at dense linear algebra. The key to accelerating FFTs is to minimize bits per datum without sacrificing accuracy. The 16-bit fixed point and IEEE float type lack sufficient accuracy for 1024- and 4096-point FFTs of data from analog-to-digital converters. We show that the 16-bit posit, with higher accuracy and larger dynamic range, can perform FFTs so accurately that a forward-inverse FFT restores the original signal perfectly. "Reversible" FFTs with posits are lossless, eliminating the need for 32-bit or higher precision. Similarly, 32-bit posit FFTs can replace 64-bit float FFTs for many HPC tasks. Speed, energy efficiency, and storage costs can thus be improved by 2× for a broad range of HPC workloads.

Keywords: Posit · Quire · FFT · Computer Arithmetic

1 Introduction

The *posit*™ number format is the rounded form of Type III universal number (unum) arithmetic [13,16]. It evolved from Type II unums in December 2016 as a hardware-friendly drop-in alternative to the floating-point IEEE Std 754™ [19]. The tapered accuracy of posits allows them to have more fraction bits in the most commonly used range, thus enabling posits to be more accurate than floating-point numbers (floats) of the same size, yet have an even larger dynamic range than floats. Posit arithmetic also introduces the *quire*, an exact accumulator for fused dot products, that can dramatically reduce rounding errors.

The computation of the Discrete Fourier Transform (DFT) using the Fast Fourier Transform (FFT) algorithm has become one of the most important and powerful tools of High Performance Computing (HPC). FFTs are investigated here to demonstrate the speed and accuracy of posit arithmetic when compared to floating-point arithmetic. Improving FFTs can potentially improve the performance of HPC applications such as CP2K [18], SpecFEM3D [20,21], and

Supported by organization A*STAR and NSCC Singapore.

WRF [31], leading to higher speed and improved accuracy. "Precision" here refers to the number of bits in a number format, and "accuracy" refers to the correctness of an answer, measured in the number of correct decimals or correct bits. Posits achieve orders of magnitude smaller rounding errors when compared to floats that have the same precision [26, 27]. Thus, the commonly-used 32-bit and 64-bit precision floats can potentially be replaced with 16-bit and 32-bit posits respectively in some applications, doubling the speed of communication-bound computations and halving the storage and power costs.

We say FFT accuracy is *lossless* when the inverse FFT reproduces the original signal perfectly; that is, the FFT is *reversible*. The rounding error of 16-bit IEEE floats and 16-bit fixed-point format adds too much noise for those formats to perform lossless FFTs, which forces programmers to use 32-bit floats for signal processing tasks. In contrast, 16-bit posits have enough accuracy for a "round trip" to be lossless at the resolution of common Analog-to-Digital Converters (ADCs) that supply the input data. Once reversibility is achieved, the use of more bits of precision is wasteful since the transformation retains all information.

The paper is organized as follow: In Sect. 2, related work on posits, fixed-point FFTs and floating-point FFTs will be shared. Background information on the posit and quire format and the FFT is provided in Sect. 3. Section 4 presents the approach used to evaluate the accuracy and performance of radix-2 and radix-4 (1024- and 4096-point) FFTs (Decimation-In-Time and Decimation-In-Frequency) using both 16-bit posits and 16-bit floats. The results of the evaluation are discussed in Sect. 5. Finally, the conclusions and plans for future work are presented in Sect. 6.

2   Related Work

Posits are a new form of computer arithmetic invented by Gustafson in December 2016. The concept was first publicly shared as a Stanford lecture seminar [16] in February 2017. The first peer-reviewed posit journal paper [15] was published in June 2017. Since then, studies on posit correctness [6], accuracy, efficiency when compared to floats [26] and various software and Field-Programmable Gate Array (FPGA) implementations [5, 24, 29] have been performed. Due to the flexibility to choose the precision required and express high dynamic range using very few bits, researchers have found posits particularly well-suited to machine learning applications. [23] has demonstrated that very low precision posits outperform fixed-point and all other tested formats for inference, thus improving speed for time-critical AI tasks such as self-driving cars.

Efforts to improve DFTs by reducing the number of operations can be traced back to the work of Cooley and Tukey [8] in 1965, whose improvements based on the algorithm of Good [12] reduced the operation complexity from $O(N^2)$ to $O(N \log_2 N)$, now called FFTs [7, p. 1667]. Additional work to further improve the FFT algorithm led to radix-2^m algorithms [9,30], the Rader-Brenner algorithm [30], the Winograd algorithm (WFTA) [35,36] and prime factor algorithms (PFA) [11,33]. In practice, radix-2, radix-4, and split-radix are the most widely adopted types.

The effect of arithmetic precision on performance has been studied [1,1]. For optimum speed, the lowest possible bit precision should be used that still meets accuracy requirements. Fixed-point as opposed to floating-point is traditionally used to implement FFT algorithms in custom Digital Signal Processing (DSP) hardware [3] due to the higher cost and complexity of floating-point logic. Fixed-point reduces power dissipation and achieves higher speed [3,25]. Custom Application-Specific Integrated Circuits (ASICs) and FPGAs allow the use of unusual and variable word sizes without a speed penalty, but that flexibility is not available in a general programming environment.

3   Background

In this section, posit format, the corresponding *quire* exact accumulator format, and the FFT algorithm are discussed.

3.1   Posits

Posits are much simpler than floats, which can potentially result in faster circuits requiring less chip area [2]. The Posit Standard (2022) The main advantages of posits over floats are:

- Higher accuracy for the most commonly-used value range
- 1-to-1 map of signed binary integers to ordered real numbers
- Bitwise reproducibility across all computing systems
- Increased dynamic range
- More information per bit (higher Shannon entropy)
- Only two exception values: zero and Not-a-Real (NaR)
- Support for associative and distributive laws

The differences among 16-bit float, fixed-point, and posit formats are displayed in Fig. 1 where each color block is a bit, i.e. 0 or 1. The colors depict the fields (sign, exponent, fraction, integer, or regime) that the bits represent.

A 16-bit float (Fig. 1a) consists of a sign bit and 5 exponent bits, leaving 10 bits for fraction after the "hidden bit". If signal data is centered about 0 so the sign bit is significant, a 16-bit float is capable of storing signed values from ADCs with up to 12 bits of output, but no larger.

Although the number of bits to the left of the radix point can be flexibly chosen for a fixed-point format (Fig. 1b), 1024-point FFTs of data in the range −1 to 1 can produce values between −32 and 32 in general. Therefore, a 16-bit fixed-point format for the FFT requires integer bits that increase from 2 to 6 with the stages of the FFT, leaving 13 to 9 bits respectively for the fraction part. At first glance, fixed-point would appear to have the best accuracy for FFTs, since it allows the maximum possible number of fraction bits. However, towards the final stage of a 1024-point FFT computation, a 16-bit float will still have 10 fraction bits (excluding the hidden bit) while fixed-point will only have

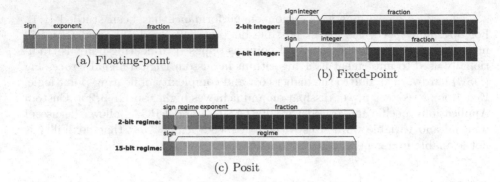

(a) Floating-point

(b) Fixed-point

(c) Posit

Fig. 1. Different number formats

9 fraction bits to accommodate the larger worst-case integer part it needs to store to avoid catastrophic overflow. For 4096-point FFTs, fixed-point will only have 8 fraction bits. Posits will have 10 to 12 fraction bits for the results of the FFT. Consequently, 16-bit fixed-point has the *lowest* accuracy among the three number formats for both 1024- and 4096-point FFTs; posits have the highest accuracy (see Fig. 2). Note also that the "twiddle factors" are trigonometric functions in the range −1 to 1, which posits represent with about 0.6 decimals greater accuracy than floats.

As with floats and integers, the most significant bit of a posit indicates the sign. The "regime" bits uses signed unary encoding requiring 2 to 15 bits (Fig. 1c). Accuracy tapers, with the highest accuracy for values with magnitudes near 1 and less accuracy for the largest and smallest magnitude numbers. Posit arithmetic hardware requires integer adders, integer multipliers, shifters, leading zero counters and AND trees very similar to those required for IEEE floats; however, posit hardware is simpler in having a single rounding mode, no internal flags, and only two exception values to deal with. Comparison operations are those of integers; no extra hardware is needed. Proprietary designs show a reduction in gate count for posits versus floats, for both FPGA and VLSI designs, and a reduction in operation latency [2].

The dynamic range for IEEE Standard 16-bit floats is from 2^{-16} to 65504, or about 6.0×10^{-8} to 6.5×10^4 (12 orders of magnitude). Floats use tapered accuracy for small-magnitude ("subnormal") values only, making their dynamic range unbalanced about 1. The reciprocal of a small-magnitude float overflows to infinity. For 16-bit posits, the use of a single eS exponent bit allows expression of magnitudes from 2^{-28} to 2^{28}, or about 3.7×10^{-9} to 2.7×10^8 (almost 17 orders of magnitude). Posit tapered precision is symmetrical about magnitude 1, and reciprocation is closed and exact for integer powers of 2. Thus, the accuracy advantage of posits does not come at the cost of reduced dynamic range.

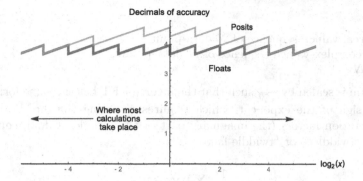

Fig. 2. Comparison of 16-bit posits and floats for accuracy

3.2   The Quire Register

The concept of the *quire* [14, pp. 80–84], a fixed-point scratch value, originates from the work of Kulisch and Miranker [22]. The quire data type is used to accumulate dot products with no rounding errors. When the accumulated result is converted back to posit form with a single rounding, the result is a "fused dot product". The quire data type is used to accumulate the addition/subtraction of a product of two posits, using exact fixed-point arithmetic. Thus, a quire data type only needs to support add and subtract operations, and obey the same rules as integer add and subtract operations (augmented with the ability to handle a NaR input value).

To store the result of a fused dot product without any rounding, a quire data type must minimally support the range $[minPos^2, maxPos^2]$, where $minPos$ is the smallest expressible real greater than zero and $maxPos$ is the biggest expressible real, for a particular n-bit posit. Since there will be a need for the quire to accumulate the results of fused dot products of long vectors, additional $n-1$ bits are prepended to the most significant bits as carry overflow protection. Thus, a 16-bit posit with a 1-bit eS (posit$\langle 16, 1\rangle$) will have a corresponding 128-bit quire, notated quire128$\langle 16, 1\rangle$.

The use of the quire reduces cumulative rounding error, as will be demonstrated in Sects. 4 and 5, and enables correctly-rounded fused dot products. Notice that the complex multiply-add in an FFT can be expressed as a pair of dot products, so all of the complex rotations in the FFT need incur only one rounding per real and imaginary part, instead of four (if all operations are rounded) or two (if fused multiply-add is used).

3.3   The FFT Algorithm

The discrete form of the Fourier transform (DFT) can be written as

$$X_k = \frac{1}{\sqrt{N}} \sum_{n=0}^{N-1} x_n e^{-2\pi i k n / N} \tag{1}$$

where

x_n is the real-valued sequence of N data-points,
X_k is the complex-valued sequence of N data-points,
k = 0, ..., N − 1

The sum is scaled by $\frac{1}{\sqrt{N}}$ such that the inverse DFT has the same form other than the sign of the exponent, which requires reversing the direction of the angular rotation factors (the imaginary part of the complex value), commonly known as "twiddles" or "twiddle factors":

$$x_n = \frac{1}{\sqrt{N}} \sum_{k=0}^{N-1} X_k e^{2\pi i k n/N}. \tag{2}$$

Following this convention, the twiddle factor $e^{2\pi i k n/N}$ will be written as w for short. While it is also possible to have no scaling in one direction and a scaling of $\frac{1}{N}$ in the other, this has only the merit that it saves one operation per point in a forward-inverse transformation. Scaling by $\frac{1}{\sqrt{N}}$ makes both forward and inverse transforms *unitary* and consistent. The forms as shown in Eqn 1 and 2 have the additional advantage that they keep intermediate values from growing in magnitude unnecessarily, a property that is crucial for fixed-point arithmetic to prevent overflow, and desirable for posit arithmetic since it maximizes accuracy. The only variant from traditional FFT algorithms used here is that the data set is scaled by 0.5 on every radix-4 pass, or every other pass of a radix-2 FFT. This automatically provides the $\frac{1}{\sqrt{N}}$ scaling while keeping the computations in the range where posits have maximum accuracy. The scaling by 0.5 can be incorporated into the twiddle factor table to eliminate the cost of an extra multiply operation.

The FFT is a form of the DFT that uses the fact that the summations can be represented as a matrix-vector product, and the matrix can be factored to reduce the computational complexity to $N \log_2 N$ operations. In this paper, two basic classes of FFT algorithms, Decimation-In-Time (DIT) and Decimation-In-Frequency (DIF), will be discussed. DIT algorithms decompose the time sequences into successively smaller subsequences while DIF algorithms decompose the coefficients into smaller subsequences [28].

Traditional analysis of the computational complexity of the FFT centers on the number of multiplications and additions. The kernel operation of an FFT is often called a "butterfly" because of its dataflow pattern (see Fig. 3). The original radix-2 algorithm performs 10 operations (6 additions and 4 multiplications) per butterfly [34, p.42], highlighted in red in Fig. 3, and there are $\frac{1}{2}N \log_2 N$ butterflies, so the operation complexity is $5N \log_2 N$ for large N. Use of radix 4 reduces this to $4.5N \log_2 N$; split radix methods are $4N \log_2 N$, and with a little more whittling away this can be further reduced to about $3.88N \log_2 N$ [32]. Operation count, however, is not the key to increasing FFT performance, since the FFT is communication-bound and not computation-bound.

Supercomputer users are often surprised by the tiny fraction of peak performance they obtain when they perform FFTs while using highly-optimized vendor libraries that are well-tuned for a particular system. The TOP500 list shows

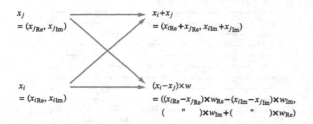

Fig. 3. A radix-1 "butterfly" calculation

many systems achieving over 80% of their peak performance for multiply-add operations in a dense linear algebra problem. FFTs, which have only multiply and add operations and predetermined data flow for a given size N, might be expected to achieve similar performances. However, traditional complexity analysis, which counts the number of operations, does a poor job of predicting actual FFT execution timings.

FFTs are thus the Achilles Heel of HPC, because they tax the most valuable resource: data motion. In an era when performance is almost always communication-bound and not computation-bound, it is more sensible to optimize the **data motion** as opposed to the **operation count**. Dense linear algebra involves order N^3 operations but only order N^2 data motion, making it one of the few HPC tasks that is still compute-bound. Dense linear algebra is one of the few workloads for which operation count correlates well with peak arithmetic performance. While some have studied the communication aspects of the FFT based on a single processor with a cache hierarchy (a valid model for small-scale digital signal processing), supercomputers are increasingly limited by the laws of *physics* and not by architecture. The communication cost for the FFT (in the limit where data access is limited by the speed of light and its physical distance) is thus **not** order $N \log_2 N$.

Figure 4 shows a typical (16-point) FFT diagram where the nodes (brown dots) and edges (lines in blue) represent the data points and communications in each stage respectively. The figure illustrates a DIT-FFT, but a DIF-FFT is simply its mirror image, so the following argument applies to either case. For any input on the left side, data travels in the y dimension by absolute distance $1, 2, 4, ..., \frac{N}{2}$ positions, a total motion of $N - 1$ positions. Simplistic models of performance assume all edges are of equal time cost, but this is not true if the physical limits on communication speed are considered. The total motion cost of $N - 1$ positions holds for each of the N data points, hence the total communication work is order N^2, the same order complexity as a DFT without any clever factoring. This assumes memory is physically placed in a line. In a real system like a supercomputer cluster covering many square meters, memory is distributed over a plane, for which the average distance between locations is order $N^{1/2}$, or in a volume, for which the average distance is order $N^{1/3}$. Those configurations result in physics-limited FFT communication complexity of order $N^{3/2}$ or $N^{4/3}$ respectively, both of which grow faster with N than does $N \log_2 N$. It is possible

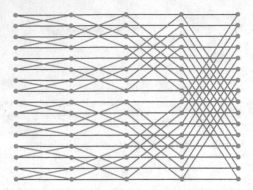

Fig. 4. A typical FFT diagram

to do all-to-all exchanges partway through the FFT to make communications local again, but this merely shifts the communication cost into the all-to-all exchange. Thus, it is not surprising that large-scale supercomputers attain only a fraction of their peak arithmetic performance when performing FFTs.

This observation points us to a different approach: reduce the *bits moved*, not the operation count. The communication cost grows linearly with the number of bits used per data item. The use of a data format, i.e. posits, that has considerably more information-per-bit than IEEE 754 floating point numbers can generate answers with acceptable accuracy using fewer bits. In the following section, 16-bit posits will be used to compute FFTs with higher accuracy than 16-bit (IEEE half-precision) floats, potentially allowing 32-bit floats to be safely replaced by 16-bit posits, doubling the speed (by halving the communication cost) of signal and image processing workloads. We speculate that similar performance doubling is possible for HPC workloads that presently use 64-bit floats for FFTs, by making them sufficiently accurate using 32-bit posits.

4   Approach

4.1   Accuracy

To test the effectiveness of posits, 1024- and 4096-point FFTs are used as the sizes most commonly found in the literature. Both radix-2 and radix-4 methods are studied here, but not split-radix [9,30]. Although modified split-radix has the smallest operation count (about $3.88N \log_2 N$), fixed-point studies [4] show it has poorer accuracy than radix-2 and radix-4 methods.

Both DIT and DIF methods are tested. The DIF approach introduces multiplicative rounding early in the processing. Intuition says this might pollute the later computations more than the DIT method where the first passes perform no multiplications. Empirical tests are conducted to check this intuition with three numerical approaches:

– 16-bit IEEE standard floats, with maximum use of fused multiply-add operations to reduce rounding error in the multiplications of complex numbers,
– 16-bit posits ($eS = 1$) with exactly the same operations as used for floats, and
– 16-bit posits using the quire to further reduce rounding error to one rounding per pass of the FFT.

For each of these 24 combinations of data-point size, radix, decimation type, and numerical approach, random uniform distribution input signals in the range $[-1, 1)$ at the resolution of a 12-bit ADC are created. The 12-bit fixed-point ADC inputs are first transformed into their corresponding 16-bit posits and floats as shown in Fig. 5. A "round-trip" (forward followed by inverse) FFT is then applied before the results are converted (with rounding) back to the 12-bit ADC fixed-point format (represented by ADC' in Fig. 5). If no errors and roundings occur, the original signal is recovered perfectly, i.e. $ADC = ADC'$.

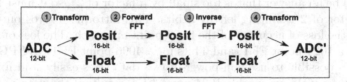

Fig. 5. A round-trip FFT for a 12-bit ADC

The absolute error of a 12-bit ADC input can thus be computed as shown in Eq. 3. This error represents the rounding errors incurred by posits and floats respectively.

$$absolute\ error = |ADC' - ADC| \tag{3}$$

To evaluate the accuracy of posits and floats, the vector of absolute errors of all ADC inputs is evaluated. Three flavors of measures, the maximum (L_∞ norm), RMS (L_2 norm) and average (L_1 norm) of the vector are computed.

To gain additional insight to the error, the units in the last place (ULPs) metric is used. As shown by Goldberg [10, p. 8], ULP error measure is superior to relative error for measuring pure rounding error. ULP error can be computed as follows as shown in Eq. 4. For a 12-bit fixed-point ADC, $ulp(ADC')$ is a constant value (2^{-11} for input in $[-1, 1)$ range).

$$ULP\ error = \frac{ADC' - ADC}{ulp(ADC')} \tag{4}$$

where $ulp(ADC')$ is one unit value of ADC' last place unit.

In the case of a posits and floats, even if an answer is correctly rounded, there will be an error of as much as 0.5 ULP. With each additional arithmetic operation, the errors accumulate. Consequently, to minimize the effect of rounding errors, it is important to minimize the error e.g. by using the quire to defer rounding as much as possible.

Because an ADC handles only a finite range of uniformly-spaced points adjusted to the dynamic range it needs to handle, a Gaussian distribution that is unbounded is deemed unsuitable for this evaluation. A uniformly-spaced distribution that is bounded to the required range is used instead. Preliminary tests were also conducted on bell-shaped distributions (truncated Gaussian distributions) confined to same range, $[-1, 1)$ representing three standard deviations from the mean at 0; they yielded results similar to those for the uniform distribution tests presented here.

For 16-bit fixed-point, we rely on analysis because it obviates experimentation. After every pass of an FFT, the FFT values must be scaled by $1/2$ to guarantee there is no overflow. For an FFT with 2^{2k} points, the result of the $2k$ scalings will be an answer that is too small by a factor of 2^k, so it must be scaled up by a factor of 2^k, shifting left by k bits. This introduces zeros on the right that reveal the loss of accuracy of the fixed-point approach. The loss of accuracy is 5 bits for a 1024-point FFT, and 6 bits for a 4096-point FFT. In FPGA development, it is possible to use non-power-of-two data sizes easily, and fixed point can be made to yield acceptable 1024-point FFT results if the data points have 18 bits of precision [25]. Since fixed point requires much less hardware than floats (or posits), this is an excellent approach for special-purpose FPGA designs. In the more general computing environment where data sizes are power-of-two bits in size, a programmer using fixed-point format has little choice but to upsize all the values to 32-bit size. The same will be shown true for 16-bit floats, which cannot achieve acceptable accuracy.

4.2 Performance

The performance of large-scale FFTs is communication bound, as pointed out in Sect. 3.3. The reduction in the size of operands not only reduces time proportionately, but also reduce *cache spill* effects. For example, a 1024-by-1024 2D-FFT computed with 16-bit posits will fit in a 4 MB cache. If the FFT was performed using 32-bit floats to achieve sufficient accuracy, the data will not fit in cache and the cache "spill" will reduce performance dramatically by a factor of more than two. This is a well-known effect.

However, there is a need to show that posit arithmetic can be as fast as float arithmetic, possibly faster. Otherwise, the projected bandwidth savings might be offset by slower arithmetic. Until VLSI processors using posits as a native type are complete, arithmetic performance comparisons between posits and floats of the same bit size can be performed with similar implementations in software.

A software library, SoftPosit, is used in this study. It is closely based on Berkeley SoftFloat [17] (Release 3d) Similar implementation and optimization techniques are adopted to enable a fair comparison of the performance of 16-bit posits versus 16-bit floats. Note: the performance results on posits are preliminary since SoftPosit is a new library; 26 years of optimization effort have been put into Berkeley SoftFloat.

Table 1. Test machine specification

Processor	Intel(R) Xeon(R) CPU E5-2699 v4
Processor Base Frequency	2.2 GHz
Max Turbo Frequency	3.6 GHz
Cores per Node	22
No. of Nodes	2
RAM	62.8 GB
OS	OpenSUSE 42.2 (x86_64)

The specification of the machine used to evaluate the performance is shown in Table 1. Both SoftPosit and SoftFloat are compiled with GNU GCC 4.8.5 with optimization level "O2" and architecture set to "core-avx2".

The arithmetic operations of $posit\langle 16,1\rangle$ and $quire128\langle 16,1\rangle$, and of IEEE Standard half-precision floats ($float\langle 16,5\rangle$) are shown in Table 2. Each operation is implemented using integer operators in C. With the exception of the fused dot product (a posit arithmetic functionality that is not in the IEEE 754 Standard), there is an equivalent posit operation for every float operation shown in Table 2.

The most significant rounding errors that influence the accuracy of DFT algorithms occur in each butterfly calculation, the bfly routine. To reduce the number of rounding errors, fused multiply-adds are leveraged. Posit arithmetic can perform fused multiply-adds, or better, leverage the fused dot products with the quire data type to further reduce the accumulation of rounding errors.

The twiddle factors are obtained using a precomputed cosine table with 1024 points to store the values of $\cos(0)$ to $\cos(\frac{\pi}{2})$. The sine and cosine values for the entire unit circle are found through indexed reflections and negations of these discrete values.

A 1D-FFT with input sizes 1024 and 4096 is used to check the computational performance with $posit\langle 16,1\rangle$ without quire, $posit\langle 16,1\rangle$ with quire, and $float\langle 16,5\rangle$ by tagging each run to the same selected core.

5   Results

5.1   Accuracy

Figure 6 shows the average RMS errors for 1024-point tests, representing hundreds of thousands of experimental data points. The RMS error bar graph for the 4096-point FFTs looks very similar but bars are uniformly about 12% higher. The vertical axis represents Units in the Last Place (ULP) at the resolution of

Table 2. Arithmetic Operations

Arithmetic operations	Posit⟨16, 1⟩ functions	Float⟨16, 5⟩ functions
Add	*p16_add*	*f16_add*
Subtract	*p16_sub*	*f16_sub*
Multiply	*p16_mul*	*f16_mul*
Divide	*p16_div*	*f16_div*
Fused multiply-add	p*16_mulAdd*	*f16_mulAdd*
Fused dot product-add	*q16_fdp_add*	Not applicable
Fused dot product-sub	*q16_fdp_sub*	Not applicable

a 12-bit ADC as described in the previous section. Besides the RMS error, L_1 and L_∞ errors are calculated and show a nearly identical pattern, differing only in the vertical scale.

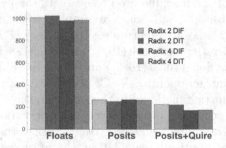

Fig. 6. RMS errors per value $\times 10^6$ for 1024-point FFTs

The obvious difference is that 16-bit posits have about 1/4 the rounding error of floats when running algorithms that round at identical places in the data flow. This follows from the fact that most of the operations occur where posits have two bits greater accuracy in the fraction part of their format. The use of the quire further reduces errors, by as much as 1.8× for the case of the radix-4 form of the FFT. (Similarly, rounding error is about 16 times less for 32-bit posits than for 32-bit floats since 32-bit posits have 28 bits in the significand for values with magnitudes between 1/16 and 16, compared with 24 bits in the significand of a standard float).

The other differences, between DIT and DIF, or between radix-2 and radix-4, are subtle but statistically significant and repeatable. For posits without the quire, radix-4 is slightly less accurate than radix-2 because intermediate calculations in the longer dot product can stray into the regions where posits have only one bit instead of two bits of greater fraction precision. However, the quire provides a strong advantage for radix-4, reducing the number of rounding events per result to only 4 per point for a 1024-point FFT, and 4 more for the inverse.

However, Fig. 6 understates the significance of the higher accuracy of posits. The original ADC signal is the "gold standard" for the correct answer. Both float or posit computations make rounding errors in performing a round-trip FFT. Additionally, we round that result again *to express it in the fixed-point format used by the ADC*, as shown in Fig. 5. Once the result is accurate to within 0.5 ULP of the ADC input format, it will round to the original value with *no* error. But if the result is more than 0.5 ULP from the original ADC value, it "falls off a cliff" and rounds to the wrong fixed-point number. Because of this insight, we focus on the number of bits wrong compared to the original signal (measured in ADC ULPs) and not measures such as RMS error or dB signal-to-noise ratios that are more appropriate when numerical errors are frequent and pervasive.

Suppose we measure and sum the absolute ULPs of error for every data point in a round-trip (radix-2, DIF) 1024-point FFT. Figure 7a shows that the massive losses produced by 16-bit floats preclude their use for FFTs.

For posits, on the other hand, 97.9% of the values make the round trip with all bits identical to the original value. Of the 2.1% that are off, they are off by only 1 ULP. While the reversibility is not mathematically perfect, it is nearly so, and may be accurate enough to eliminate the need to use 32-bit data representation. The bar chart shows 16-bit posits to be about 36 times as accurate as 16-bit floats in preserving the information content of the original data. The ratio is similar for a 4096-point FFT, shown in Fig. 7b; they are almost indistinguishable except for the vertical scale.

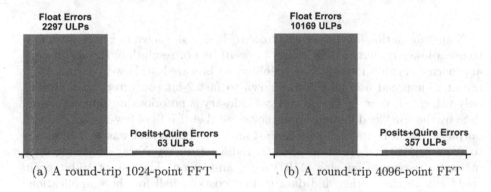

(a) A round-trip 1024-point FFT   (b) A round-trip 4096-point FFT

Fig. 7. Total ULPs of error

Figure 8a shows another way to visualize the error, plotting the error in ULPs as a function of the data point (real part errors in blue, and imaginary part errors in orange). The errors are as large as six ULPs from the original data, and 68% of the round-trip values are incorrect. An error of six ULPs represents a worst-case loss of 1.8 decimals of accuracy (a one-bit loss represents about 0.3 decimal loss), and 16-bit floats only have about 3.6 decimals to begin with. Figure 8b shows the results when using posits and the quire, with just a few scattered points that do not lie on the x-axis. The information loss is very slight.

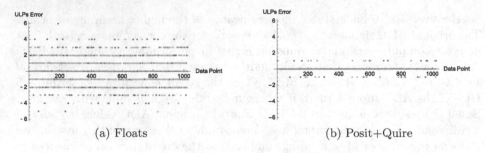

Fig. 8. ULPs error, 1024-point round-trip FFT

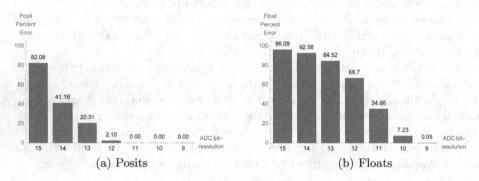

Fig. 9. Percent round-trip errors versus ADC bit resolution for 1024-point FFTs

Can information loss be reduced to *zero*? It can, as shown in Fig. 9. If we were to use a lower-resolution ADC, with 11 or 10 bits of resolution, the 16-bit posit approach can result in perfect reversibility; no bits are lost. Low-precision ADCs are in widespread use, all the way down to fast 2-bit converters that produce only values −1, 0, or 1. The oil and gas industry is notorious for moving seismic data by the truckload, literally, and they store their FFTs of low-resolution ADC output in 32-bit floats to protect against any loss of data that was very expensive to acquire. A similar situation holds for radio astronomy, X-ray crystallography, magnetic resonance imaging (MRI) data, and so on. The use of 16-bit posits could cut all the storage and data motion costs in half for these applications. Figure 9 shows that the insufficient accuracy of 16-bit floats forces the use of 32-bit floats to achieve lossless reversibility.

5.2   Performance

The performance of arithmetic operations, add, subtract, multiply and divide, from SoftPosit and SoftFloat are computed exhaustively by simulating all possible combinations of the inputs in the range $[-1, 1]$ where most of the FFT calculations occur. Fused multiply-add and fused dot product will require from days to weeks to be exhaustively tested on the selected machine. Consequently, the tests are simplified by reusing function arguments, i.e. restricting the test to run only two nested loops exhaustively instead of three. Ten runs for each operation were performed on a selected core to eliminate performance variations between cores and remove the variation caused by operating system interrupts and other interference.

In the selected input range, float$\langle 16, 5 \rangle$ and posit$\langle 16, 1 \rangle$ have 471951364 and 1073807361 bit patterns respectively. Thus posit$\langle 16, 1 \rangle$ has more accuracy than float$\langle 16, 5 \rangle$. One of the reasons why floats$\langle 16, 5 \rangle$ have fewer than half the bit patterns compared to posits$\langle 16, 1 \rangle$ is due to the reserved 2048 bit-patterns for "non-numbers", i.e. when all exponent bits are 1s. "Non-numbers" represent positive and negative infinity and not-a-number (NaN). In comparison, posits do not waste bit patterns and have only one Not-a-Real (NaR) bit pattern, 100...000, and only one representation for zero, 000...000. Additionally, posits have more values close to ± 1 and to 0 than do floats.

The performance in operations per second for arguments in the range of $[-1, 1]$ is shown in Fig 10.

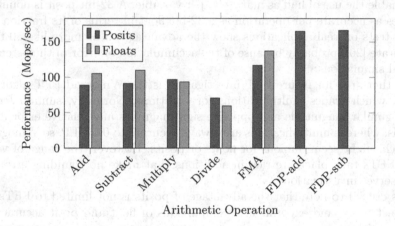

Fig. 10. Posit$\langle 16, 1 \rangle$ versus float$\langle 16, 5 \rangle$ performance in range $[-1, 1]$

The results show that posits have slightly better performance in multiply and divide operations while floats have slightly better performance in add, subtract and FMA operations. "FDP-add" and "FDP-sub" are additions and subtractions of products using the quire when computing a fused dot product. They show higher performance than FMA due to the fact that one of the arguments, the quire, does not require additional shifting before adding/subtracting the dot product of two other posit arguments. It also does not need to perform rounding until it completes all accumulations, which saves time. When appropriately used, quires can potentially improve performance while minimizing rounding errors.

6   Conclusions and Future Work

We have shown that 16-bit posits outperform 16-bit floats and fixed-points in accuracy for radix-2 and radix-4, 1024- and 4096-point FFTs for both DIT and DIF classes. To have accuracy similar to that of 16-bit posits, 32-bits floats would have to be used. When ADC inputs are 11-bits or smaller, 16-bit posits can compute completely lossless "round-trip" FFTs. 16-bit posits have comparable computation performance to that of 16-bit floats, but approximately twice the performance on bandwidth bound tasks such as the FFT. Because posit arithmetic is still in its infancy, the performance result shown here using an in-house software emulator, SoftPosit, is preliminary.

While we here studied examples from the low-precision side of HPC, the advantages of posits should also apply to high-precision FFT applications such as *ab initio* computational chemistry, radar cross-section analysis, and the solution of partial differential equations (PDEs) by spectral methods. For some users, posits might be desirable to increase accuracy using the same precision, instead of to enable the use of half as many bits per variable. A 32-bit posit is nominally 16 times as accurate per operation as a 32-bit float in terms of its fraction bits, though tests on real applications show the advantage to be more like 50 times as accurate [26], probably because of the accumulation of error in time-stepping physical simulations.

Another area for future FFT investigation is the Winograd FFT algorithm [35, 36], which trades multiplications for additions. Normally, summing numbers of similar magnitude and opposite sign magnifies any relative error in the addends, whereas multiplications are always accurate to 0.5 ULP, so Winograd's approach might seem dubious for floats or posits. However, the range of values where FFTs take place are rich in additions that make no rounding errors, so this deserves investigation.

It is crucial to note that the advantage of posits is not limited to FFTs and we expect to expand experimental comparisons of float and posit accuracy for other algorithms such as linear equation solution and matrix multiplication, for both HPC and machine learning (ML) purposes. One promising area for 32-bit posits is weather prediction (which frequently relies on FFTs that are typically performed with 64-bit floats).

Large-scale simulations typically achieve only single-digit percentages of the peak speed of an HPC system, which means the arithmetic units are spending most of their time waiting for operands to be communicated to them. Hardware bandwidths have been increasing very slowly for the last several decades, and there has been no steep trend line for bandwidth like there has been for transistor size and cost (Moore's law). High-accuracy posit arithmetic permits use of reduced data sizes, which promises to provide dramatic speedups not just for FFT kernels but for the very broad range of bandwidth-bound applications that presently rely on floating-point arithmetic.

References

1. Bouziane, R., et al.: Optimizing FFT precision in optical OFDM transceivers. IEEE Photonics Technol. Lett. **23**(20), 1550–1552 (2011). https://doi.org/10.1109/LPT.2011.2164059
2. Buddhiram, C.R., et al.: Parameterized posit arithmetic generator (2018). Submitted to ICCD 2018
3. Chang, W.H., Nguyen, T.Q.: On the fixed-point accuracy analysis of FFT algorithms. IEEE Trans. Signal Process. **56**(10), 4673–4682 (2008). https://doi.org/10.1109/TSP.2008.924637
4. Chang, W.H., Nguyen, T.Q.: On the fixed-point accuracy analysis of FFT algorithms. IEEE Trans. Signal Process. **56**(10), 4673–4682 (2008)
5. Chen, J., Al-Ars, Z., Hofstee, H.P.: A matrix-multiply unit for posits in reconfigurable logic using (Open) CAPI. ACM (2018)
6. Chung, S.Y.: Provably correct posit arithmetic with fixed-point big integer. ACM (2018)
7. Cochran, W.T., et al.: What is the fast Fourier transform? Proc. IEEE **55**(10), 1664–1674 (1967). https://doi.org/10.1109/PROC.1967.5957
8. Cooley, J.W., Tukey, J.W.: An algorithm for the machine calculation of complex Fourier series. Math. Comput. **19**, 297–301 (1965)
9. Duhamel, P., Hollmann, H.: 'Split radix' FFT algorithm. Electron. Lett. **20**(1), 14–16 (1984). https://doi.org/10.1049/el:19840012
10. Goldberg, D.: What every computer scientist should know about floating-point arithmetic
11. Good, I.: The interaction algorithm and practical Fourier analysis. J. Roy. Stat. Soc. Ser. B (Methodol.) 361–372 (1958)
12. Good, I.: The interaction algorithm and practical Fourier analysis: an addendum. J. Roy. Stat. Soc. Ser. B (Methodol.) 372–375 (1960)
13. Gustafson, J.L.: The End of Error: Unum Computing. Chapman & Hall/CRC Computational Science, CRC Press (2015)
14. Gustafson, J.L.: Posit arithmetic (2017). Mathematica notebook
15. Gustafson, J.L., Yonemoto, I.: Beating floating point at its own game: posit arithmetic. Supercomput. Front. Innov. **4**(2) (2017). https://doi.org/10.14529/jsfi170206
16. Gustafson, J.L., Yonemoto, I.: Beyond floating point: next generation computer arithmetic (2017). https://www.youtube.com/watch?v=aP0Y1uAA-2Y
17. Hauser, J.R.: Berkeley SoftFloat (2018). http://www.jhauser.us/arithmetic/SoftFloat.html
18. Hutter, J., Iannuzzi, M., Schiffmann, F., VandeVondele, J.: CP2K: atomistic simulations of condensed matter systems. Wiley Interdisc. Rev.: Comput. Mol. Sci. **4**(1), 15–25 (2014)
19. Kahan, W.: IEEE standard 754 for binary floating-point arithmetic. Lect. Notes Status EEE **754**(94720–1776), 11 (1996)
20. Komatitsch, D., Tromp, J.: Spectral-element simulations of global seismic wave propagation-I. Validation. Geophys. J. Int. **149**(2), 390–412 (2002). https://doi.org/10.1046/j.1365-246X.2002.01653.x
21. Komatitsch, D., Tromp, J.: Spectral-element simulations of global seismic wave propagation–II. Three-dimensional models, oceans, rotation and self-gravitation. Geophys. J. Int. **150**(1), 303–318 (2002)

22. Kulisch, U.W., Miranker, W.L.: The arithmetic of the digital computer: a new approach. SIAM Rev. **28**(1), 1–40 (1986). https://doi.org/10.1137/1028001, http://dx.doi.org/10.1137/1028001

23. Langroudi, S.H.F., Pandit, T.N., Kudithipudi, D.: Deep learning inference on embedded devices: fixed-point vs posit. In: Energy Efficiency Machine Learning and Cognitive Computing for Embedded Applications (EMC^2) (2018). https://sites.google.com/view/asplos-emc2/program

24. Lehoczky, Z., Szabo, A., Farkas, B.: High-level.NET software implementations of unum type I and posit with simultaneous FPGA implementation using Hastlayer. ACM (2018)

25. Li, M., et al.: Evaluation of variable precision computing with variable precision FFT implementation on FPGA. In: 2016 International Conference on Field-Programmable Technology (FPT), pp. 299–300 (2016). https://doi.org/10.1109/FPT.2016.7929560

26. Lindstrom, P., Lloyd, S., Hittinger, J.: Universal coding of the reals: alternatives to IEEE floating point. In: Conference for Next Generation Arithmetic. ACM (2018)

27. Mallasén, D., Murillo, R., Barrio, A.A.D., Botella, G., Piñuel, L., Prieto-Matias, M.: Percival: open-source posit RISC-V core with quire capability. IEEE Trans. Emerg. Top. Comput. **10**(3), 1241–1252 (2022). https://doi.org/10.1109/TETC.2022.3187199

28. Oppenheim, A.V., Schafer, R.W.: Discrete-Time Signal Processing, Second Edition. Prentice-Hall (1998)

29. Podobas, A.: Accelerating POSIT-based computations using FPGAs and OpenCL (2018). https://posithub.org/conga/2018/techprogramme#invitedtalk2

30. Rader, C., Brenner, N.: A new principle for fast Fourier transformation. IEEE Trans. Acoust. Speech Signal Process. **24**(3), 264–266 (1976). https://doi.org/10.1109/TASSP.1976.1162805

31. Skamarock, W.C., Klemp, J.B., Dudhia, J.: Prototypes for the WRF (weather research and forecasting) model. In: Preprints, Ninth Conf. Mesoscale Processes, J11–J15, American Meteorological Society, Fort Lauderdale, FL (2001)

32. Soni, M., Kunthe, P.: A General comparison of FFT algorithms (2011). http://pioneerjournal.in/conferences/tech-knowledge/9th-national-conference/3471-a-general-comparison-of-fft-algorithms.html

33. Thomas, L.: Using a computer to solve problems in physics. Appl. Digit. Comput. **458**, 44–45 (1963)

34. Weinstein, C.J.: Quantization effects in digital filters. Technical report, MIT Lexington Lincoln Lab (1969)

35. Winograd, S.: On computing the discrete Fourier transform. Math. Comput. **32**(141), 175–199 (1978)

36. Winograd, S.: On the multiplicative complexity of the discrete Fourier transform. Adv. Math. **32**(2), 83–117 (1979). https://doi.org/10.1016/0001-8708(79)90037-9, http://www.sciencedirect.com/science/article/pii/0001870879900379

Bedot: Bit Efficient Dot Product for Deep Generative Models

Nhut-Minh Ho[1]([✉]), Duy-Thanh Nguyen[2], John L. Gustafson[3], and Weng-Fai Wong[1]

[1] National University of Singapore, Singapore, Singapore
{minhhn,wongwf}@comp.nus.edu.sg
[2] Kyung Hee University, Seoul, South Korea
dtnguyen@khu.ac.kr
[3] Arizona State University, Tempe, USA
jlgusta6@asu.edu

Abstract. This paper presents an optimization method to build the smallest possible integer mapping unit that can replace a conventional multiply-and-accumulate unit in deep learning applications. The unit is built using a hardware-software co-design strategy that minimizes the set of represented real values and energy consumed. We target larger and more complex deep learning applications domains than those explored in previous related works, namely generative models for image and text content. Our key result is that using our proposed method, we can produce a set as small as 4 entries for an image enhancement application, and 16–32 entries for the GPT2 model, all with minimal loss of quality. Experimental results show that a hardware accelerator designed using our approach can reduce the processing time up to $1.98\times/3.62\times$ and reduce computation energy consumed up to $1.7\times/8.4\times$ compared to 8-bit integer/16-bit floating-point alternatives, respectively.

Keywords: Number format · Deep learning · Generative Adversarial Networks · Generative Models · Energy Efficient Machine Learning

1 Introduction

Deep learning has permeated a wide variety of computer applications ranging from image recognition to the more creative uses of *generative adversarial networks* (GAN) and generative models in general to produce realistic artifacts like images and text. Performing inference for these models as efficiently as possible is crucial to promoting their wider adoption, for example, on edge devices. For example, low quality video can be upscaled to higher quality at the monitor end using deep learning based upscaling. To this end, compressing large models by reducing the number of bits used to represent model parameters has garnered considerable interest. This technique has been frequently used for more popular networks such as *convolutional neural networks* (CNN). However, applying it to

J. Gustafson et al. (Eds.): CoNGA 2023, LNCS 13851, pp. 19–37, 2023.
https://doi.org/10.1007/978-3-031-32180-1_2

more recent networks such as OpenAI's GPT models for language modelling as well as GANs is not straightforward. While CNN inference can be done with a very few number of bits, the state-of-the-art for language models' bit requirements remain at 8 bits [1]. Similarly, while quantization mechanisms have been marginally explored for GANs, they are inefficient, require re-training, and are only able to represent weights [2]. Moreover, a systematic method of obtaining the quantization levels can be beneficial for extending the technique to even newer models. In this paper, we apply a new multiply-accumulate (MAC) approach for the emerging neural networks (the deep generative models) for which the output and error metrics are vastly different from the most popular classification tasks in the literature.

Depending on the number of bits required to represent the model, different types of hardware can be used. Traditional MAC units with accumulators of various sizes have been used in many studies to date. Approaches that use lookup tables have been scarcely studied due to the complexities involved with large table sizes that increase the look-up time. However, when the number of bits needed are significantly reduced, custom tables can be used to speed-up execution. Furthermore, by implementing efficient lookup mechanisms, the circuitry required for traditional MACs can also be replaced by integer mappings, bringing about substantial energy savings.

Our contributions in this work are as follows.

- We reduce the number of bits required to 2–3 bits for weights and 2–5 bits for activation on large generative models such as GPT2 using our optimizing algorithm.
- We implement a new, highly efficient MAC method that uses integer summation of mapped inputs.
- We propose an architecture to perform exact dot products with much higher performance and energy efficiency than fixed-point or floating-point architectures.

2   Background and Related Work

2.1   Neural Networks and Emerging Architectures

Deep neural networks (DNNs) have recently achieved enormous success in a variety of domains, such as image classification, object detection, image segmentation, language, and media-related tasks. Initial efforts focused primarily on classification and detection. More recently, research interest has shifted to designing neural networks to address an even more complex challenge: *content generation*. Content generation tasks range from simple image style transfer, colorization, and super resolution to generating deepfake videos, synthetic voice and text which utilize GANs. In GANs, the input is either a random vector (for random data generation) or an original image (for style transfer or image enhancement). Graphic output introduces another challenge for low-precision

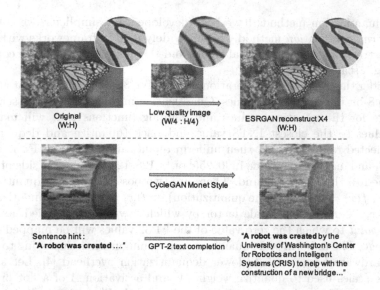

Fig. 1. Overview of some generative models used in this paper

approaches; in contrast with image classification where the output are only a vector of N values for N classes being classified, the outputs of GANs are image pixels. For example, an image of size $512 \times 512 \times 3$ needs all 786432 values to be in the output layers instead of 1000 real values in the output layer of ImageNet classification DNNs. Pixel values also need to remain in high precision to construct output images, e.g. 8 bits per channel for high quality color output. Figure 1 shows some samples of the tasks that will be optimized in this paper.

Previous work on quantization of Convolutional Neural Networks (CNNs) for image classification can reduce the required precision of parameters down to 4–8 bits with minimal loss of accuracy, with the help of quantization-aware training. However, the current retraining method is difficult to apply since training data is not available in some models (training settings for GPT2 and GPT-3 are proprietary). Another obstacle of this approach is the cost and time associated with training. Millions of dollars are required to train the latest GPT models. They are trained with non-disclosed training data to be a general model for various language-related tasks. For other GANs, fine-tuning methods are still not easy and training is difficult to converge [3]. Thus, in this paper, we present a method to optimize both weights and activations of these models without fine-tuning. The techniques of fine-tuning to enhance the output quality can always be applied on top of our method.

2.2   Quantization and Table Lookup

Two predominant approaches exist to reduce the bitwidths of parameters for low-precision neural network inference: Applying quantization functions to high-precision values, and looking up corresponding low-precision values from a table.

Several quantization methods have been developed; for simplicity, we consider the *uniform quantization* method which is widely used in frameworks with 8-bit tensor instructions since the actual values and the quantized values are convertible using a scale s.

Consider the quantization operation of mapping 32-bit floating-point (FP32) values to 8-bit integer (INT8) values. Quantization in this case involves selecting the range for the quantized values and defining functions that will map the FP32 values to the closest INT8 value and back (quantize and dequantize). If the selected range is $[\alpha, \beta]$, then uniform quantization takes an FP32 value, $x \in [\alpha, \beta]$ and maps it to a value in $[0, 255]$ or $[-128, 127]$. Values outside of $[\alpha, \beta]$ are clipped to the nearest bound. There are two possible uniform quantization functions: $f(x) = s \cdot x + z$ (affine quantization) or $f(x) = s \cdot x$ (scale quantization) where $s, x, z \in R$; s is the scale factor by which x will be multiplied, and z is the *zero-point* to which the zero value of the FP32 values will be mapped in the INT8 range. The uniform scale quantization is common when deploying to INT8 tensor hardware because of its lower dequantization overhead [4]. Let s_1 and s_2 be the scales used to quantize weight W and activation A of a dot product operation ($\otimes$). The scale quantized dot product result R' can be dequantized by using the appropriate factor:

$$R' = W' \otimes A' = \sum_{1}^{K} w_i \times s_1 \times a_i \times s_2$$

$$R = \sum_{1}^{K} w_i \times a_i = R'/(s_1 \times s_2)$$

For our new MAC approach, we allow the numerical inputs to be **anywhere** in $\mathbb{R}$. Instead of requiring N-bit integer multiplier logic, we use a low-precision integer form of logarithm and antilogarithm mappings that *need not produce rounding error*. Instead of filling out a two-dimensional multiplication table of size 2^{N+M} where M is the number of w_i values and N is the number of a_i values, we map inputs to low-precision unsigned integers that are added and the resulting sum mapped to a (potentially exact) fixed-point product that can be accumulated. This eliminates "decoding" of a bit format into sign, exponent, and fraction fields, and any need for an integer multiplier in the MAC unit. In this paper we show that by allowing the precision of the fixed-point product to be 10–16 bits and optimizing the "vocabulary" of input real values, the sizes of M and N can be as low as 2 or 3 bits.

There are four main enhancements in Bedot compared to conventional INT8 quantization in current general-purpose tensor core architectures (see Fig. 2):

1. Activation of the previous layers are kept at fixed point while the weights are kept at as small as 3-bit pointers to our carefully chosen real-valued weights.
2. The product of two operands is obtained by integer mapping instead of traditional multiplier hardware.
3. The accumulator is smaller than 32 bits, and optimized to preserve dot product correctness (no rounding).

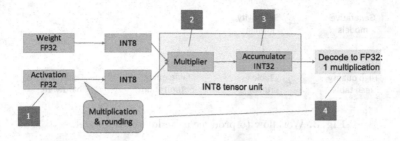

Fig. 2. A conventional integer quantization architecture for inference and the main differences in Bedot

4. We introduce *rounding hints*. This enhancement yields additional tuning knobs for improving output quality compared to the conventional round-to-nearest.

This motivates the first part of our paper to search for the smallest number set (vocabulary) possible while maintaining high output quality. The search results will be used for customized hardware design with the details in Sect. 5.

2.3 Related Work

Due to the high energy consumption of single precision floating point arithmetic, there have been many proposals to use lower precision arithmetic such as fixed point [5–7], half precision and mixed precision [8–11], posit [12,13] for general applications. In the specific domain of deep learning, there have been several proposals to optimize both inference and training phases. Our work is specific to inference optimization. This method can be considered as the last-step optimization after all other optimizations have been applied (e.g. network pruning, retraining, fine-tuning). Regardless of how the model was trained and optimized, our technique produces a high-efficiency model that is ready to deploy.

There are several approaches to quantizing network models to lower bitwidths, mainly in the area of image classification with well organized surveys in [14,15]. Notably, recent works have explored hardware-friendly nonuniform quantization methods with the restriction being that quantized values are additive power-of-two [16]. More recently, next generation arithmetic such as Posit plays an important role in neural network training and inference [12,17,18]. However, most of these methods are not directly applicable to more complex generative models such as GPT and GANs. Most analytical methods for quantization target the convolutional layer and rely on RELU activation and a softmax layer when deriving cross-layer relationships and error formulae [19,20]. Unfortunately, activation and network architectures vary greatly in recent systems. INT8 quantization has been used for emerging neural networks include transformer architectures [1,21]. The current standard method for quantization of deep generative models that can be easily reproduced is to use INT8 inference module on Pytorch and Nvidia TensorRT. These frameworks provide standard

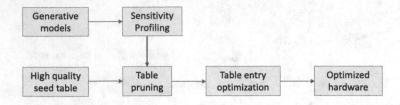

Fig. 3. Workflow to produce a Bedot-ready model.

methods for quantizing image classification models, with support for language and generative models in experimental mode. To the best of our knowledge, we are the first to attempt ultra-low-bitwidth tuning of the GPT2 model.

On the hardware design front, Eyeriss [22] is a systolic array system for CNNs. [23] proposes a systolic array engine using table lookup instead of a multiplier. Their table lookup unit uses 4-bit addresses. To ensure high output quality, their architecture also requires higher precision (8–16 bit) data. Most designs focus on CNNs for image classification or normal applications. Current widely-used hardware for generative model inference is still GPGPU-based. Our work uses the multiply-accumulate design but with very low bitwidth. It is possible because our software module detects accuracy-sensitive layers so the rest of the layers can use 2–3 bit inputs for most models.

3   Overview of Bedot

Our work consist of two components working in synergy: software to find the smallest possible real number set that preserves answer quality, and hardware based on those sets. Given a neural network and a specified output quality, our software framework runs inference many times to find the smallest set of real values for w_i and a_i that works and optimize the set entries using our proposed algorithm (Fig. 3).

The set is then used in the hardware module to speed up the actual inference of the network for low energy environments (e.g. edge devices). Because we aggressively reduce the set size in our software module, the MAC task becomes simple integer-to-integer mapping that can be implemented using combinational logic instead of addressed ROM. This yields a massive performance and efficiency gain compared to both conventional low-precision units and table lookup approaches for neural network inference. In the trade-off for energy gain, we have to sacrifice the flexibility of the hardware module. Our target application is edge devices designed for a limited number of applications. For example, in image super resolution for TVs, the video can be transferred using low quality to conserve bandwidth and the higher resolution video can be reconstructed efficiently by our module for display.

4   Set Construction

4.1   Detecting the Sensitive Layers

Generating the minimal real number sets that preserve quality is the main focus of our work. This is particularly difficult given that the applications we target are diverse, large, and complex. We need to address *error sensitivity*. For example, quantization pixel color channel of sensitive GAN's layer to below 8 bits will likely result in a loss of information in the input image and incorrect colors in the output. Typically, reduced-precision designs use higher precision for the first and last layers of a CNN. Although this heuristics can be applied to generative models, we found that more layers needed to be excluded to preserve quality than conventional CNNs. We apply a low-precision format (e.g. floating-point 8-bit [24]) to each layer in turn, while maintaining the rest at full 32-bit precision, and then measuring the output quality to quantify the sensitivity of a layer to precision reduction. Using this method, we found that the number of high-sensitive layers varies among models.

For image generative models, the *structural similarity index measure* (SSIM) identifies sensitive outliers; a 1% drop of SSIM is the outlier threshold. For GPT2, we use *perplexity* (PPL) as the quality metric since it is widely used for text models. It is difficult to tell what amount of increase in PPL is "too high." Thus, for GPT2 we use an outlier detection method, the Boxplot method using *inter-quartile range* (IQR) [25,26]. Let $Q1$ and $Q3$ be the first and third quartiles of the data (25th and 75th percentiles). The IQR $= Q3 - Q1$ is computed and thresholds $Q3 + 3 \times$ IQR and $Q1 - 3 \times$ IQR are used to detect extreme sensitive outliers. As a result, we exclude three layers ($17^{th}, 141^{th}$, and 145th) out of the 145 layers in GPT2 model. For ESRGAN, the first layer and the last five layers were excluded. For other models, two layers are excluded (the first and last layers). We use fixed-point 16-bit for these excluded layers.

4.2   Building Optimized Real Number Sets

In the next step, we construct a single set of real magnitudes for both positive and negative numbers, to reduce hardware cost. The sign bit of the product is simply the XOR of the two input sign bits. We start with a large set that yields high output quality (e.g. FP16 [27]). However, because the set of possible 16-bit values is large, building a smaller set from such large set by testing every possible value is very time-consuming. Instead, we use smaller sets of numbers that are known to be good for inference. For this purpose, we chose the best among posit [18,28,29] and [24] floating-point formats (64–128 unsigned entries) as the starting sets. We simply try different configurations with 7 or 8 bits, and choose the configuration with the fewest bits that yields acceptable quality (which in our experiment means 'less than 1% quality drop'). For the rest of this paper, the set represents magnitudes and will be used along with the sign bit of the original value for dot product computation.

4.3   Fast Derivation of the Small Set from a Seed Set

After obtaining a seed set yielding good quality, we turn to reducing its size. Our algorithm halves the set size in rounds. From 128 unsigned entries, to find a set with only eight entries, we need to perform four rounds: $128 \rightarrow 64 \rightarrow 32 \rightarrow 16 \rightarrow 8$. At each step, we loop over the L entries of the set, record the output quality of the neural network after removing *each* entry. We then sort the output quality array to find the $L/2$ entries with the *least impact* on output accuracy. We remove these from the set and repeat the process. Assuming we want to reduce set size from 2^A to 2^B, $B < A$, the algorithm stops after $A - B$ iterations. The threshold ε is chosen based on our desired output quality. Since output quality will be improved in the next step by our set optimization algorithm, we actually select ε *below* the desired threshold. Based on our experiments, the search algorithm can improve accuracy up to 10%, thus we can pick ε about 10% worse quality than desired before running the optimization algorithm in the next Section.

Note that, removing the entries one by one (like a Jenga game) instead of deleting half of the set in line 13 will give a slightly better set with the same number of entries. However, the advantage is minimal when applying our optimizing algorithm afterwards while incurring huge additional overhead (from $A - B$ iterations to $2^{(A-B)}$ iterations). Thus, we chose to execute this phase batch by batch.

4.4   Enhancing Output Quality

The next step iteratively tunes each *value* in the set to improve output quality. The pseudocode can be seen in Algorithm 1. Each iteration measures the effect of changing each entry by δ in both directions. Let $O'[i]$ be the current value of an entry, the algorithm tests the result quality for $O'[i] \pm \delta \cdot O'[i]$. The algorithm then picks the best candidate (lines 21–28). If the best candidate improves the results compared to the previous iteration, the original set value is replaced by the best candidate and the algorithm continues with the same rate of change (δ). If all candidates worsen output quality, we reduce δ by half. The δ value will thus decrease rapidly and eventually converge when δ becomes too small (<1% change). Note that, in Algorithm 1, there is only one set to be optimized. We concatenate the weight and activation sets into a single set to optimize.

The $Test(O')$ function in lines 11 and 17 in Algorithm 1 is where we assess the output quality of the current set (O') with a separate representative dataset, different from that used to optimize set entries. The representative dataset is different for each model. If the model has multiple recommended evaluation datasets, we pick one for tuning and test against all others. For example, for ESRGAN, we pick Set14 for our tuning process but at the end of the optimization process measure the output quality of another test set (Set5). Both results will be presented in our Sect. 6. The result of $Test(O')$ is in form of the metric for measuring output quality. The default setting in Algorithm 1 assumes the higher metric indicates better results. For models with the lower-better metric (i.e. Perplexity of GPT2), we simply pass $-Test(O')$ to line 11 and 17 and other parts of the algorithm can remain the same. The complexity of this algorithm

---

Algorithm 1. Algorithm for optimizing set entries

1: **Input** Table I : $[I_1 \ldots I_N]$ // Input unoptimized set entries, sorted in ascending order
2: **Output** Table O : $[O_1 \ldots O_N]$
3: $O \leftarrow I$
4: $\delta \leftarrow 0.5$ // Initialize changing rate, 50% of each table entry's value
5: $Q_{curr} = Test(O)$ // Initialize the table
6: **while** $\delta \geq 0.01$ **do**
7:     $Inc \leftarrow [0 \ldots 0]$ // Store output quality when increasing table entries
8:     **for** $i = 1$ to N **do**
9:         $O' \leftarrow copy(O)$
10:        $O'[i] \leftarrow O'[i] + O'[i] \times \delta$
11:        $Inc[i] \leftarrow Test(O')$
12:    **end for**
13:    $Dec \leftarrow [0 \ldots 0]$ // Store output quality when decreasing table entries
14:    **for** $i = 1$ to N **do**
15:        $O' \leftarrow copy(O)$
16:        $O'[i] \leftarrow O'[i] - O'[i] \times \delta$
17:        $Dec[i] \leftarrow Test(O')$
18:    **end for**
19:    $Inc\_idx \leftarrow \max(Inc)$ // Get the index of the entry having maximum output quality in **Inc**
20:    $Dec\_idx \leftarrow \max(Dec)$ // Get the index of the entry having maximum output quality in **Dec**

21:    **if** $\max(\max(Inc), \max(Dec)) > Q_{curr}$ **then**
22:        **if** $\max(Inc) > \max(Dec)$ **then**
23:            $O[Inc\_idx] \leftarrow O[Inc\_idx] + O[Inc\_idx] \times \delta$ // Increase the corresponding table entry
24:            $Q_{curr} = \max(Inc)$
25:        **else**
26:            $O[Dec\_idx] \leftarrow O[Dec\_idx] - O[Dec\_idx] \times \delta$ // Decrease the corresponding table entry
27:            $Q_{curr} = \max(Dec)$
28:        **end if**
29:    **else**
30:        Quality not improved, decrease changing rate by half
31:        $\delta \leftarrow \delta/2$
32:    **end if**
33: **end while**

---

is low because halving the changing rate δ converges quickly. For the longest experiment we ran (GPT2), it cost $33 + 6$ iterations as demonstrated in Fig. 4 (6 more iterations where the condition in line 30 is met, δ is decreased).

4.5 The Rounding Hint Table and Its Effect

There are several ways to convert any real value to one of our set's entries. Initially, we use round-to-nearest. Consider a value x and the set $O[O_1..O_N]$ with N entries from Algorithm 1, sorted in ascending order. Let $M[M_1..M_N]$ be the set of midpoints. The round-to-nearest mode can be implemented by comparing the absolute value $|x|$ against the midpoints and taking the index of the entry with its midpoint just below $|x|$:

$$M[i] = \begin{cases} (O[i] + 0)/2 & \text{if } i = 1 \\ (O[i] + O[i-1])/2 & \text{if } i > 1 \end{cases}$$

$$\text{Encode}(x) = i \text{ where } \max_i M[i] \leq |x| \tag{1}$$

During our experiments, we realized these comparison points can be *tuned*. Better "midpoints" can improve the output quality of the model with no additional hardware overhead. Naive round to nearest requires a comparison unit.

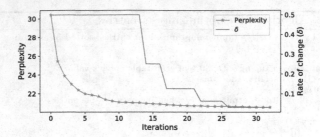

Fig. 4. Sample run of Algorithm 1 on GPT2. A lower perplexity metric on the left y-axis indicates better output.

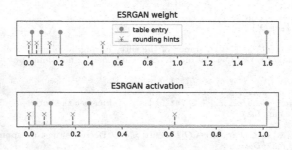

Fig. 5. Tuning of rounding hints for ESRGAN

In rounding in the range $[O[i], O[i-1]]$, we can replace the midpoint with any real value $M[i]$ (a *rounding hint*) that is in the same range:

$$M[i] = \begin{cases} 0 \leq M[i] \leq O[i] & \text{if } i = 1 \\ O[i-1] \leq M[i] \leq O[i] & \text{if } i > 1 \end{cases}$$

Note that in the actual implementation, the index will begin with 0 instead of 1. The initial rounding hints table is set to be mid-points (round to nearest mode) and concatenated with the set entries. The whole table will be used in Algorithm 1 for optimization. To support efficient hardware implementation, the optimized rounding hints are rounded to a fixed-point format with lower bitwidth with the hardware design in Sect. 5.5. Figure 5 shows set entries and rounding hints after optimizing the ESRGAN model. The effect of rounding hints will be presented in Sect. 6.

5 Set Mapping Based Inference

5.1 Processing Element Utilizing Table Lookup

The number of weight and activation entries is reduced significantly by our algorithms. We can use a "wired ROM" to create a MAC based on the integer mappings. In this paper, we introduce and evaluate the wired ROM unit implemented with combinational logic, and show that the design has smaller area,

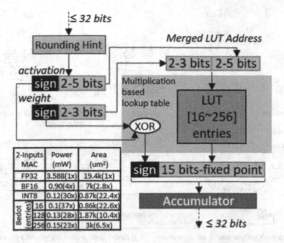

Fig. 6. Set mapping unit to find the product of weight and activation, and comparison of the power and area size of a two-input MAC for several input formats.

lower cost, and higher speed per watt than MAC hardware based on integer multipliers or addressed lookup tables.

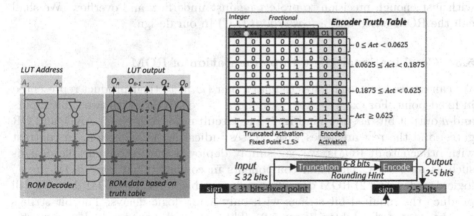

Fig. 7. An example design of our lookup unit with 2-bit inputs and example Rounding Hint module of ESRGAN

5.2 Wired ROM Logic for Multiplication

For each neural network, after we obtain the optimized values from Algorithm 1, conventional table lookup units would decode the weights and activations to fixed-point numbers before multiplication. However, we pre-compute the exact Cartesian products of the weights and activations at full precision and find integer mappings with the same Cartesian sum ranking as the Cartesian products,

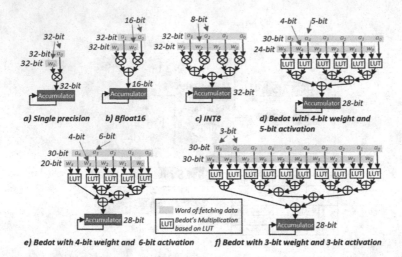

Fig. 8. 32-bit SIMD MAC architecture to compute dot product of 2 N-element vectors

like a low-precision logarithm table. Analogously, the "inverse logarithm" can then be a rounding-free map to the fixed-point product as shown in Fig. 6. For inference, a table lookup using the combined weight and activation bits yields the exact fixed-point product. The result is accumulated exactly in fixed-point with just enough precision to protect against underflow and overflow. We shall call the ROM-based unit a *lookup unit* (LU) in our design.

5.3   Combinational Logic Implementation of ROM

We can derive basic logic gates to map a pair (w, a) to their product represented in fixed-point. For example, we can build a "wired ROM" with two 2-bit inputs and n output bits as shown in Fig. 7. The circuit needs only NOT, AND, and OR gates, and the rest are wires with crosses indicating a connection. In contrast with other circuit ROMs, we can simply deploy it into reconfigurable designs such as an FPGA. The main components in combinational logic ROM are 1) logic decoder, and 2) ROM data. For each possible input, the ROM decoder will produce the required bit strings with only a few logic delays. The bit strings are the integer "log tables" (Sect. 5.2). This approach has very high energy efficiency compared to FP32, BF16, and the state-of-the-art INT8 inference. For our MAC unit, we estimate the energy using 45 nm CMOS at 200 MHz. Our ROM designs with 16/128/256 entries achieve significantly higher speed and lower power consumption than INT8, FP32 and BF16, as shown in Fig. 6.

5.4   SIMD MAC Unit Utilizing Our Lookup Units

With the LU as the multiplier, we can design a dot product engine to perform the dominant operation in neural networks. Besides the dot product, simpler operations such as scaling, pooling, and averaging can be performed using fixed-point

Table 1. Normalized GOPs/W and area reduction of 32-bit SIMD MAC design for each design in Fig. 8 for 45 nm CMOS at 200 MHz. FP32 is used as baseline.

Design	Power, mW	Dot-product Speedup	GOPs/W (improvement)	Area μm^2 (reduction)
FP32	3.80	1×	0.11 (1×)	19.4k (1×)
BF16	1.49	2×	0.53 (4.81×)	12.48k (1.56×)
INT8	0.57	4×	2.81 (25.18×)	3.2k (6×)
Bedot 16 entries	0.79	10×	5.04 (45.14×)	4.3k (4.5×)
Bedot 128 entries	0.67	6×	3.55 (31.8×)	8.7k (2.2×)
Bedot 256 entries	0.68	5×	2.93 (26.27×)	12.51k (1.55×)

units. We focus only on the dot product engine in this paper since it accounts for >95% of the energy. Note that any activation function can be implemented with *zero cost* by incorporating it into the rounding hints step.

Each LU multiplies a weight by an activation. A conventional *floating-point multiply-accumulate* (FMA) instruction requires fetching 32-bit FP32 operands. Each such fetch is equivalent to fetching multiple inputs in parallel if we use BF16, INT8, or our Bedot design instead. As shown in Fig. 8, with different precisions for weights and activations, we can speed up the dot product by 2× to 10× compared to a 32-bit FMA because of this parallelism. As mentioned in Sect. 5.4, our combinational logic ROMs consume the same power as a 2-input MAC design; however, Bedot (Fig. 8) is more energy efficient (GOPs/W) than other formats because of the lower number of bits, as shown in Table 1.

5.5 The Implementation of Rounding Hints

Encoded weights are pre-computed, but activations must be encoded back to 2–5 bits at runtime via rounding. Rounding hints can be implemented by a few logic gates found by Karnaugh maps (K-map). For example, the set of rounding hints is $\{0, 0.0625, 0.1875, 0.625\}$ for activation for the ESRGAN applications and it is applied to the encoded two-bit activation set. For this set, we only need a $(1, 5)$ (1-bit integer, 5-bit fraction) fixed-point number to represent the rounding hint values, as shown in Fig. 7. Hence, we only need to truncate the raw activations to this $(1, 5)$-fixed-point. We then simply solve the K-map problems to provide the encoder logic circuit for activation data. As a result, the rounding hint can be implemented using just a few logic gates (14 AND/OR gates), negligible compared to the MAC.

6 Experiments

In this section, we provide the experimental results of our software and hardware modules. For the software module, we tested different applications from text generation to style transfer and image super resolution. For the hardware module, we estimate the 32-bit MAC design specs as discussed in Sect. 5.4 to evaluate Bedot.

Table 2. Output quality of models used in our experiment. There are two or three columns for each model. The first column is the tuning data used to test for output quality and guide the search in Algorithm 1. The remaining column(s) is the testing data that has not been used in the tuning process. Entries with two numbers show "SSIM/PSNR (dB)".

Model Name	ESRGAN		Horse to Zebra		Van Gogh Style		Monet Style		GPT2-large		
Dataset	Set14	Set5	h2z	h2z	v2p	v2p	m2p	m2p	Wiki-2 (19.1)	Wiki-2 (19.44)	Wiki-103 (19.09)
Bedot	0.932/30.9	0.925/31.9	0.928/28.3	0.928/28.1	0.930/27.9	0.928/27.9	0.947/30.8	0.945/30.4	20.552	20.969	20.539
Bedot+H	0.954/33.2	0.956/34.7	**0.938/29.9**	**0.938/29.9**	**0.935/28.4**	**0.932/28.4**	**0.951/31.1**	**0.949/30.4**	20.435	20.828	20.367
INT8	**0.975/34.5**	**0.987/40.7**	0.726/24.4	0.645/22.6	0.773/21.3	0.775/21.4	0.627/19.7	0.623/19.3	**20.229**	**20.629**	**20.235**
Metric(s)	S/P	S/P	S/P	S/P	S/P	S/P	S/P	S/P	PPL	PPL	PPL

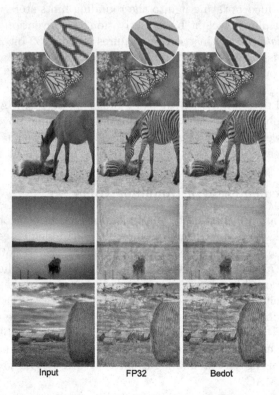

Input   FP32   Bedot

Fig. 9. Sample visual outputs of models. From top to bottom: Image super-resolution using ESRGAN, Horse-2-Zebra transform, Monet Style transform, Van Gogh Style transform. A live demo for ESRGAN is available at [30].

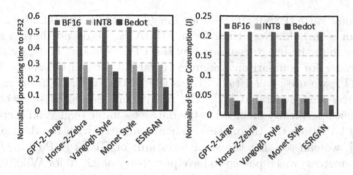

Fig. 10. Processing time and processing energy for several deep generative models using a 32-bit SIMD MAC design

6.1   Table Configurations and Accuracy

The software module (with rounding hints enabled) is developed and tested using our extension Qtorch+ [31] based on the design of QPytorch library [32]. We test our software module to optimize five emerging applications including GANs and GPT2. The Horse2Zebra model is used to transform an image of a horse to a zebra. The Van Gogh and Monet style models are used to transform a photo to a drawing mimicking the styles of those artists. These image transforming tasks use the custom datasets described in the original paper [33] (h2z: Horse2zebra dataset, v2p: VanGogh2photo dataset, m2p: Monet2photo dataset in Table 2). The *image superresolution* model (ESRGAN) was introduced in [34] with *Set14* and *Set5* datasets [35,36]. We also process a language model for text generation. For this task, we choose OpenAI's GPT2-large (762 million parameters) model [37] for Wikitext-2, Wikitext-103 datasets [38]. Note that only the *model* is released by OpenAI. Input pre-processing and measurement parameters affect the perplexity results but are not publicly released. So perplexity is measured using the guide from [39] which closely matches the result reported in the original OpenAI paper. For comparison, we use all available INT8 quantization in both the quantization module of Pytorch [40] and Nvidia's TensorRT [4]. Because each of these frameworks and quantization modes has their own limitations in the supported models and layer types, they also produce different output quality as the hyper parameters need to be manually chosen. We present only the highest output quality obtained after trying many possible variants of the configurations described in these frameworks. These configurations include: Pytorch quantization, TensorRT with different calibrations for *amax*: max, histogram, entropy, percentile and mse. We tried 99.9 and 99.99 as percentile and 2 and 10 images for the number of calibration images. Apart from trying these manual configurations, we use their automatic quantization modules with all default settings.

For image generation tasks, we use the *structural similarity index* metric (SSIM [41]), a standard way to measure image quality by comparison with a reference image. The highest quality is SSIM = 1.0. We also included the *peak signal-to-noise ratio* (PSNR) metrics for image-related tasks. The best result in each column is in bold. Note that, for most GANs, we do not have a reference image other than the image generated by the FP32 version. Thus, we use FP32 as the reference for comparison[1]. Sample visual output can be seen in Fig. 9.

For GPT2, we use *perplexity* (PPL) as the metric, where a lower value indicates a better text generated [42]. The results are presented in Table 2 with FP32 reference perplexity included in the dataset's name (e.g. WikiText-2: FP32 achieves 19.1 PPL on the tuning set). When compared with the data published by OpenAI, we can see that the smaller variant of GPT2 (GPT2-medium 345 million parameters) was reported to have perplexity of 22–26 for WikiText tasks. Bedot only need a 3-bit table to encode weights while having better perplexity. Bedot can reduce the parameters size to $32/4 = 8\times$ (1 more bit for the sign of weight) compared to FP32. In the table, 'Bedot+H' means rounding hints are enabled for tuning. Tuning the rounding hints can improve the output quality by up to 3% in ESRGAN. In general, quality decreases only slightly when testing datasets other than the tuning dataset. We obtained mixed results when comparing Bedot with uniform INT8 quantization in the different standard frameworks. In general, INT8 uniform quantization works better than Bedot when the range is tight, and worse than Bedot when the dynamic range required is high.

6.2   Performance and Energy Estimation

We estimate the processing time of deep generative applications. For the GPT2 and Horse-2-Zebra, we use Bedot with 128 entries. For the ESRGAN, we use Bedot with 16 entries. For the Van Gogh and Monet styles, we use Bedot with 256 entries. We assume a deep learning system that has only one MAC unit with speed and power as shown in Table 1, with the other operations performed sequentially at 200 MHz. Bedot reduces processing time by up to $1.98\times$ and $3.62\times$ compared to INT8 and BF16, respectively. For energy consumption, we only consider computation and do not include the register file, SRAM and DRAM accessing energy. Bedot also reduces the computation energy by $1.7\times$ and $8.4\times$ compared to INT8 and BF16, respectively. All results are in Fig. 10.

7   Conclusion

We have introduced a suite of methods from software to hardware to realize an accelerator for emerging deep generative models based on a novel approach to the MAC operation. With the table optimization algorithm, we successfully deliver high quality output with only four lookup entries for image resolution upscaling. For other more difficult tasks, the table has to be larger but never exceeds 32 (5-bit) entries. We believe our approach will empower future devices to perform difficult deep learning tasks with very low energy consumption.

---

[1] ESRGAN can compare its output against the original images. For Set5, the model achieves a PSNR of 30.8/28/29/30.3 dB on FP32/Bedot/Bedot+H/INT8. The reduction in quality has the same trend when we compare against FP32. Thus we also use FP32 images in Table 2 for a consistent comparison.

Acknowledgements. This research/project is supported in part by the Ministry of Education, Singapore, under the Academic Research Fund Tier 1 (FY2018) and the Next Generation Arithmetic grant from the National Supercomputing Centre, A*STAR, Singapore.

References

1. Lin, Y., Li, Y., Liu, T., Xiao, T., Liu, T., Zhu, J.: Towards fully 8-bit integer inference for the transformer model. arXiv preprint arXiv:2009.08034 (2020)
2. Wang, P., et al.: QGAN: quantized generative adversarial networks. arXiv preprint arXiv:1901.08263 (2019)
3. Salimans, T., Goodfellow, I., Zaremba, W., Cheung, V., Radford, A., Chen, X.: Improved techniques for training GANs. Adv. Neural. Inf. Process. Syst. **29**, 2234–2242 (2016)
4. Wu, H., Judd, P., Zhang, X., Isaev, M., Micikevicius, P.: Integer quantization for deep learning inference: principles and empirical evaluation. arXiv preprint arXiv:2004.09602 (2020)
5. Kim, S., Kum, K.-I., Sung, W.: Fixed-point optimization utility for C and C++ based digital signal processing programs. IEEE Trans. Circuits Syst. II: Analog Digit. Signal Process. **45**(11), 1455–1464 (1998)
6. Kum, K.-I., Kang, J., Sung, W.: AUTOSCALER for C: an optimizing floating-point to integer C program converter for fixed-point digital signal processors. IEEE Trans. Circuits Syst. II: Analog Digit. Signal Process. **47**(9), 840–848 (2000)
7. Cong, J., Liu, B., Neuendorffer, S., Noguera, J., Vissers, K., Zhang, Z.: High-level synthesis for FPGAs: from prototyping to deployment. IEEE Trans. Comput. Aided Des. Integr. Circuits Syst. **30**(4), 473–491 (2011)
8. Ho, N.-M., Wong, W.-F.: Exploiting half precision arithmetic in Nvidia GPUs. In: 2017 IEEE High Performance Extreme Computing Conference (HPEC), pp. 1–7. IEEE (2017)
9. Higham, N.J., Mary, T.: Mixed precision algorithms in numerical linear algebra. Acta Numer. **31**, 347–414 (2022)
10. Ho, N.-M., Manogaran, E., Wong, W.-F., Anoosheh, A.: Efficient floating point precision tuning for approximate computing. In: 22nd Asia and South Pacific Design Automation Conference (ASP-DAC), pp. 63–68. IEEE (2017)
11. De Silva, H., Santosa, A.E., Ho, N.-M., Wong, W.-F.: Approxsymate: path sensitive program approximation using symbolic execution. In: Proceedings of the 20th ACM SIGPLAN/SIGBED International Conference on Languages, Compilers, and Tools for Embedded Systems, pp. 148–162 (2019)
12. Gustafson, J.L., Yonemoto, I.T.: Beating floating point at its own game: posit arithmetic. Supercomput. Front. Innov. **4**(2), 71–86 (2017)
13. Ciocirlan, S.D., Loghin, D., Ramapantulu, L., Ṭăpuș, N., Teo, Y.M.: The accuracy and efficiency of posit arithmetic. In: 2021 IEEE 39th International Conference on Computer Design (ICCD), pp. 83–87. IEEE (2021)
14. Gholami, A., Kim, S., Dong, Z., Yao, Z., Mahoney, M.W., Keutzer, K.: A survey of quantization methods for efficient neural network inference. arXiv preprint arXiv:2103.13630 (2021)
15. Krishnamoorthi, R.: Quantizing deep convolutional networks for efficient inference: a whitepaper. arXiv preprint arXiv:1806.08342 (2018)
16. Li, Y., Dong, X., Wang, W.: Additive powers-of-two quantization: an efficient non-uniform discretization for neural networks. arXiv preprint arXiv:1909.13144 (2019)

17. Cococcioni, M., Rossi, F., Ruffaldi, E., Saponara, S., de Dinechin, B.D.: Novel arithmetics in deep neural networks signal processing for autonomous driving: challenges and opportunities. IEEE Signal Process. Mag. **38**(1), 97–110 (2020)

18. Ho, N.-M., Nguyen, D.-T., De Silva, H., Gustafson, J.L., Wong, W.-F., Chang, I.J.: Posit arithmetic for the training and deployment of generative adversarial networks. In: 2021 Design, Automation & Test in Europe Conference & Exhibition (DATE), pp. 1350–1355. IEEE (2021)

19. Zhou, Y., Moosavi-Dezfooli, S.-M., Cheung, N.-M., Frossard, P.: Adaptive quantization for deep neural network. In: Thirty-Second AAAI Conference on Artificial Intelligence (2018)

20. Li, Y., et al.: BRECQ: pushing the limit of post-training quantization by block reconstruction. arXiv preprint arXiv:2102.05426 (2021)

21. Zafrir, O., Boudoukh, G., Izsak, P., Wasserblat, M.:Q8BERT: quantized 8bit BERT. arXiv preprint arXiv:1910.06188 (2019)

22. Chen, Y.-H., Krishna, T., Emer, J.S., Sze, V.: Eyeriss: an energy-efficient reconfigurable accelerator for deep convolutional neural networks. IEEE J. Solid-State Circuits **52**(1), 127–138 (2016)

23. Ramanathan, et al.: Look-up table based energy efficient processing in cache support for neural network acceleration. In: 2020 53rd Annual IEEE/ACM International Symposium on Microarchitecture (MICRO), pp. 88–101. IEEE (2020)

24. Sun, X., et al.: Hybrid 8-bit floating point (HFP8) training and inference for deep neural networks. Adv. Neural. Inf. Process. Syst. **32**, 4900–4909 (2019)

25. Tukey, J.W., et al.: Exploratory Data Analysis, vol. 2. Reading, Mass. (1977)

26. Dawson, R.: How significant is a boxplot outlier? J. Stat. Educ. **19**(2) (2011)

27. Micikevicius, P., et al.: Mixed precision training. arXiv preprint arXiv:1710.03740 (2017)

28. Langroudi, H.F., Karia, V., Gustafson, J.L., Kudithipudi, D.: Adaptive posit: Parameter aware numerical format for deep learning inference on the edge. In: Proceedings of the IEEE/CVF Conference on Computer Vision and Pattern Recognition Workshops, pp. 726–727 (2020)

29. Lu, J., Fang, C., Xu, M., Lin, J., Wang, Z.: Evaluations on deep neural networks training using posit number system. IEEE Trans. Comput. **70**(2), 174–187 (2020)

30. Anonymous: Anonymous demo (2021). https://colab.research.google.com/drive/1mT-tBy5gpn8lassGIlYwS9q1cAW9O5ot?usp=sharing

31. Ho, N.-M., De Silva, H., Gustafson, J.L., Wong, W.-F.: Qtorch+: next Generation Arithmetic for Pytorch Machine Learning. In: Gustafson, J., Dimitrov, V. (eds.) CoNGA 2022. LNCS, vol. 13253, pp. 31–49. Springer, Cham (2022). https://doi.org/10.1007/978-3-031-09779-9_3

32. Zhang, T., Lin, Z., Yang, G., De Sa, C.: QPyTorch: a low-precision arithmetic simulation framework. arXiv preprint arXiv:1910.04540 (2019)

33. Zhu, J.-Y., Park, T., Isola, P., Efros, A.A.: Unpaired image-to-image translation using cycle-consistent adversarial networks. In: Proceedings of the IEEE International Conference on Computer Vision, pp. 2223–2232 (2017)

34. Wang, X., et al.: Esrgan: Enhanced super-resolution generative adversarial networks. In: Proceedings of the European Conference on Computer Vision (ECCV) Workshops (2018)

35. Bevilacqua, M., Roumy, A., Guillemot, C., Alberi-Morel, M.L.: Low-Complexity Single-Image Super-Resolution Based on Nonnegative Neighbor Embedding. BMVA Press (2012)

36. Zeyde, R., Elad, M., Protter, M.: On single image scale-up using sparse-representations. In: Boissonnat, J.-D., et al. (eds.) Curves and Surfaces 2010. LNCS, vol. 6920, pp. 711–730. Springer, Heidelberg (2012). https://doi.org/10. 1007/978-3-642-27413-8_47
37. Radford, A., et al.: Language models are unsupervised multitask learners. OpenAI Blog 1(8), 9 (2019)
38. Stephen, M., Caiming, X., James, B., Socher, R.: The wikitext long term dependency language modeling dataset (2016)
39. Wolf, T., et al.: Hugging face's transformers: state-of-the-art natural language processing. arXiv preprint arXiv:1910.03771 (2019)
40. Krishnamoorthi, R., James, R., Min, N., Chris, G., Seth, W.: Introduction to Quantization on PyTorch (2020). https://pytorch.org/blog/introduction-to-quantization-on-pytorch/
41. Wang, Z., Bovik, A.C., Sheikh, H.R., Simoncelli, E.P.: Image quality assessment: from error visibility to structural similarity. IEEE Trans. Image Process. 13(4), 600–612 (2004)
42. Bahl, L.R., Jelinek, F., Mercer, R.L.: A maximum likelihood approach to continuous speech recognition. IEEE Trans. Pattern Anal. Mach. Intell. 2, 179–190 (1983)

A Paradigm for Interval-Aware Programming

Moritz Beutel$^{(\boxtimes)}$ and Robert Strzodka

Institute of Computer Engineering (ZITI), Ruprecht-Karls-Universität Heidelberg,
Heidelberg, Germany
{moritz.beutel,robert.strzodka}@ziti.uni-heidelberg.de

Abstract. Interval arithmetic is a well-known method for obtaining exact bounds on computational results even with inexact input data and numerical error introduced by finite-precision numerics. The *posit* format, which aims to surpass the precision efficiency of the conventional IEEE 754 floating-point format, is accompanied by *valids*, an adaption and generalisation of interval arithmetic. A calculation can be performed either with posits or with valids, yielding either an approximate result with high computational efficiency or rigorous lower and upper bounds on the result. However, Boolean relational predicates such as $a < b$ are ambiguous when applied to overlapping intervals, leading to logical inconsistency no matter how the ambiguity is resolved. A numerical routine which has data-dependent branches can thus return incorrect results when applied to intervals or valids.

This paper proposes to define relational predicates for interval types as set-valued predicates instead of Boolean predicates. The proposed relational predicates are logically consistent and have intuitive projections to the two-element Boolean algebra. Using these predicates, we can express a calculation with data-dependent branches such that it can operate either on numbers or on intervals, while easily constraining interval-valued comparands by the branch condition. With such *interval-aware* code we can obtain either an approximate result or good interval bounds. We have developed a C++ library which implements the proposed concepts for traditional interval arithmetic. Furthermore, we have adapted it to a posit and valid implementation, demonstrating the viability of the concept with both traditional and more recent interval formats.

Keywords: Interval arithmetic · Posits · Valids · Set-valued predicates · Reliable computing

1 Introduction

Numerical calculations often involve and result in quantities whose exact value is not known. This can have a variety of reasons: some numbers cannot be represented exactly by the finite-precision number formats used for a calculation; some numerical methods yield only approximate results; and sometimes the input values are not known exactly.

© The Author(s), under exclusive license to Springer Nature Switzerland AG 2023
J. Gustafson et al. (Eds.): CoNGA 2023, LNCS 13851, pp. 38–60, 2023.
https://doi.org/10.1007/978-3-031-32180-1_3

The desire to propagate exact lower and upper bounds through a calculation led to the development of *interval arithmetic* [4,13,14]. The underlying idea is that, for a routine which operates on real numbers and yields a real number as a result, an *interval extension* of the routine can be constructed which operates on lower and upper bounds of real numbers and yields a lower and upper bound of the result. For example, let us consider the real-valued function

$$f(a, b) := a + b. \tag{1}$$

Given two values $\tilde{a}$ and $\tilde{b}$ which are not known precisely but can be constrained with known lower and upper bounds, $\tilde{A}^- \leq \tilde{a} \leq \tilde{A}^+$ and $\tilde{B}^- \leq \tilde{b} \leq \tilde{B}^+$, we would like to infer lower and upper bounds on $f(\tilde{a}, \tilde{b})$. To this end, we construct an interval extension of f,

$$F(A, B) := A + B. \tag{2}$$

where $A \equiv [A^-, A^+]$, $B \equiv [B^-, B^+]$ denote real-valued intervals, and where interval-valued addition is defined as

$$A + B = [A^-, A^+] + [B^-, B^+] := [A^- + B^-, A^+ + B^+]. \tag{3}$$

The interval extension of f now gives a bounding interval for $f(\tilde{a}, \tilde{b})$:

$$f(\tilde{a}, \tilde{b}) \overset{!}{\in} F(\tilde{A}, \tilde{B}) \equiv F([\tilde{A}^-, \tilde{A}^+], [\tilde{B}^-, \tilde{B}^+]). \tag{4}$$

Interval extensions can be obtained for all elementary arithmetic operations. Additionally, as stated by the 'Fundamental Theorem of Interval Arithmetic' [1,11], interval extensions are composable: given some closed-form real-valued arithmetic expression, an interval-valued variant of the expression can be obtained with a syntactical transformation by replacing every real-valued function or operator with its interval extension. For example, if the interval extensions of negation, scalar multiplication, negation, addition, and exponentiation are known, then an interval extension of an expression like $x^2 - 2x$ can be obtained by syntactically replacing every real-valued operation with its interval extension, $X^2 - 2X$, where $X \equiv [X^-, X^+]$ are bounds of $x \in X$.

The propagation of lower and upper bounds with interval arithmetic can be automated by taking advantage of the composability of interval extensions. Several software packages for interval arithmetic exist [e.g. 6,7] which supply the interval extensions of elementary arithmetic operations as building blocks, often overloading arithmetic operators to allow for a natural syntactical representation which resembles the original real-valued calculation.

Despite the availability of a general mapping of scalar-valued expressions to interval-valued expressions, it would be unreasonable to expect that regular scalar code could automatically be extended to intervals. Even when an automatic transformation is possible, the results are often worse—that is, they yield intervals wider than necessary—compared to an interval-specific implementation, largely due to the *dependency problem*, discussed in Appendix A.1.

Another reason why scalar code may be unfit for intervals is the ambiguity of relational predicates. Even a simple routine, such as an implementation of the max function

$$\max(a,b) := \begin{cases} b & \text{if } a < b \\ a & \text{otherwise,} \end{cases} \tag{5}$$

may have data-dependent branches, usually conditioned on Boolean relational predicates such as $a < b$. For real numbers a and b, such a relational predicate is either *true* or *false*. However, it is not clear how relational predicates for intervals would be interpreted. Given two intervals $A := [A^-, A^+]$ and $B := [B^-, B^+]$, the predicate $A < B$ might reasonably be *true* or *false* if the intervals are disjoint; but the relational predicate becomes ambiguous for overlapping intervals. If $A^- < B^+$ but $A^+ > B^-$, then for some values $a \in A$ and $b \in B$ the predicate $a < b$ holds *true*, but $a' < b'$ is *false* for other values $a' \in A$ and $b' \in B$.

Most software packages which implement interval arithmetic define Boolean relational predicates for intervals, resolving this ambiguity by settling for a particular interpretation. The two obvious interpretations are often referred to as 'certainly' and 'possibly' [e.g. 6,7,16], where 'certainly' uses the definition

$$A \sim B :\Leftrightarrow \forall a \in A, b \in B : a \sim b \tag{6}$$

and 'possibly' is defined by

$$A \sim B :\Leftrightarrow \exists a \in A, b \in B : a \sim b, \tag{7}$$

with '$\sim$' representing a comparison: $=, \neq, <, \leq, >, \geq$.

However, opting for just one interpretation of the relational operators has several unfortunate consequences. Resembling the scalar relational operators syntactically, they are easy to mistake for equivalence relations or total orderings which are usually defined by relational operators $=, <$, or $\leq$, thus leading to undefined behaviour when used with common algorithms and data structures. Their inherent and unavoidable logical inconsistencies lead to brittle code, the semantics of which can be inadvertently altered by seemingly innocuous transformations. In fact, this problem is not specific to interval arithmetic. A similar problem appears already with the relational predicates for IEEE 754 floating-point types, which define a special value NaN ('not a number') that has no ordering relation with real-valued or infinite floats.

In Sect. 2, we study the relational predicates commonly defined for floats, intervals, and type III unums (posits and valids), pointing out their shortcomings and exploring some of the consequences. In Sect. 3, we propose an alternative definition of set-valued relational predicates, which we then employ to write *interval-aware code*, that is, code which can operate either on scalars or on intervals, by taking advantage of the expressive freedom of the C++ programming language. In Sect. 4, we demonstrate how interval bounds can be tightened by inferring constraints from relational predicates, and how this technique can be used to obtain better bounds. Finally, in Sect. 5 we briefly discuss our reference implementation and further applications of the technique.

2 Relational Predicates

The set of real numbers $\mathbb{R}$ is totally ordered by the $\leq$ relation. This does not necessarily hold true for sets of floating-point values, which are often used to approximately represent real numbers in numerical calculations. However, the fact that the ordering is only partial is often ignored by programmers, leading to surprising and misleading results when dealing with unordered values.

2.1 IEEE 754 Floating-Point Numbers

The most prominent example of a set of floating-point values not totally ordered by the $\leq$ relation is the IEEE 754 floating-point format [2]. In addition to a finite subset of the real numbers, an IEEE 754 floating-point value, referred to as 'float' henceforth, can represent positive and negative infinity as well as a range of special values subsumed under the term 'not a number' (NaN). These values, which emerge for example as the result of undefined arithmetic operations such as $0 \div 0$, have no ordering relation with real-valued or infinite floats; they are unordered values in the partially ordered set of floats. NaN values tend to have 'contagious' semantics: according to the IEEE 754 standard, an arithmetic operation that involves at least one NaN value should produce a NaN as output value [2, §6.2.3]. Although the philosophical and practical value of NaNs has been disputed—some authors have called it a 'logical error [to assign] a number to something that is, by definition, not a number' [10]—, their contagious nature helps by propagating arithmetic undefinedness, clearly marking the result of a calculation invalid if it comprises an invalid operation or operates on invalid input, and thereby preventing oversight of mathematical or logical mistakes.

Unlike floats, integral and Boolean data types usually have no representation of an invalid value. Therefore, a NaN cannot be propagated to an integral or Boolean result. To avoid sweeping errors under the rug, the IEEE 754 standard specifies that attempting to convert a NaN value to an integer type without a NaN representation shall cause an invalid operation exception [2, §5.8]. Likewise, the standard defines *unordered-signaling predicates* $=, >, \geq, <, \leq$, 'intended for use by programs *not* written to take into account the possibility of NaN operands' [2, §5.11], which cause an invalid operation exception if either operand is NaN.

Unfortunately, many implementations do not obey the IEEE 754 standard with regard to float-to-integer conversion and relational predicates. Most C and C++ compilers (e.g. GCC, Clang, Microsoft Visual C++) do not raise an invalid operation exception when converting a NaN value to an integer type, and the relational operators $=, >, \geq, <, \leq$ for floats are usually taken to be the *unordered-quiet predicates* which evaluate to *false* if either operand is NaN. With NaNs, the negations of unordered-quiet predicates $>, \geq, <, \leq$ are not equivalent to their inversion: for instance, the predicate $x > \text{NaN}$ is *false*, and thus its logical negation $\neg(x > \text{NaN})$ is *true*; but the inverse predicate $x \leq \text{NaN}$ is also *false*, and therefore $\neg(x > y)$ and $x \leq y$ are not equivalent.

The consequences are most easily observed with the mundane library function `max`, of which a possible definition is given in Listing 1.1. This definition of the `max` function has two flaws: it is not strictly commutative, and it does not always propagate NaN values. Both flaws are readily demonstrated by evaluating `max(0.f, NAN)` and `max(NAN, 0.f)`, which yields `0.f` and `NaN`, respectively. The flaws can both be attributed to the non-equivalence of negated and inverted relational predicates: the `else` clause, which amounts to a logical negation of the `if` condition in Line 2, has the semantic meaning '$a \geq b$ or a, b unordered', which differs from the semantic meaning '$a \geq b$' that was intended by the programmer.

One possibility of rectifying these flaws would be to explicitly check for a partial ordering. We instead opt to express the function with a default value and *without using logical negations*, cf. Listing 1.2. Instead of expressing the piecewise function definition as the usual `if-else` chain, we use independent `if` statements with the understanding that *none of them might be executed*, in which case the default value `empty` is returned.

Expressing the relational conditions without logical negations resulted in the desired semantics in this case; but the actual rules for NaN-sensitive programming are necessarily more complicated. A NaN-aware program may employ logical negations but must place them carefully to ensure that a NaN argument ends up 'on the correct side' of a relational predicate. For example, let an interval $[a, b]$ be defined by the two numbers a and b with $a \leq b$. We could ensure that two floats `a`, `b` define a valid interval with the following runtime check:

```
1 if (!(a <= b)) throw std::invalid_argument("no interval");
```

This code appears to be unnecessarily convoluted, and an unsuspecting maintainer might be tempted to 'simplify' it:

```
1 if (a > b) throw std::invalid_argument("no interval");
```

But this apparent simplification changes the semantics of the code with regard to NaN arguments: the first version throws an exception if either `a` or `b` is NaN, whereas the second version does not.

Both examples highlight the inherent brittleness of NaN-sensitive code. Additionally, the fact that the unordered-quiet flavour of the equality predicate evaluates to *false* if either argument is NaN is often overlooked but has confusing implications of its own. A NaN value does not compare equal with itself, implying that negated self-comparison can evaluate to *true*:

```
1 if (a != a) throw std::invalid_argument("a is NaN");
```

Being non-reflexive, the equality predicate thus cannot be an equivalence relation, which undermines an elementary assumption commonly made for regular types. For general-purpose algorithms and data structures which rely on an equivalence relation (e.g. hash sets), or which require that an equivalence relation can be obtained from the relational predicate `<` using logical negation and the identity $a = b \Leftrightarrow \neg(a < b \lor a > b)$ (e.g. sort, binary search), the occurrence of NaNs thus silently causes undefined behaviour, which may become manifest in 'impossible' runtime actions or seemingly inexplicable corruption of data structures.

To formalise our observations: a set of relational predicates $=, \neq, <, \leq$ shall be called *logically consistent* if the following identities hold for all values a, b:

$$a = b \;\Leftrightarrow\; \neg\,(a \neq b)\,, \tag{8}$$

$$a < b \;\Leftrightarrow\; \neg\,(b \leq a)\,, \tag{9}$$

$$a = b \;\Leftrightarrow\; \neg\,(a < b \vee b < a)\,. \tag{10}$$

The unordered-quiet predicates for floats are not logically consistent, as neither of the three identities holds true in the presence of the NaN value. NaN-sensitive code thus must not rely on either of these identities.

2.2   Posits

Posits, also known as *type III unums*, are an alternative number format proposed by Gustafson [10], among other things designed to be simpler than IEEE 754 floats both conceptually and in terms of the required implementation effort. One of the key differences in the initial proposal was that '[there] are no "NaN" (not-a-number) bit representations with posits; instead, the calculation is interrupted, and the interrupt handler can be set to report the error and its cause, or invoke a workaround and continue computing' [10, §2.4], although more recent revisions of the posit specification have revised the stance that invalid calculations must cause an interrupt [3]. Posits can represent one special value which is not a real number. This value is usually designated as complex infinity, $\pm\infty$. The revised posit specification subsumes the special value under the umbrella term 'not a real' (NaR) and states the following guiding principle for it: 'If an operation usually produces real-valued output, any NaR input produces NaR output', making NaR semantically equivalent to the 'quiet NaN' value in IEEE 754 floating-point arithmetic, that is, a special value which propagates the state of invalidity through calculations.

However, for the purpose of comparisons the posit specification treats the special value as negative infinity, $-\infty$: according to [10, §2.4], '[posits] share the same $a < b$ relation as signed integers', and because the special value is represented as the bit pattern with only the most significant bit set, it corresponds to the smallest representable integer in a two's complement representation, and is thus considered 'less than' any other representable value, a corollary explicitly confirmed by the posit specification [3].

A conforming posit implementation which interprets the special value as negative infinity will exhibit no surprising behaviour with relational comparisons: the relational predicates are logically consistent as per Eqs. (8–10), the equality predicate $=$ defines an equivalence relation, and the predicates $<$ and $\leq$ define a strict and a non-strict total order, respectively, on the set of all posit values. A `max` function implemented as in Listing 1.1 remains commutative in the face of NaRs; however, it does not promote invalidity: if only one argument is NaR, the other argument, which always compares greater than NaR, will be returned.

Diverging from the posit specification, some implementations of posits [e.g. 15] do away with the ambivalent interpretation of the NaR value and consistently take it to be complex infinity, defining the ordering predicate $<$ as *false* if either operand is $\pm\infty$. With this interpretation, the set of relational predicates is not logically consistent, and the incongruence discussed for NaN floats in Sect. 2.1 will arise.

2.3   Valids and Intervals

In [10], posits were introduced along with *valids*, defined as 'a pair of equal-size posits, each ending in a ubit', with the ubit indicating 'whether a real number is an exact float or lies in the open interval between adjacent floats'. Arguing that posits and IEEE 754 floats were designed to be 'cheap, fast and "good enough" for an established set of applications', valids were proposed as the rigorous counterpart of posits, allowing determination of exact lower and upper bounds of numerically computed quantities, as can be achieved for floating-point numbers with traditional interval arithmetic.

A *valid* usually represents an open, half-open, or closed interval of real numbers. Unlike posits, valids have not yet been defined exactly by Gustafson in [9]. However, a formal definition of valids has been suggested by Schärtl [15], who also developed an implementation of posits and valids—to our knowledge, the only existing and publicly accessible implementation of valids at this time—as part of the *aarith* library [12]. The definition of valids given by [15] adheres to the principle of having all possible bit patterns correspond to legitimate value representations which had been upheld in the definition of posits and was reinforced with regard to valids in [9]. With this definition, a valid can represent the following types of sets:

- the *empty set* $\varnothing$;
- the *full set* $\mathbb{R} \cup \{\text{NaR}\}$;
- *regular valids*, that is, unit sets containing a single real value $\{a\}$, the proper intervals $[a, b]$, $(a, b]$, $[a, b)$, (a, b), and the improper intervals $(-\infty, b]$, $(-\infty, b)$, $[a, \infty)$, (a, ∞), and $(-\infty, \infty) = \mathbb{R}$, where $a, b \in \mathbb{R}$, $a < b$;
- *irregular valids*, the complements of regular valids, that is, the set difference $(\mathbb{R} \cup \{\text{NaR}\}) \setminus V$ of the full set and a given regular valid $V \subsetneq \mathbb{R}$; among them a unit set $\{\text{NaR}\}$ containing the NaR value.

Valids are conceptually similar to intervals in traditional interval arithmetic, but can be considered superior in several ways, in particular because half-open and open intervals can be represented, whereas traditional interval arithmetic is defined only for closed intervals.

Lacking a formal definition, the exact semantics originally envisioned for valids, in particular the semantics of the relational predicates for valids, are not known. However, valids are modelled after *ubounds* [cf. 9, §3.6], an interval-like construct based on type I unums; and '[for] a ubound u to be less than a ubound v, the maximum of u must be less than the minimum of v' [8, §8.1]. The ubound interpretation of relational ordering thus corresponds to 'certainly' semantics of Eq. (6). In the implementation of Schärtl [15], the same semantics had been

Table 1. Results of the generic max function in Listing 1.1 for different interval arguments assuming either 'possibly' or 'certainly' semantics for relational predicates, compared to fiducial results as per Eq. (11). Wrong results are highlighted with red background, excessive results (i.e. resulting intervals which contain but also exceed the fiducial result) are highlighted with yellow background.

		fiducial result	'possibly' semantics		'certainly' semantics	
A	B	$\text{Max}(A,B)$	$\text{max}(A,B)$	$\text{max}(B,A)$	$\text{max}(A,B)$	$\text{max}(B,A)$
$[0,2]$	$[3,6]$	$[3,6]$	$[3,6]$	$[3,6]$	$[3,6]$	$[3,6]$
$[2,4]$	$[3,6]$	$[3,6]$	$[3,6]$	$[2,4]$	$[2,4]$	$[3,6]$
$[4,5]$	$[3,6]$	$[4,6]$	$[3,6]$	$[4,5]$	$[4,5]$	$[3,6]$

chosen for valids, with the caveat that the NaR value is treated as complex infinity, and thus as unordered with regard to real numbers.

Gustafson [8] also discusses predicates for equality and inequality. Given two valids X, Y, an obvious candidate for an equality relation would be set equality, which is an equivalence relation. However, as noted in [8, §8.2], a different notion of equality, there referred to as 'not nowhere equal', is often more useful. This notion matches the 'possibly' interpretation of Eq. (7). Unlike the set equality relation, it does not constitute an equivalence relation because it is not transitive. Likewise, one could also define an equality relation with 'certainly' semantics; in this interpretation, two sets would be considered 'certainly equal' only if either set is empty or if both sets are identical single-element sets, and the $=$ relation would not be an equivalence relation because it is not reflexive.

Whichever interpretation of the relational predicates is chosen, it can easily be verified that the set of interval predicates $=, \neq, <, \leq$ cannot be logically consistent. Checking the definitions of Eqs. (8–10) with the counterexample $a = b = [0,1]$, we find all three identities invalid using either the 'certainly' or the 'possibly' semantics for relational predicates. The consequences are similar to those discussed for floats with NaN values in Sect. 2.1. To illustrate, let us consider how the generic implementation of the max function given in Listing 1.1 would behave if the relational predicates adhered to 'certainly' or 'possibly' semantics. A fiducial max function for set arguments could be defined as

$$\text{Max}(X,Y) := \{\max(x,y) \mid x \in X, y \in Y\}. \tag{11}$$

For either 'certainly' or 'possibly' semantics, the generic implementation of the max function is not correct, and not even commutative, as is evident from the results in Table 1.

3   Set-Valued Logic

According to [9], posits and valids are considered 'two modes of operation, selectable by the user'. Although the referenced work acknowledges that 'algorithms for valids are often quite different from the ones for floats, and vice versa', it implies that valids and posits should be exchangeable to some extent, for instance in the recommendation that 'valids are for where you need a provable bound on the answer. Or when you are still developing an algorithm and debugging its numerical behavior'. Traditional interval arithmetic has often been used in a similar manner, relying on the 'Fundamental Theorem of Interval Arithmetic' discussed in Sect. 1. Defining relational predicates seems to be worthwhile and even necessary to allow writing generic code which can work with either scalar values or with intervals or valids. This section explores how to define relational predicates in a way that retains logical consistency and avoids the pitfalls discussed in Sect. 2.

3.1   Set-Extended Relational Predicates

Although Boolean relational predicates can be and have been defined for floats with NaNs, for intervals, and for valids, in the preceding sections we have seen that they are logically inconsistent, which makes them error-prone even in targeted use. Moreover, they lack properties commonly expected from relational predicates in generic code such as reflexivity and transitivity, and thus easily lead to unexpected or undefined behaviour.

The core of the problem is the definition of relational predicates as Boolean predicates. For real numbers, the Boolean relational predicates $=, \neq, <, \leq$ are intuitive, well-defined, and logically consistent; $=$ is an equivalence relation, $<$ defines a strict total order, and $\leq$ defines a non-strict total order. But let us consider how floats with NaNs would be represented mathematically. A float can be either some real number or 'not a number'; in mathematical terms, it is either a unit set $\{x\}$ containing a real number $x \in \mathbb{R}$, or the empty set. Likewise, valids can represent certain subsets of $\mathbb{R} \cup \{\text{NaR}\}$, including the empty set. But if floats and intervals represent sets of real numbers, then relational predicates of floats or intervals should represent sets of Booleans. Given a Boolean predicate $\sim \colon \mathbb{R} \times \mathbb{R} \to \mathbb{B}$, where $\mathbb{B} = \{\mathit{false}, \mathit{true}\}$ denotes the two-element Boolean algebra, we can thus define a general set extension of the predicate as

$$F_\sim(A, B) := \begin{cases} \{\mathit{false}\}, & \text{if } \exists a \in A, b \in B : \neg(a \sim b) \\ \varnothing, & \text{otherwise,} \end{cases}$$

$$T_\sim(A, B) := \begin{cases} \{\mathit{true}\}, & \text{if } \exists a \in A, b \in B : a \sim b \\ \varnothing, & \text{otherwise,} \end{cases}$$

$$A \sim B := F_\sim(A, B) \cup T_\sim(A, B) \tag{12}$$

for any two subsets $A, B \subseteq \mathbb{R}$.

Although it looks complicated, the definition is intuitive. To assemble the relational predicate $A \sim B$, we start with an empty set. Then, if any pair of elements $a \in A$, $b \in B$ exists for which the Boolean relational predicate $a \sim b$ does not hold true, we insert false into the set. Likewise, if any pair of elements $a \in A$, $b \in B$ exists for which the Boolean relational predicate $a \sim b$ holds true, we insert true into the set. We end up with one of the following sets: $\varnothing$, $\{\mathit{false}\}$,

Table 2. Truth tables for conjunction, disjunction, and negation in the $\mathcal{P}(\mathbb{B})$ logic as per Eqs. (14–16).

$A \wedge B$		B				$A \vee B$		B			
		None	*False*	*True*	*Both*			*None*	*False*	*True*	*Both*
	None	*None*	*None*	*None*	*None*		*None*	*None*	*None*	*None*	*None*
A	*False*	*None*	*False*	*False*	*False*	A	*False*	*None*	*False*	*True*	*Both*
	True	*None*	*False*	*True*	*Both*		*True*	*None*	*True*	*True*	*True*
	Both	*None*	*False*	*Both*	*Both*		*Both*	*None*	*Both*	*True*	*Both*

A	$\neg A$
None	*None*
False	*True*
True	*False*
Both	*Both*

Table 3. Truth tables for Boolean projections from $\mathcal{P}(\mathbb{B})$ as per Eqs. (17–20).

A	POSSIBLY A	ALWAYS A	CONTINGENT A	VACUOUS A
None	*false*	*true*	*false*	*true*
False	*false*	*false*	*false*	*false*
True	*true*	*true*	*false*	*false*
Both	*true*	*false*	*true*	*false*

$\{true\}$, or $\{false, true\}$, in other words: with an element of the *powerset of the two-element Boolean algebra*, $\mathcal{P}(\mathbb{B})$, which itself is a 4-valued logic. We identify its elements with the following intuitive names:

$$None \equiv \varnothing, \quad False \equiv \{false\}, \quad True \equiv \{true\}, \quad Both \equiv \{false, true\}. \quad (13)$$

We can infer the truth tables for the $\mathcal{P}(\mathbb{B})$ logic, reproduced in Table 2, by defining their logical operators $\wedge$, $\vee$, $\neg$ as set extensions of the corresponding Boolean operators:

$$U \wedge V := \{u \wedge v \mid u \in U, v \in V\}, \quad (14)$$

$$U \vee V := \{u \vee v \mid u \in U, v \in V\}, \quad (15)$$

$$\neg U := \{\neg u \mid u \in U\} \quad (16)$$

for any two subsets of the Boolean powerset logic $U, V \in \mathcal{P}(\mathbb{B})$. When defined as a set extension as per Eq. (12), the relational predicates $=, \neq, <, \leq$ are logically consistent because the identities given in Eqs. (8–10) hold.

Programs usually employ relational predicates to make binary choices: to jump or not to jump, tertium non datur. Thus, if relational predicates are $\mathcal{P}(\mathbb{B})$-valued instead of $\mathbb{B}$-valued, a program must be able to interpret them as Boolean value somehow. We thus need to define suitable projections. Following up on the previous attempts to define relational predicates for intervals, we find the two intuitive projections POSSIBLY and ALWAYS, defined as

$$\text{POSSIBLY}\, U := \textit{true} \in U, \tag{17}$$

$$\text{ALWAYS}\, U := \textit{false} \notin U \tag{18}$$

for any set-valued element $U \in \mathcal{P}(\mathbb{B})$. We emphasise that, by virtue of its anti-symmetric definition, the ALWAYS projection yields vacuous truth for an empty set U. We go on to define two more useful projections:

$$\text{CONTINGENT}\, U := (U \equiv \textit{Both}), \tag{19}$$

$$\text{VACUOUS}\, U := (U \equiv \varnothing). \tag{20}$$

Truth tables for all four projections are shown in Table 3.

With the POSSIBLY and ALWAYS projections, we can interpret a given relational predicate as having either 'possibly' or 'certainly' semantics. But unlike in previous attempts at defining relational predicates for intervals, the semantic interpretation is not attached to the predicate itself. A projection can be applied to a more complex logical expression as well, such as POSSIBLY $(x < -1 \vee x > 1)$ or ALWAYS $(a \leq x < b)$, allowing for intuitive expressive freedom. Because the relational operators do not evaluate to Boolean values, they are not directly compatible with algorithms or data structures expecting Boolean predicates, thereby forcing the user to explicitly choose a particular projection.

3.2   Writing NaN-Aware Code

We revisit the precondition-checking examples from Sect. 2.1. Given two scalar numbers a and b, we want to verify that they define a valid interval by asserting that $a \leq b$. If floats were considered sets containing either a single real number or nothing to indicate NaN ('not a number'), and if the relational operators for floats were defined according to Eq. (12) and returned $\mathcal{P}(\mathbb{B})$ values, we would write the check as

```
1 if (!possibly(a <= b)) {
2     throw std::invalid_argument("no interval");
3 }
```

If either `a` or `b` was NaN, the predicate `a <= b` would evaluate to `None`, and `possibly(None)` is `false`; therefore, a NaN value will trigger the exception.

The check can be simplified to avoid the negation. However, the negation of a Boolean condition is not the same as a logical negation of the set-valued predicate. Thanks to the Boolean projections, the difference is evident: $\neg\text{POSSIBLY}\, U$ is clearly a different logical statement than POSSIBLY $\neg U$. We find that the following intuitive identities hold among projections:

$$\neg\text{ALWAYS}\,U \quad \Leftrightarrow \quad \text{POSSIBLY}\,\neg U \tag{21}$$

$$\neg\text{POSSIBLY}\,U \quad \Leftrightarrow \quad \text{ALWAYS}\,\neg U \tag{22}$$

$$\text{CONTINGENT}\,U \quad \Leftrightarrow \quad \text{POSSIBLY}\,U \wedge \text{POSSIBLY}\,\neg U \tag{23}$$

$$\text{VACUOUS}\,U \quad \Leftrightarrow \quad \text{ALWAYS}\,U \wedge \text{ALWAYS}\,\neg U \tag{24}$$

Using Eq. (22), we can thus rewrite the check as

```
if (always(!(a <= b))) {
    throw std::invalid_argument("no interval");
}
```

and, taking advantage of logical consistency, we can get rid of the negation by inverting the relational operator with the identity Eq. (9):

```
if (always(a > b)) {
    throw std::invalid_argument("no interval");
}
```

which is as close as possible to the simplest but NaN-ignorant condition $a > b$ in Sect. 2.1.

3.3   Writing Interval-Aware Code

Based on the ideas presented in Sect. 3.1, we now demonstrate how to express a routine like the max function such that it yields correct results for floats, posits, intervals, and valids (and also for floats with NaNs if the C++ language actually allowed redefining their built-in comparison operators).

In Listing 1.3 we give a new definition of a generic max function. The function signature is identical to the first definition in Listing 1.1, but the function was restructured in a fashion similar to the version in Listing 1.2: instead of if–else chains, if branches are expressed independently with the understanding that *none, one, or multiple branches might be executed*. Instead of directly returning a result, values are now accumulated in a local result variable, which is initialised with some generic empty value, empty, which equals NaN for floats, NaR for posits, an empty set for valids, or an uninitialised value for float-valued intervals. The branch condition $a < b$ is assumed to be set-valued, $(a < b) \in \mathcal{P}(\mathbb{B})$, and hence a Boolean projection has to be used to make a branching decision.

For multi-valued arguments a or b (i.e. intervals or valids), the two Boolean conditions possibly(a < b) and possibly(a >= b) are not necessarily exclusive: if both arguments overlap, both conditions evaluate to *true*, and both branches are executed. To avoid that an assignment from the previous branch is over-written, conditional assignment must be performed with a function assign_par tial which *integrates* the given value in the destination variable. For floats or posits, assign_partial(x, a) asserts that x is still empty and then executes the assignment x = a. For intervals and valids, assign_partial(x, a) widens the set represented by x such that it encloses a.

```
1 template <typename T>
2 T max(T a, T b) {
3     if (a < b) return b;
4     else return a;
5 }
```

Listing 1.1. Definition of a generic max function (Eq. (5)) in C++.

```
1 constexpr float empty = NAN;
2 template <std::floating_point T>
3 T max(T a, T b) {
4     T x = empty;
5     if (a < b) x = b;
6     if (a >= b) x = a;
7     return x;
8 }
```

Listing 1.2. NaN-aware definition of the max function in C++.

```
1 template <typename T>
2 T max2(T a, T b) {
3     T x = empty;
4     if (possibly(a < b)) assign_partial(x, b);
5     if (possibly(a >= b)) assign_partial(x, a);
6     return x;
7 }
```

Listing 1.3. Interval-aware definition of a generic max function in C++.

```
1 template <typename T>
2 T max3(T a, T b) {
3     T x = empty;
4     auto c = (a < b);
5     if (possibly(c)) {
6         auto bc = constrain(b, c);
7         assign_partial(x, bc);
8     }
9     if (possibly(!c)) {
10        auto ac = constrain(a, !c);
11        assign_partial(x, ac);
12    }
13    return x;
14 }
```

Listing 1.4. Optimal interval-aware definition of a generic max function in C++.

Some results for the revised `max2` function of Listing 1.3 are shown in Table 4. The `max` routine is now commutative and returns correct results for all cases, although some results are too wide.

We emphasise that the C++ language does not allow to redefine operators such as `==` and `<` for built-in data types such as `float`. Therefore, when calling the revised `max2` function with arguments of type `float`, relational comparisons would in reality exhibit the traditional *unordered-quiet* behaviour. To actually obtain the results for NaN floats in Table 4, a user-defined data type would have to be created which wraps `float` but has set-valued relational operators.

Table 4. Results of the revised interval-aware generic max function in Listing 1.3 for different interval arguments, compared to fiducial results as per Eq. (11). Excessive results (that is, resulting intervals which contain but also exceed the fiducial result) are highlighted with yellow background. For floats and intervals, NaN is considered semantically equivalent to the empty set. For posits and valids, NaR is treated as negative infinity. Intervals cannot represent the empty set, but our interval datatype permits an uninitialised state. With '3](6' we denote the irregular valid $(\mathbb{R} \cup \{\text{NaR}\}) \setminus (3, 6]$.

			fiducial result	experimental results	
domain type	A	B	$\text{Max}(A, B)$	$\texttt{max2}(A, B)$	$\texttt{max2}(B, A)$
floats	NaN	0	NaN	NaN	NaN
posits	NaR	0	0	0	0
posits	NaR	NaR	NaR	NaR	NaR
intervals	$[0, 2]$	$[3, 6]$	$[3, 6]$	$[3, 6]$	$[3, 6]$
intervals	$[0, 2]$	$[3, 6]$	$[3, 6]$	$[3, 6]$	$[3, 6]$
intervals	$[2, 4]$	$[3, 6]$	$[3, 6]$	$[2, 6]$	$[2, 6]$
intervals	$[4, 5]$	$[3, 6]$	$[4, 6]$	$[3, 6]$	$[3, 6]$
valids	NaR	0	0	0	0
valids	NaR	NaR	NaR	NaR	NaR
valids	$[2, 4]$	$(3, \infty)$	$(3, \infty)$	$[2, \infty)$	$[2, \infty)$
valids	$[2, 4]$	$[-\infty, 6]$	$[2, 6]$	$[-\infty, 6]$	$[-\infty, 6]$
valids	$[2, 4]$	$3](6$	$[2, \infty)$	$[-\infty, \infty)$	$[-\infty, \infty)$

4   Constraints

To understand why some of the results returned by `max2` are wider than necessary, consider the example of $a = [2, 4]$, $b = [3, 6]$. Because the two intervals overlap, both relational predicates $a < b$ and $a \geq b$ evaluate to *Both*, which is then mapped to *true* by the POSSIBLY projection. The `assign_partial(x, b)` statement in the first branch finds x uninitialised and thus initialises it with the value of b, $[3, 6]$. In the second branch, the statement `assign_partial(x, a)` widens the interval x such that it encloses all of a.

This behaviour is clearly suboptimal. Although not obvious in this case, it is also wrong, as can be demonstrated with `clampedSqrt`, a simple function which uses its branch conditions to retain its well-definedness for all real arguments. A conventional definition is given in Listing 1.5, and an attempt at crafting an interval-aware variant is shown in Listing 1.6. It is clear from the conventional definition that the function is well-defined for both negative and non-negative arguments. However, when passing the interval $[-1, 4]$ to the `clampedSqrt2` function, both branches are executed, and the `sqrt` function, which is not defined for negative arguments, is thus called with an interval argument $[-1, 4]$.

As expressed by its branch predicate, the first branch of the `clampedSqrt2` function should contribute to the result only for arguments ≥ 0. Thus, an

Table 5. Results of the revised interval-aware generic max function in Listing 1.4 for different interval arguments, compared to fiducial results as per Eq. (11). Results which are now optimally tight are highlighted with green background.

domain type	A	B	fiducial result Max(A,B)	experimental results max3(A,B)	max3(B,A)
intervals	$[2,4]$	$[3,6]$	$[3,6]$	$[3,6]$	$[3,6]$
intervals	$[4,5]$	$[3,6]$	$[4,6]$	$[4,6]$	$[4,6]$
valids	$[2,4]$	$(3,\infty)$	$(3,\infty)$	$(3,\infty)$	$(3,\infty)$
valids	$[2,4]$	$[-\infty,6]$	$[2,6]$	$[2,6]$	$[2,6]$
valids	$[2,4]$	$3](6$	$[2,\infty)$	$[2,\infty)$	$[2,\infty)$

interval-aware function needs to constrain its arguments inside branches according to the respective branch conditions. More generally, inside a branch with a Boolean predicate of the form POSSIBLY $P(A,B)$ where P is some $\mathcal{P}(\mathbb{B})$-valued logical predicate which itself is the interval extension of a logical predicate $p(a,b)$, the interval value A can be constrained as

$$A|P(A,B) := \{a \in A \,|\, \exists b \in B : p(a,b)\}. \qquad (25)$$

It turns out that constraints can be inferred from branch predicates, and that this process can be automated. For automatic derivation of constraints, we only impose the practical requirement that a given branch condition must be composed of *linear* relational predicates: a constraint can be inferred for an interval or valid x only if it appears in the branch condition as $x \sim \xi$ or $\xi \sim x$, where $\sim$ is one of the relational operators and ξ stands for an arbitrary real-valued, interval-valued, or valid-valued expression. As an example, no constraint for x could be inferred from the relation $x^2 \leq 1$; to permit automatic constraint inference, the condition would have to be expressed in linear form, $x \geq -1 \land x \leq 1$. Relational predicates can then be arbitrarily combined with other logical expressions using the logical operators $\land$, $\lor$, and $\neg$.

We note that the requirement of linearity is imposed only for practical reasons; it could be overcome by an implementation capable of symbolically solving the predicate expression for the variable to be constrained. In the above example, the inequality $x^2 \leq 1$ would first need to be solved for x symbolically before deriving a constraint with the rules for automatic inference.

The automatic inference of constraints is demonstrated in the final revisions of the max and clampedSqrt functions in Listings 1.4 and 1.7. The updated results for the max3 function are presented in Table 5. In both code listings, the logical condition is stored in a variable c, from which the constrain function then infers which constraints the given interval can be subjected to. In max3, Line 6, the constrain function imposes the constraint $a < b$ on the variable b and returns its constrained value; for example, if a and b are closed intervals, $a \equiv [A^-, A^+]$, $b \equiv [B^-, B^+]$, then constrain(b,c) infers the constrained interval

$$[B_c^-, B_c^+] = \begin{cases} (A^-, B^+] & \text{if } A^- \geq B^- \\ [B^-, B^+] & \text{otherwise,} \end{cases} \tag{26}$$

in the first case omitting the part of the interval $[B^-, A^-]$ for which the condition can never be fulfilled. Because traditional interval arithmetic does not represent half-open intervals, the slightly excessive closed interval $[A^-, B^+]$ is produced instead of the correct interval $(A^-, B^+]$. With valids, the half-open interval can be represented correctly, and hence more accurate constraints are possible.

Thanks to inference of constraints, both `max3` and `clampedSqrt3` are well-defined interval extensions returning optimal results. In Listing 1.8, we also demonstrate how the technique applies to multiple branches, specifically for linear interpolation,

$$y(x) = \begin{cases} y_1 & \text{if } x < x_1 \\ y_1 + \frac{x-x_1}{x_2-x_1}(y_2 - y_1) & \text{if } x_1 \leq x \leq x_2 \\ y_2 & \text{if } x > x_2, \end{cases} \tag{27}$$

also yielding optimal results. The inferred constraint ensures that the quotient $(x - x_1)(x_2 - x_1)$ in the $x_1 \leq x < x_2$ branch never exceeds $[0, 1]$.

5 Implementation

We have developed a C++ library, aptly named *intervals* [5], which implements traditional interval arithmetic along with $\mathcal{P}(\mathbb{B})$-valued relational predicates, Boolean projections, and automatic inference of constraints.

The library defines a class template `interval<T>`, which represents a closed interval of floating-point numbers of type `T`, and a class template `set<B>` which represents an element of the powerset of the type `B`. The elementary arithmetic operations and most standard mathematical functions are overloaded for `interval<T>`; and the logical operators &, |, and ! (but not the short-circuiting variants && and ||) are overloaded for `set<bool>`. Additional function definitions such as `possibly`, `constrain`, `assign_partial` are provided to enable interval-aware programming as demonstrated in Listings 1.4, 1.7, and 1.8. When instantiated for non-interval types, these functions degenerate to trivial operations and introduce no runtime overhead, in particular `possibly(c)` becomes c, `constrain(x,c)` becomes x, and `assign_partial(y,x)` becomes y = x.

Taking the interval-awareness paradigm further, the library also supports interval arithmetic with integral numbers and random-access iterators, which the `interval<T>` class template can be instantiated with as well. Algorithms such as `lower_bound` (implementing binary search) can then be defined for interval-valued arguments, returning intervals of iterators, demonstrated with a piecewise linear interpolation routine in Appendix A.3.

```
1 float clampedSqrt(float x) {
2     if (x >= 0) return sqrt(x);
3     else return 0;
4 }
```

Listing 1.5. Definition of a clamped square root function in C++.

```
1 template <typename T>
2 T clampedSqrt2(T x) {
3     T y = empty;
4     if (possibly(x >= 0)) assign_partial(y, sqrt(x));
5     if (possibly(x < 0)) assign_partial(y, 0);
6     return y;
7 }
```

Listing 1.6. Interval-aware but ill-defined clamped square root function in C++.

```
1 template <typename T>
2 T clampedSqrt3(T x) {
3     T y = empty;
4     auto c = (x >= 0);
5     if (possibly(c)) {
6         auto xc = constrain(x, c);
7         assign_partial(y, sqrt(xc));
8     }
9     if (possibly(!c)) {
10        assign_partial(y, 0);
11    }
12    return y;
13 }
```

Listing 1.7. Corrected interval-aware clamped square root function in C++.

```
1 template <typename T, typename FloatT>
2 T interpolateLinear(T x,
3         FloatT x1, FloatT x2, FloatT y1, FloatT y2) {
4     T y = empty;
5     auto below = (x < x1);
6     if (possibly(below)) assign_partial(y, y1);
7     auto above = (x > x2);
8     if (possibly(above)) assign_partial(y, y2);
9     auto c = !below & !above;
10    if (possibly(c)) {
11        auto xc = constrain(x, c);
12        assign_partial(y,
13            y1 + (xc - x1)/(x2 - x1)*(y2 - y1));
14    }
15    return y;
16 }
```

Listing 1.8. Interval-aware linear interpolation in C++.

Based on the posit and valid implementation developed by Schärtl [15] as part of the *aarith* library [12], we also ported the interval-aware infrastructure of the *intervals* library to posits and valids, demonstrating that *valid-aware programs* can be written using the same principles. The multitude of possible combinations of closed, half-open, open intervals and irregular valids renders constraint inference much more complicated than for the closed intervals of traditional interval arithmetics, but in reward the inferred constraints can be more precise than with traditional interval arithmetic.

Although our prototype implementation has been written in C++, we emphasise that the proposed paradigm is not specific to this language. In fact, the handling of logical constraints and branch assignment with `constrain` and `assign_partial`, while consistent and straightforward, is still verbose in our implementation; a domain-specific language aware of set-valued logical predicates and relational constraints could provide more concise syntax and automatically infer and apply constraints, possibly even non-linear constraints, inside branches.

6   Conclusion

In this work we have discussed the shortcomings of traditional definitions of relational predicates for IEEE 754 floating-point types, intervals, and valids. Pursuing the goal of writing *interval-aware code*, that is, code that can work either with numbers or with intervals, we have proposed a set-valued definition of relational predicates as a better alternative, overcoming the logical inconsistencies inherent to Boolean relational predicates on intervals and allowing for intuitive expression of conditionals with intervals. We have demonstrated that branch conditions composed from relational predicates can be used to constrain interval arguments inside the branch, and that the inference of constraints from a logical predicate can be automated. We have tested the viability of the proposed ideas by developing a library, *intervals*, which implements the proposed techniques for traditional interval arithmetic. Additionally, we have augmented an existing implementation of valids with the proposed set-valued relational predicates and worked out the corresponding constraint inference logic for valids, showing that the same principles can be applied to write *valid-aware code*, allowing for more accurate constraints since valids can also represent half-open or open intervals.

Acknowledgements. We would like to thank Cornelis P. Dullemond and Charlotte Boys for valuable feedback and useful discussions, and Andreas Schärtl and Oliver Keszöcze for granting us access to their implementation of posits and valids. This work is funded by the Deutsche Forschungsgemeinschaft (DFG, German Research Foundation) under Germany's Excellence Strategy EXC 2181/1-390900948 (the Heidelberg STRUCTURES Excellence Cluster).

A   Appendix

A.1   The Dependency Problem

The *dependency problem* [e.g. 8, §16.2f], is a fundamental limitation of interval arithmetic which is rooted in the fact that correlations or dependencies between quantities cannot be represented in their bounding intervals, resulting in unnecessarily loose bounds. The problem becomes apparent already in the simple example given in Sect. 1.

Let us first define some elementary interval operations as

$$[X^-, X^+]^2 := \begin{cases} [0, (\max\{-X^-, X^+\})^2] & \text{if } 0 \in X \\ [(X^-)^2, (X^+)^2] & \text{if } X^- > 0 \\ [(X^+)^2, (X^-)^2] & \text{if } X^+ < 0 \end{cases} \tag{28}$$

$$a[X^-, X^+] := \begin{cases} [aX^-, aX^+] & \text{if } a \geq 0 \\ [aX^+, aX^-] & \text{if } a < 0 \end{cases} \tag{29}$$

$$-[X^-, X^+] := [-X^+, -X^-] \tag{30}$$

$$X + Y := [X^- + Y^-, X^+ + Y^+]. \tag{31}$$

We only state the definitions for closed intervals for simplicity, but analogous definitions for half-open and open intervals are known.

Now, as per the Fundamental Theorem of Interval Arithmetic [1,11], an interval extension of the algebraic expression

$$x^2 - 2x \tag{32}$$

can be obtained as the composition of interval extensions of the constituting operations,

$$X^2 - 2X, \tag{33}$$

where $X \equiv [X^-, X^+]$ denotes an interval. Inserting the interval $X = [0, 1]$ into Eq. (33), we obtain

$$[0, 1]^2 - 2[0, 1] = [0, 1] - [0, 2] = [-2, 1]. \tag{34}$$

However, if we first recast the expression in Eq. (32) as

$$(x - 1)^2 - 1, \tag{35}$$

then inserting $X = [0, 1]$ into its syntactic interval extension $(X - 1)^2 - 1$ yields the much narrower and, in fact, optimal interval bounds $[-1, 0]$. The two scalar expressions of Eqs. (32) and (35) may be equivalent, but their syntactic interval extensions are not.

```
1  // C++ Standard Library
2  #include <array>
3  #include <cmath>
4  #include <ranges>
5  #include <cassert>
6  #include <cstddef>
7  #include <concepts>
8  #include <algorithm>
9  namespace ranges = std::ranges;
10 using std::sqrt;
11 using index = std::ptrdiff_t;
12 using dim = std::ptrdiff_t;
13
14 // intervals
15 #include <intervals/set.hpp>
16 #include <intervals/interval.hpp>
17 #include <intervals/algorithm.hpp>
18 using namespace intervals;
```

Listing 1.9. Common prefix code for all C++ examples which use the *intervals* library.

A.2 Code Dependencies

To avoid redundancy, the `#include` statements and some other declarations needed to compile the code were omitted in our listings. Listing 1.9 shows the statements and declarations that need to be prepended to each of the listings in this paper.

A.3 Piecewise Linear Interpolation

The linear interpolation example in Listing 1.8 can be generalised to a piecewise linear interpolation between ordered sampling points $x_1, \ldots, x_n$ and associated sampling values $y_1, \ldots, y_n$, given in Listing 1.10. By taking advantage of the monotonically increasing order of sampling points, $x_i < x_{i+1} \forall i \in \{1, \ldots, n-1\}$, for a given value x we can locate the appropriate segment i in $\mathcal{O}(\log n)$ steps with binary search using the `lower_bound` algorithm from the C++ Standard Library.

To make piecewise linear interpolation interval-aware, as has been done in Listing 1.11, we use the `lower_bound` implementation from the *intervals* library. When called with an interval argument, it returns a set of predicates `preds` and an interval of lower-bound iterators `pos`. An interval of segment indices `i` can then be obtained by subtraction. By iterating over the elements `j` of the interval of overlapping segment indices `i` and by constraining the argument `x` with the segment predicate `preds[j]` of the j-th segment, we can compute all piecewise contributions to the result. The same code can also be instantiated for normal floating-point types, in which case it is equivalent to the code in Listing 1.10 because the loop over j collapses to a single iteration with $j = i$.

```
1  template <std::floating_point T>
2  T
3  interpolate_linear(
4          ranges::random_access_range auto&& xs,
5          ranges::random_access_range auto&& ys,
6          T x) {
7      dim n = ranges::ssize(xs);
8      assert(n >= 2);
9      assert(ranges::ssize(ys) == n);
10
11     auto pos = ranges::lower_bound(xs, x);
12     index i = pos - ranges::begin(xs);
13
14     auto result = T{ };
15     bool below = (i == 0);
16     if (below) {
17         result = ys[0];
18     }
19     bool above = (i == n);
20     if (above) {
21         result = ys[n-1];
22     }
23     if (!below && !above) {
24
25
26         auto x0 = xs[i-1];
27         auto x1 = xs[i];
28         auto y0 = ys[i-1];
29         auto y1 = ys[i];
30
31         result =
32             y0 + (x-x0)/(x1-x0)*(y1-y0);
33
34     }
35     return result;
36 }
37 // usage:
38 // auto xs = std::array{ 1., 2., 4., 8.};
39 // auto ys = std::array{ 1., 3., 9., -3. };
40 // double x = ...;
41 // auto y = interpolate_linear(xs, ys, x);
```

Listing 1.10. C++ implementation of piecewise linear interpolation for scalar types.

```
1  template <typename T>
2  T
3  interpolate_linear (
4          ranges::random_access_range auto&& xs,
5          ranges::random_access_range auto&& ys,
6          T x) {
7      dim n = ranges::ssize(xs);
8      assert(n >= 2);
9      assert(ranges::ssize(ys) == n);
10
11     auto [preds, pos] = intervals::lower_bound(xs, x);
12     auto i = pos - ranges::begin(xs);
13
14     auto result = T{ };
15     auto below = (i == 0);
16     if (possibly(below)) {
17         assign_partial(result, ys[0]);
18     }
19     auto above = (i == n);
20     if (possibly(above)) {
21         assign_partial(result, ys[n-1]);
22     }
23     if (auto c = !below & !above; possibly(c)) {
24         auto ic = constrain(i, c);
25         for (index j : enumerate(ic)) {
26             auto x0 = xs[j-1];
27             auto x1 = xs[j];
28             auto y0 = ys[j-1];
29             auto y1 = ys[j];
30             auto xc = constrain(x, preds[j]);
31             assign_partial(result,
32                 y0 + (xc-x0)/(x1-x0)*(y1-y0));
33         }
34     }
35     return result;
36 }
37 // usage:
38 // auto xs = std::array{ 1., 2., 4., 8.};
39 // auto ys = std::array{ 1., 3., 9., -3. };
40 // auto x = ...; // scalar or interval value
41 // auto y = interpolate_linear(xs, ys, x);
```

Listing 1.11. C++ implementation of piecewise linear interpolation as a generic function which can be used for scalar types and for interval types.

References

1. IEEE Standard for Interval Arithmetic. IEEE Std 1788-2015, pp. 1–97 (2015). https://doi.org/10.1109/IEEESTD.2015.7140721
2. IEEE Standard for Floating-Point Arithmetic. IEEE Std 754-2019 (Revision of IEEE 754-2008), pp. 1–84 (2019). https://doi.org/10.1109/IEEESTD.2019.8766229
3. Standard for Posit Arithmetic (2022). Posit Working Group (2022)

4. Alefeld, G., Herzberger, J.: Introduction to Interval Computation. Academic Press (2012). Google-Books-ID: rUsX5x0OqUcC
5. Beutel, M.: Intervals: simple C++ library for interval arithmetic (2022). https://github.com/mbeutel/intervals
6. Brönnimann, H., Melquiond, G., Pion, S.: The design of the Boost interval arithmetic library. Theor. Comput. Sci. **351**(1), 111–118 (2006). https://doi.org/10.1016/j.tcs.2005.09.062
7. Goualard, F.: GAOL (Not Just Another Interval Library) (2015). https://frederic.goualard.net/#research-software-gaol
8. Gustafson, J.L.: The End of Error: Unum Computing. Chapman and Hall/CRC, New York (2017). https://doi.org/10.1201/9781315161532
9. Gustafson, J.L.: Posit Arithmetic (2017)
10. Gustafson, J.L., Yonemoto, I.: Beating floating point at its own game: posit arithmetic. Supercomput. Front. Innov. **4**(2), 16 (2017)
11. Hickey, T., Ju, Q., Van Emden, M.H.: Interval arithmetic: from principles to implementation. J. ACM **48**(5), 1038–1068 (2001). https://doi.org/10.1145/502102.502106
12. Keszöcze, O., Brand, M., Witterauf, M., Heidorn, C., Teich, J.: Aarith: an arbitrary precision number library. In: Proceedings of the 36th Annual ACM Symposium on Applied Computing, SAC 2021, pp. 529–534. Association for Computing Machinery, New York (2021). https://doi.org/10.1145/3412841.3442085
13. Moore, R.E.: Interval Analysis (1966)
14. Moore, R.E., Kearfott, R.B., Cloud, M.J.: Introduction to interval analysis. Soc. Ind. Appl. Math. (2009). https://doi.org/10.1137/1.9780898717716
15. Schärtl, A.: Unums and Posits: A Replacement for IEEE 754 Floating Point? M.Sc. thesis, p. 111 (2021)
16. Sun Microsystems Inc.: C++ Interval Arithmetic Programming Reference (2001). Forte Developer 6 update 2 (Sun WorkShop 6 update 2)

Decoding-Free Two-Input Arithmetic for Low-Precision Real Numbers

John L. Gustafson[1], Marco Cococcioni[2] , Federico Rossi[2(✉)] ,
Emanuele Ruffaldi[3] , and Sergio Saponara[2]

[1] Arizona State University, Tempe, AZ, USA
[2] University of Pisa, Pisa, Italy
{marco.cococcioni,federico.rossi,sergio.saponara}@unipi.it
[3] MMI s.p.a, Pisa, Italy
eruffaldi@mmimicro.com

Abstract. In this work, we present a novel method for directly computing functions of two real numbers using logic circuits without decoding; the real numbers are mapped to a particularly-chosen set of integer numbers. We theoretically prove that this mapping always exists and that we can implement any kind of binary operation between real numbers regardless of the encoding format. While the real numbers in the set can be arbitrary (rational, irrational, transcendental), we find practical applications to low-precision posit^{TM} number arithmetic. We finally provide examples for decoding-free 4-bit Posit arithmetic operations, showing a reduction in gate count up to a factor of 7.6× (and never below 4.4×) compared to a standard two-dimensional tabulation.

Keywords: decoding-free arithmetic · posit format · low-precision arithmetic · tabulated functions

1 Introduction

For nearly a century, the method to expressing real numbers on digital computers has been with scientific notation: some form of significant digits (fixed-size storage representing a signed integer) scaled by a base number raised to a signed integer power, also in fixed-size storage. The IEEE 754 standard gave guidance for the details of this two-integer approach.

The artificial intelligence (AI) sector has been pushing the boundaries of Machine Learning (ML) and inference, which has reignited the debate over what is the appropriate representation for real numbers. The bandwidth and storage requirements of 32-bit IEEE standard floats, in particular, have prompted academics to consider 16-bit (and smaller, even down to 2-3-4 bits for extremely quantized neural networks [1]) alternatives to represent the numbers required for AI. According to the IEEE 754 standard, the half precision (binary16) format has 5 exponent bits and 10 fraction bits.

The posit^{TM} number system, which was introduced in 2017, deviates from all previous fixed-field floating-point forms. It features the quire fixed-point accumulator, which is comparable to the Kulisch accumulator [2–4]. The AI Group on

Research supported by Horizon H2020 projects EPI-SGA2 and TextaRossa.

J. Gustafson et al. (Eds.): CoNGA 2023, LNCS 13851, pp. 61–76, 2023.
https://doi.org/10.1007/978-3-031-32180-1_4

Facebook employs posits with the Logarithmic Number System kind of binade [5]. We focus on posits in this paper, but the method is applicable to any collection of $2N$ real-valued values represented by N bits. Posits are particularly well-suited to the approach, as we shall demonstrate in the next sections.

We propose an optimum method for mapping real numbers to integers, allowing us to execute exact two-input arithmetic operations on real numbers with simply integer addition. This significantly reduces hardware complexity (in terms of AND-OR gates), particularly when just a few bits are required to describe the two inputs. We employ a non-linear variant of integer linear programming to get the best mapping. Unlike traditional circuit designs that require decoding a format bit string into the scale (exponent) and significand in order to operate on floats and their variations, our solution just requires an integer mapping (two logic levels), an unsigned integer addition, and another integer mapping. The approach reaches its limit when the integer sizes get too large, but we demonstrate that it works for posit precision adequate for ML and inference.

The paper is organised as follows: i) In Sect. 2 we summarise the posit format and its key properties, ii) in Sect. 3 we recap the standard way to perform binary mathematical operations between real numbers, iii) in Sect. 4 we present the mathematical foundation for the proposed approach, iv) in Sect. 5 we present the problem formulation and the feasibility of finding a solution for such problem, iv) in Sect. 6 we show the application of the proposed approach to the Posit$\langle 4, 0 \rangle$ format and we report some quality metrics for the provided solution.

2   The Posit Format

The mapping method we describe in this paper can be applied to any set of real values, including algebraic and transcendental values, simply by assigning each real value to a natural number. Our method can be applied to the legacy floating-point formats (floats), but IEEE Standard floats lack a mapping to integers that is one-to-one and onto, and redundant bit patterns make them inefficient at low precision. The IEEE Standard also specifies ten different exception categories and makes asymmetric use of tapered precision, complicating the use of our approach. For these reasons, we will focus on the *posit* format for encoding real values.

The posit format for real numbers was introduced in 2017 [4]. The format is n bits in length, $n \geqslant 2$. There are only two exception values, 0 represented by $00 \cdots 0$ and Not-a-Real (NaR) represented by $10 \cdots 0$. Non-exception values have four fields as shown in Figs. 1 and 2, with color coding for clarity:

- Sign field: A single bit with digit value s
- Regime field: variable length, composed of a run of $k + 1$ 1 bits or $-k$ 0 bits, ended by the opposite bit or by the end of the number
- Exponent field: es bits (bits beyond the end have value 0) representing an exponent e as an unsigned integer
- Fraction field: fraction f with up to $n - es - 3$ significant bits.

The real value r represented by the encoding is

$$r = (1 - 3s + f) \times 2^{(1-2s) \times (2^{es}k+e+s)}.$$

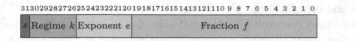

Fig. 1. Bit fields of a posit$\langle 32, 6 \rangle$ data type.

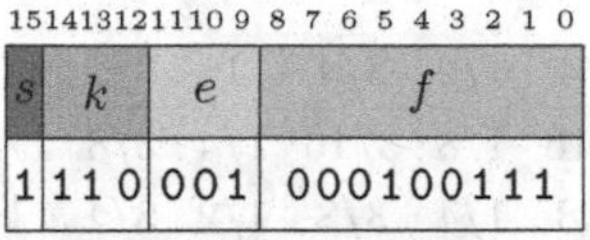

15 14 13 12 11 10 9 8 7 6 5 4 3 2 1 0

s	k	e	f
1	11 0	001	000100111

Fig. 2. An example of a 16-bit posit with 3 bits for the exponent size ($n = 16$, $es = 3$). The sign is simply the bit value, $s = 1$. The regime has $(k+1) = 2$ bits equal to 1 (pair 11) in its run before terminating in a 0 bit, so $k = 1$. The exponent value (unsigned integer) is $e = 1$. The nine fraction bits represent $39/2^9 = 39/512$. The associated real value is therefore $(1 - 3 \cdot 1 + 39/512) \times 2^{(1-2 \cdot 1) \times (8 \cdot 1 + 1 + 1)} = -1.923828125 \times 2^{-10} \approx -0.0018787$.

While the formula may be non-intuitive, the posit format provides a monotonic mapping of reals to 2's complement signed integers with symmetric dynamic range and symmetric accuracy tapering. It also eliminates non-mathematical complications like "negative zero."

3   Standard Two-Input Arithmetic for Reals

Consider a very simple case, that of Posit$\langle 4, 0 \rangle$ format. The sixteen values are shown in Table 1.

Table 1. Posit$\langle 4, 0 \rangle$ binary representations (bistrings) and corresponding real values

Posit	Value	Posit	Value
1000	NaR	0000	0
1001	-4	0001	1/4
1010	-2	0010	1/2
1011	$-3/2$	0011	3/4
1100	-1	0100	1
1101	$-3/4$	0101	3/2
1110	$-1/2$	0110	2
1111	$-1/4$	0111	4

Notice that the mapping is a *bijection*, and if the posit representation is interpreted as a 2's complement integer, the mapping is also monotone. The Posit Standard treats NaR as "less than" any real value, so posits are ordered. We focus on posit format instead of float format because float format is not a bijection, not monotone, and not ordered, which makes mathematical formalizations awkward and complicated.

Table 2 shows the multiplication table for positive values from the Posit$\langle 4, 0 \rangle$ set. Note that the table entries are exact (not rounded to the nearest posit value).

Table 2. Multiplication table, positive Posit$\langle 4, 0 \rangle$ values.

×	1/4	1/2	3/4	1	3/2	2	4
1/4	1/16	1/8	3/16	1/4	3/8	1/2	1
1/2	1/8	1/4	3/8	1/2	3/4	1	2
3/4	3/16	3/8	9/16	3/4	9/8	3/2	3
1	1/4	1/2	3/4	1	3/2	2	4
3/2	3/8	3/4	9/8	3/2	9/4	3	6
2	1/2	1	3/2	2	3	4	8
4	1	2	3	4	6	8	16

The table is symmetric because multiplication is commutative and the input row and input column are the same set; the method described here generalizes to non-commutative functions (like division, as shown later) and to inputs from different sets of real values. Two of the entry values are colour-coded (3/8 and 4) to make clear that arithmetic tables can be many-to-one, where several pairs of inputs result in the same value. This is key to understanding the mathematical formalization in the Sections that follow.

The classical hardware implementation of an arithmetic operation on two real arguments in binary float or posit format consists of the following four steps:

1. Test for exception cases using OR or AND trees on the bit fields, and trap to the appropriate output if an exceptional case is detected.
2. Otherwise, decode each argument into its significand and scale factor (exponent), each stored as a signed integer using the usual positional notation.
3. Operate, using traditional circuits for integer operations such as shift, add/-subtract, multiply, and count leading zeros. For example, argument multiplication involves the addition of the integer scale factors and integer multiplication of the significands.
4. Encode the result into the format using rounding rules, which for round-to-nearest, tie-to-even requires an OR tree of some of the truncated bits and other logic, and an integer increment if the rounding is upward.

The decoding and encoding are costly for time, circuit resources, and electrical energy compared to the task of simply adding two unsigned integers. The first two steps can be done concurrently (speculatively) to save time, at the cost of wasting additional energy on the path not needed. The stages lend themselves to pipelining to improve throughput, but pipelining slightly increases the latency because of latching the result of each stage.

4   Mapping Method and Mathematical Formalization

Let $X, Y \subset \mathbb{R}$ be two finite sets of real numbers, and $X^*, Y^* \subset \mathbb{N}$ be the sets of bit strings that digitally encode them. The encodings are bijective maps (as an example taken from Table 1, $x_i = \frac{3}{4} \in X$ is encoded as $x_i^* = 0011 \in X^*$). Let ∇ be any operation on an element of X and an element of Y. Let $Z \subset \mathbb{R}$ be the set of values obtainable as $z_{i,j} = x_i \nabla y_j$, where $x_i \in X$, $y_j \in Y$. The number of elements in Z, $|Z|$, can be as high as $|X| \cdot |Y|$, when every $x_i \nabla y_j$ is unique. In general, $1 \leqslant |Z| \leqslant |X| \cdot |Y|$.

Let us introduce the ordered sets of distinct natural numbers $L^x \equiv \{L_i^x\}, L^y \equiv \{L_j^y\}$, (hence $L^x, L^y \subset \mathbb{N}$) and let us suppose that $\exists f^x : X \longmapsto L^x$, f^x being a bijective mapping from the reals in X encoded by X^* to the naturals in L^x. Similarly, let us suppose that $\exists f^y : Y \longmapsto L^y$, f^y being a bijective mapping from the reals in Y encoded by Y^* to the naturals in L^y. Under such hypotheses, each x_i will be uniquely mapped into the corresponding value L_i^x. The same happens for the y_i, which are uniquely associated to L_i^y.

Let L^z be the set of all distinct sums of elements in L^x and L^y: $L^z \equiv \{L_k^z\}$, $L^z = \text{distinct}\{L_{i,j}^z\}, L_{i,j}^z = L_i^x + L_j^y$ and let f^z be a mapping between the natural numbers in L^z and Z: $f^z : L^z \longmapsto Z$.

When choosing the values for the sets L^x and L^y, we must ensure that whenever $x_i \nabla y_j$ and $x_p \nabla y_q$ differ, the same must happen for the values $L_i^x + L_j^y$ and $L_p^x + L_q^y$:

$$x_i \nabla y_j \neq x_p \nabla y_q \Rightarrow L_i^x + L_j^y \neq L_p^x + L_q^y \tag{1}$$

In Sect. 5 we formulate the optimization problem to solve this task, i.e., we show a constructive way on how to build f^x, f^y and f^z (more precisely, on how to obtain the ordered sets L^x, L^y and the function f^z).
If (1) holds, then for any pair of elements $x_i \in X$, $y_j \in Y$, we have that:

$$z_{i,j} = x_i \nabla y_j = f^z(f^x(x_i) + f^y(y_j)) \tag{2}$$

where $+$ is simply the addition between natural numbers, something digital computers can perform perfectly within a finite range using the Arithmetic Logic Unit. Figure 3 summarizes the approach.

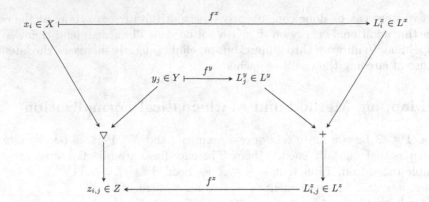

Fig. 3. Mapping between the product of reals and sum of natural numbers. Note that we can generalize it to any kind of operation if we are able to provide the appropriate $f^x()$, $f^y()$ and $f^z()$ functions. All the three functions can be implemented using one-dimensional look-up tables and $f^x()$, $f^y()$ are bijective functions.

As a recap, instead of implementing a full-fledged hardware processing unit for a given format (e.g., a Floating Point Unit), this approach aims to find **once** the three functions $f^x()$, $f^y()$ and $f^z()$ as shown before. These functions can be straightforwardly implemented as one-dimensional look-up tables and enables us to perform real number arithmetic using only the Arithmetic Logic Unit (ALU). Furthermore, these functions always exist and the optimal mapping can be obtained as shown in Sect. 5.

4.1   A Note on the Z Set

As said before, Z can be obtained as the set of values obtainable as $z_{i,j} = x_i \nabla y_j$, where $x_i \in X$, $y_j \in Y$. Since we want to be able to represent $z_{i,j}, \forall i,j$ for the given format, we are limited by its dynamic range and decimal accuracy. The representable values of the format are equivalent to the set X (and Y, since in all practical implementations $Y \equiv X$).

This means that the following phenomena occur when constructing the Z set:

- Overflow: the result $z_{i,j} = x_i \nabla y_j > \max(X) = \max(Y)$. Saturation can occur, forcing $z_{i,j} = \max(X) = \max(Y)$.
- Underflow: the result $0 < z_{i,j} < min(|x_i|, x_i \in X), z_{i,j} > 0$. The underflow can be forced to $z_{i,j} = min(|x_i|, x_i \in X)$. The same holds for $z_{i,j} < 0$ and the underflow occurs to $-min(|x_i|, x_i \in X)$.
- Rounding: in general $z_{i,j}$ may not be representable – i.e. $z_{i,j}$ does not belong to X. Depending on the format, a rounding scheme must be applied. As an example, the rounding scheme of Posit numbers is *round to nearest even*.

If we apply the three previous rules (overflow handling, underflow handling and rounding scheme, overall named "casting") we get a new set $\hat{Z} = \{\text{distinct}(\text{cast}(z_{i,j}))\} = \{\hat{z}_t\}$, $\hat{Z} \subseteq X$. Let $|\hat{Z}|$ be the cardinality of such set. Since it can be sorted, we will indicate it as $\tilde{Z} = \{\hat{z}_1, ..., \hat{z}_t, ..., \hat{z}_{|\hat{Z}|}\}$.

For the purposes of this work, this new set $\hat{Z}$ is even more relevant than Z itself, as shown in the following sections.

5   Obtaining the Mapping: Problem Formulation and Its Solvability

The general problem of finding the mapping can be formulated as the integer programming problem in (3).

$$
\begin{aligned}
\min \quad & \sum_i L_i^x + \sum_j L_j^y \\
\text{s.t.} \quad & L_1^x \geq 0 \\
& L_1^y \geq 0 \\
& L_{i_1}^x \neq L_{i_2}^x && \forall i_1 \neq i_2 \\
& L_{j_1}^y \neq L_{i_2}^y && \forall j_1 \neq j_2 \\
& L_i^x + L_j^y \neq L_p^x + L_q^y && \forall i,j,p,q \ s.t. \ x_i \nabla y_j \neq x_p \nabla y_q \\
& L_i^x, L_j^y \in \mathbb{Z} && \forall i, \forall j
\end{aligned}
\tag{3}
$$

Since the *not-equals* constraints introduce disjoint domains for the solution, to ease the solver computation, we can exploit characteristics of the specific operation to specialize said constraints.

Let us consider an operation that is non-decreasing monotonic and commutative (e.g. sum and multiplication).

$$
\begin{aligned}
\min \quad & \sum_i L_i^x + \sum_j L_j^y \\
\text{s.t.} \quad & L_1^x \geq 0 \\
& L_1^y \geq 0 \\
& L_i^x \geq L_j^x + 1 && i > j \\
& L_i^y \geq L_j^y + 1 && i > j \\
& L_i^x + L_j^y = L_j^x + L_i^y && \forall i, \forall j \\
& L_i^x + L_j^y + 1 \leq L_p^x + L_q^y && \forall i,j,p,q \ s.t. \ x_i \nabla y_j < x_p \nabla y_q \\
& L_i^x, L_j^y \in \mathbb{Z} && \forall i, \forall j
\end{aligned}
\tag{4}
$$

This integer programming formulation is more tractable, since now the domain is a single polyhedron and not the disjunction of multiple ones. In addition, it can be constructively proved that its feasible region is not empty (see the procedure described in the Appendix 7). Furthermore, the minimization problem is bounded from below, since the variables must stay on the first quadrant and the coefficients of the objective function are all positive.

Under these assumptions, *the problem always admits a minimum for its objective value* [6], although its solution is not guaranteed to be unique. The latter means that different optimal sets L^x and L^y might exist, but they will be associated to the same (optimal) value of the objective function $\sum_i L_i^x + \sum_j L_j^y$.

6   Application: Posit$\langle 4, 0 \rangle$

In this section we show an application of the aforementioned method with a low-precision Posit$\langle 4, 0 \rangle$ format. We applied the method to derive the mapping for the four algebraic operations: $+, -, \times, /$. For each operation we report the $f^x(\cdot), f^y(\cdot)$ and $f^z(\cdot)$ mappings as well as the resulting look-up tables and the respective logic functions that implement the mapping. The four different problems were solved enforcing different policies on the values that L^x and L^y sets can contain. These policies help the solving algorithm to converge to the solution faster. Table 3 summarise the policies adopted for the solution.

Table 3. Policies for the solver algorithm. All policies are to be intended as monotonic.

	L^x	L^y
SUM	Increasing	Increasing
MUL	Increasing	Increasing
SUB	Decreasing	Increasing
DIV	Increasing	Decreasing

We run the solver for the problems defined in Sect. 5 obtaining, for each operation, the following outputs:

- The L^x, L^y and L^z sets.
- The f^x, f^y and f^z functions (or one-dimensional look-up tables) for that perform the mapping between the $X, Y, \hat{Z}$ and, respectively, the L^x, L^y, L^z sets.

Table 4. L^x and L^y sets for Posit$\langle 4, 0 \rangle$ ($X \equiv Y \equiv \{ \frac{1}{4}, \frac{1}{2}, \frac{3}{4}, 1, \frac{3}{2}, 2, 4 \}$)

operation	L^x	L^y
+	$\{0, 1, 2, 3, 5, 6, 11\}$	$\{0, 1, 2, 3, 5, 6, 11\}$
$\times$	$\{0, 2, 3, 4, 5, 6, 8\}$	$\{0, 2, 3, 4, 5, 6, 8\}$
$-$	$\{0, 1, 2, 3, 5, 6, 7\}$	$\{15, 14, 13, 12, 10, 8, 0\}$
/	$\{0, 2, 3, 4, 5, 6, 8\}$	$\{8, 6, 5, 4, 3, 2, 0\}$

The first step consists in obtaining the mapping between the two Posit$\langle 4, 0\rangle$ operands and, respectively, the L^x and L^y sets. Table 4 shows the obtained mapping $(f^x(\cdot), f^y(\cdot))$ for the four different operations. As stated at the beginning of this section, we enforced different L^x, L^y policies for the different operations. Indeed, we can see that, for addition and multiplication, the L^x, L^y sets are identical and monotonic increasing. This reflects the commutative properties of the addition and multiplication. On the other hand, for subtraction and division, the L^x, L^y sets are different: for the division, the two sets have the same elements, but the ordering is different, with L^x being monotonic increasing and L^y monotonic decreasing; for the subtraction the two sets are different, while preserving the same properties of the division ones – i.e. one being monotonic increasing and the other being monotonic decreasing.

Table 5. Cross-sum of the L^x, L^y sets, producing the $L^z_{i,j}$ elements for multiplication (left) and addition (right)

L^x L^y	0	2	3	4	5	6	8
0	0	2	3	4	5	6	8
2	2	4	5	6	7	8	10
3	3	5	6	7	8	9	11
4	4	6	7	8	9	10	12
5	5	7	8	9	10	11	13
6	6	8	9	10	11	12	14
8	8	10	11	12	13	14	16

L^x L^y	0	1	2	3	5	6	11
0	0	1	2	3	5	6	11
1	1	2	3	4	6	7	12
2	2	3	4	5	7	8	13
3	3	4	5	6	8	9	14
5	5	6	7	8	10	11	16
6	6	7	8	9	11	12	17
11	11	12	13	14	16	17	22

Table 6. Cross-sum of the L^x, L^y sets, producing the $L^z_{i,j}$ elements for division (left) and subtraction (right)

L^x L^y	8	6	5	4	3	2	0
0	8	6	5	4	3	2	0
2	10	8	7	6	5	4	2
3	11	9	8	7	6	5	3
4	12	10	9	8	7	6	4
5	13	11	10	9	8	7	5
6	14	12	11	10	9	8	6
8	16	14	13	12	11	10	8

L^x L^y	15	14	13	12	10	8	0
0	15	14	13	12	10	8	0
1	16	15	14	13	11	9	1
2	17	16	15	14	12	10	2
3	18	17	16	15	13	11	3
5	20	19	18	17	15	13	5
6	21	20	19	18	16	14	6
7	22	21	20	19	17	15	7

Once we obtained the L^x, L^y sets, the $L^z_{i,j}$ elements can be obtained by computing the cross-sum between the two sets, with all the sum between each pair of elements of L^x and L^y. Table 5 shows the result for multiplication and addition. Due to symmetry properties of the two operations there are several duplicated values. The same holds for division and subtraction operations in Table 6.

As said above, the set L^z can be found as: $L^z = \text{distinct}\{L^z_{i,j}\}$. Such set will have $|L^z|$ entries, and therefore we can represent it as a ordered set of values in the following way:

$$L^z = \{L^z_1, ..., L^z_k, ..., L^z_{|L^z|}\}$$

having indicated with L^z_k its k-th element and $L^z_1 < L^z_2 < ... < L^z_{|L^z|}$. Let us now introduce the vector $\boldsymbol{w}$, having size equal to the cardinality of L^z. We will indicate it as $\boldsymbol{w} = (w_1, ..., w_k, ..., w_{|L^z|})$. Each component of the vector belongs to $\hat{Z}$. In particular, $w_k = \hat{z}_{i,j}$, if i and j are such that $L^z_{i,j}$ is equal to the k-th value in L^z.

Hereafter we show what we obtained for the *Posit* $\langle 4, 0 \rangle$ multiplication:

Ordered sets of real numbers

$X = \{\frac{1}{4}, \frac{1}{2}, \frac{3}{4}, 1, \frac{3}{2}, 2, 4\}$
$Y \equiv X$
$\hat{Z} = \{\frac{1}{4}, \frac{1}{2}, \frac{3}{4}, 1, \frac{3}{2}, 2, 4\}$ (in general $\hat{Z} \subseteq X$, but in this case we obtained
$\hat{Z} \equiv X$)

Ordered sets of natural numbers

$L^x = \{0, 2, 3, 4, 5, 6, 8\}$
$L^y = \{0, 2, 3, 4, 5, 6, 8\}$
$L^z = \{0, 2, 3, 4, 5, 6, 7, 8, 9, 10, 11, 12, 13, 14, 16\}$

Vector $\boldsymbol{w}$

$\boldsymbol{w} = (\frac{1}{4}, \frac{1}{4}, \frac{1}{4}, \frac{1}{4}, \frac{1}{4}, \frac{1}{2}, \frac{3}{4}, 1, \frac{3}{2},\ 2,\ 2,\ 4,\ 4,\ 4,\ 4)$

The correspondence among the values of $z_{i,j}$, $\hat{z}_{i,j}$, $L^z_{i,j}$, L^z_k and w_k is shown in Table 7.

Table 7. *Posit* $\langle 4, 0 \rangle$ *multiplication*: correspondence among $z_{i,j}$, $\hat{z}_{i,j}$, $L_{i,j}^z$, L_k^z and w_k values. On the left we report the first part, and on the right the second part (to save space).

$z_{i,j}$	$\hat{z}_{i,j}$	$L_{i,j}^z$ $(= L_i^x + L_j^y)$	L_k^z	w_k
1/16	1/4	0	**0**	**1/4**
1/8	1/4	2	**2**	**1/4**
1/8	1/4	2		
3/16	1/4	3	**3**	**1/4**
3/16	1/4	3		
1/4	1/4	4	**4**	**1/4**
1/4	1/4	4		
1/4	1/4	4		
3/8	1/4	5	**5**	**1/4**
3/8	1/4	5		
3/8	1/4	5		
3/8	1/4	5		
1/2	1/2	6	**6**	**1/2**
1/2	1/2	6		
1/2	1/2	6		
1/2	1/2	6		
9/16	1/2	6		
3/4	3/4	7	**7**	**3/4**
3/4	3/4	7		
3/4	3/4	7		
3/4	3/4	7		
1	1	8	**8**	**1**
1	1	8		
1	1	8		
1	1	8		
1	1	8		
9/8	1	8		
9/8	1	8		

$z_{i,j}$	$z\hat{_{i,j}}$	$L_{i,j}^z$ $(= L_i^x + L_j^y)$	L_k^z	w_k
3/2	3/2	9	**9**	**3/2**
3/2	3/2	9		
3/2	3/2	9		
3/2	3/2	9		
2	2	10	**10**	**2**
2	2	10		
2	2	10		
2	2	10		
9/4	2	10		
3	2	11	**11**	**2**
3	2	11		
3	2	11		
3	2	11		
4	4	12	**12**	**4**
4	4	12		
4	4	12		
6	4	13	**13**	**4**
6	4	13		
8	4	14	**14**	**4**
8	4	14		
16	4	16	**16**	**4**

We also report some multiplications using 4-bit posit in Table 8 (we do not report all the combinations for the sake of the space). Note that we are employing the standard rounding scheme for posit numbers, therefore values that are not represented by the posit domain are rounded to the nearest value.

Table 8. Example of multiplication for $Posit\langle 4,0\rangle$ using the L^x, L^y, L^z values, for some (x_i, y_j) pairs.

x_i	L_i^x	y_j	L_j^y	$L_{i,j}^z$ $(= L_i^x + L_j^y)$	$z_{i,j}$ $(= x_i \times y_j)$	$\hat{z}_{i,j}$ $(= \texttt{cast}(x_i \times y_j)$
$\frac{1}{2}$	2	$\frac{1}{4}$	0	2	$\frac{1}{8}$ $\bullet$	$\frac{1}{4}$
$\frac{1}{2}$	2	$\frac{1}{2}$	2	4	$\frac{1}{4}$	$\frac{1}{4}$
$\frac{1}{2}$	2	$\frac{3}{4}$	3	5	$\frac{3}{8}$	$\frac{1}{4}$
$\frac{1}{2}$	2	$\frac{3}{2}$	5	7	$\frac{3}{4}$	$\frac{3}{4}$
$\frac{1}{2}$	2	2	6	8	1	1
$\frac{1}{2}$	2	4	8	10	2	2

Finally we report in Table 9 the L^z sets for the different operations and the associated w vectors for $Posit\langle 4,0\rangle$.

Table 9. L^z ordered sets and the associated w vectors for $Posit\langle 4,0\rangle$ for the four arithmetic operations.

Op	L^z set	Associated w vector
×	$\{0,2,3,4,5,6,7,8,9,10,11,12,13,14,16\}$	$(\frac{1}{4},\frac{1}{4},\frac{1}{4},\frac{1}{4},\frac{1}{2},\frac{3}{4},1,\frac{3}{2},2,2,4,4,4,4)$
+	$\{0,1,2,3,4,5,6,7,8,9,10,11,12,13,14,16,17,22\}$	$(\frac{1}{2},\frac{3}{4},1,1,\frac{3}{2},\frac{3}{2},2,2,2,2,4,4,4,4,4,4)$
/	$\{0,2,3,4,5,6,7,8,9,10,11,12,13,14,16\}$	$(\frac{1}{4},\frac{1}{4},\frac{1}{4},\frac{1}{4},\frac{1}{2},\frac{3}{4},1,\frac{3}{2},2,2,4,4,4,4)$
−	$\{0,1,2,3,5,6,7,8,9,10,11,12,13,14,15,16,17,18,19,20,21,22\}$	$(\{\frac{1}{4}$ repeated 14 times$\},2,\frac{1}{2},2,1,2,4,4,4)$

As a final remark, observe how the function $f^z()$ described in Sect. 4 (in particular, in Eq. (2)), is easily obtainable using the values in the vector w. Indeed, the $f^z : L^z \longmapsto \hat{Z}$ we are looking for is the one-dimensional lookup table having entries (L_k^z, w_k). An example of such a lookup table is given by the last two columns of Table 7.

6.1   Quality Metrics

When evaluating the results produced by the solver we want to have a baseline benchmark to compare our results. Let us have a $Posit\langle N, E\rangle$, if we think about a look-up table to accommodate the results of an operation, the simplest approach we can have is a 2-dimensional look-up table indexed by the elements of the integer sets X^*, Z^* that digitally encode the respective real values contained in the set X, Y. Each cell of the table has N bits for the output while the address of the look-up table is just the concatenation of the integer representations, thus on $2 \cdot N$ bits. Therefore the table has $2^{2 \cdot N}$ entries of N bits. Table 10 shows this *naïve* approach for a 4-bit posit with the multiplication operation. As we said before, such table has $2^{2 \cdot N} = 2^8 = 256$ entries with 4-bit wide cells, totalling to $256 \cdot 4 = \mathbf{1024\ bits}$. An optimized version of this table may operate just on the positive part of the domain, reducing the number of entries to $2^{2 \cdot (N-1)} = 2^6 = 64$ with 3-bit wide cells, totalling to $64 \cdot 3 = \mathbf{192\ bits}$.

Table 10. Naïve look-up table for the multiplication for $Posit \langle 4.0 \rangle$.

	Naïve $L_{i,j}^z$ $(=L_i^x+L_j^y)$	Posit encoding of $\hat{z}_{i,j}$	$\hat{z}_{i,j}$
row 1	0000*0000*	0000	0
	...	...	...
row 16	0000*1111*	0000	0
row 17	0001*0000*	0000	0
	...	...	...
row 32	0001*1111*	1111	$-1/4$
row 33	0010*0000*	0000	0
	...	...	...
row 48	0010*1111*	1111	$-1/4$
row 49	0011*0000*	0000	0
	...	...	...
row 64	0011*1111*	1111	$-1/4$
row 65	0100*0000*	0000	0
	...	...	...
row 80	0100*1111*	1111	$-1/4$
row 81	0101*0000*	0000	0
	...	...	...
row 96	0101*1111*	1111	$-1/4$
row 97	0110*0000*	0000	0
	...	...	...
row 113	0110*1111*	1110	$-1/2$
	...	...	...
	...	...	...
row 240	1111*0000*	0000	0
	...	...	...
row 256	1111*1111*	0001	$1/4$

When we obtain a solution to the problem of mapping we need to compare it at least against to the baseline solution to see if it actually introduces an improvement. Such improvement can be in the number of entries of the look-up(s) table(s), in the number of output bits or in the combination of the two factors. Moreover, we may also consider that, for low-precision format, we can derive a combinatorial logic function that performs the f^x, f^y, f^z mappings.

Since we deal with a 4-bit format, it is worth to consider the gate count of a combinatorial solution to the problem. Suppose that, instead of implementing the mapping with a look-up table, we implement the mapping using a combinatorial logic function of the input bits. We can evaluate the cost of this solution in terms of number of AND-OR gates (ignoring the cost of NOT gates, as usually done). Table 11 shows the gate cost for each operation and the comparison with the naïve solution presented before as a baseline benchmark.

Table 11. Total gate count AND-OR for each operation for Posit$\langle 4,0 \rangle$.

	Total gates for L^x	Total gates for L^y	Total gates for L^z	Grand total gates	Grand total gates of the naïve solution	Gate reduction
+	10	10	11	**31**	138	4.4×
×	7	7	9	**23**	138	6×
−	8	5	5	**18**	138	7.6×
/	7	7	9	**23**	138	6×

7 Conclusions

In this paper, we described a novel method for directly computing functions of two real numbers without decoding using logic circuits; the real numbers are mapped to a specially chosen set of integer values. We demonstrated that this mapping exists all the time and that we can implement any type of binary operation between real numbers independent of encoding scheme. In particular, we applied this method to the 4-bit posit format, obtaining the mapping for all the 4 algebraic operations. Finally, we compared the obtained solution to a baseline benchmark in terms of number of look-up table entries and gates count. We showed how our approach can produce mapping tables that are smaller than a traditional look-up table solution with logic functions that implement the mappings having a lower AND-OR gate count when compared to the baseline solution.

Acknowledgments. Work partially supported by H2020 projects EPI2 (grant no. 101036168, https://www.european-processor-initiative.eu/ and TextaRossa (grant no. 956831, https://textarossa.eu/).

Appendix: How to Build an Initial Feasible Solution

An initial feasible solution (useful to speedup Matlab `intlinprog` function) can be constructed as shown below. We will focus on the positive values in X, different both from NaR (notice that we are excluding the zero as well). Let us call this set $\mathcal{X}$. Let us indicate with $x_i^* \in \mathcal{X}$ the corresponding bistring (in the next we will refer to the *Posit* $\langle 4,0 \rangle$ case, as an example). Therefore, the bistrings will be the ones of *Posit* $\langle 4,0 \rangle$ without its most significant bit (see Table 1).

- Each $x_i \in \mathcal{X}$ is mapped to the natural number $L_i^x = x_i^* \cdot 2^n$, n being the maximum number of bits needed for representing the x_i (in the case of *Posit* $\langle 4,0 \rangle$, $n = 3$)
- Each $y_j \in \mathcal{Y}$ is mapped to the natural number $L_j^y = y_j^*$

Therefore, we obtain the L^x, L^y sets: $L^x : \{x_1^* \cdot 2^n, \ldots, x_{|\mathcal{X}|}^* \cdot 2^n\}$ and $L^y : \{y_1^*, \ldots, y_{|\mathcal{Y}|}^*\}$. Each $L_{i,j}^z \in L^z$ is obtained by the concatenation of the bit strings x_i^*, y_j^* (or equivalently, as $L_{i,j}^z = L_i^x + L_j^y$, as shown in Table 12).

Table 12. Example of a feasible solution for positive values of $Posit\langle 4, 0\rangle$. Notice that $L_i^x = x_i^* \cdot 2^3$ and $L_j^y = y_j^*$.

x_i	x_i^*	L_i^x	y_j	y_j^*	L_j^y	$L_{i,j}^z$	$L_{i,j}^z$	L_k^z	w_k
	(base 10)	(base 2)		(base 10)	(base 2)	(base 2)	(base 10)	(base 10)	
1/4	1	001000	1/4	1	001	001001	9	9	1/4
1/4	1	001000	1/2	2	010	001010	10	10	1/4
1/4	1	001000	3/4	3	011	001011	11	11	1/4
1/4	1	001000	1	4	100	001100	12	12	1/4
1/4	1	001000	3/2	5	101	001101	13	13	1/4
1/4	1	001000	2	6	110	001110	14	14	1/2
1/4	1	001000	4	7	111	001111	15	15	1
1/2	2	010000	1/4	1	001	010001	17	17	1/4
1/2	2	010000	1/2	2	010	010010	18	18	1/4
1/2	2	010000	3/4	3	011	010011	19	19	1
1/2	2	010000	1	4	100	010100	20	20	1
1/2	2	010000	3/2	5	101	010101	21	21	3/4
1/2	2	010000	2	6	110	010110	22	22	1
1/2	2	010000	4	7	111	010111	23	23	2
3/4	3	011000	1/4	1	001	011001	25	25	1/4
3/4	3	011000	1/2	2	010	011010	26	26	1/4
3/4	3	011000	3/4	3	011	011011	27	27	1/2
3/4	3	011000	1	4	100	011100	28	28	3/4
3/4	3	011000	3/2	5	101	011101	29	29	1
3/4	3	011000	2	6	110	011110	30	30	3/2
3/4	3	011000	4	7	111	011111	31	31	2
1	4	100000	1/4	1	001	100001	33	33	1/4
1	4	100000	1/2	2	010	100010	34	34	1/2
1	4	100000	3/4	3	011	100011	35	35	3/4
1	4	100000	1	4	100	100100	36	36	1
1	4	100000	3/2	5	101	100101	37	37	3/2
1	4	100000	2	6	110	100110	38	38	2
1	4	100000	4	7	111	100111	39	39	4
3/2	5	101000	1/4	1	001	101001	41	41	1/4
3/2	5	101000	1/2	2	010	101010	42	42	3/4
3/2	5	101000	3/4	3	011	101011	43	43	1
3/2	5	101000	1	4	100	101100	44	44	3/2
3/2	5	101000	3/2	5	101	101101	45	45	2
3/2	5	101000	2	6	110	101110	46	46	2
3/2	5	101000	4	7	111	101111	47	47	4
2	6	110000	1/4	1	001	110001	49	49	1/2
2	6	110000	1/2	2	010	110010	50	50	1
2	6	110000	3/4	3	011	110011	51	51	3/2
2	6	110000	1	4	100	110100	52	52	2
2	6	110000	3/2	5	101	110101	53	53	2
2	6	110000	2	6	110	110110	54	54	4
2	6	110000	4	7	111	110111	55	55	4
4	7	111000	1/4	1	001	111001	57	57	1
4	7	111000	1/2	2	010	111010	58	58	2
4	7	111000	3/4	3	011	111011	59	59	2
4	7	111000	1	4	100	111100	60	60	4
4	7	111000	3/2	5	101	111101	61	61	4
4	7	111000	2	6	110	111110	62	62	4
4	7	111000	4	7	111	111111	63	63	4

We now prove that this solution satisfies the constraint given in Eq. (1):

- Since there are no conflicting encodings of the real numbers in $\mathcal{X}$ and $\mathcal{Y}$, we can guarantee that different real numbers have different bit-strings that digitally encode them. Therefore, $L_i^x \neq L_j^x, \forall i \neq j$ and $L_p^y \neq L_l^y, \forall k \neq l$.
- Since all the encodings in L^x, L^y are different from each other, also the concatenation of any pair L_i^x, L_j^y is unique. Therefore, $L_{i,j}^z \neq L_{k,q}^z$, if $x_i \nabla y_j \neq X_j \nabla Y_q$ (with ∇ we indicate the generic operation for which we are finding the mapping).
- Being the values $L_{i,j}^z$ unique (no duplicates), we can easily obtain the ordered set L^z, by sorting them.
- the k-element vector $\boldsymbol{w}$ can be trivially obtained as $\texttt{cast}(x_i \nabla y_j)$, when $i \cdot 2^n + j = k$.

An example of feasible solution for the multiplication of *Posit* $\langle 4, 0 \rangle$ numbers is reported in Table 12.

References

1. Cococcioni, M., Rossi, F., Ruffaldi, E., Saponara, S.: Small reals representations for deep learning at the edge: a comparison. In: Gustafson, J., Dimitrov, V. (eds.) CoNGA 2022. LNCS, vol. 13253, pp. 117–133. Springer, Cham (2022). https://doi.org/10.1007/978-3-031-09779-9_8
2. Gustafson, J.L.: The End of Error: Unum Computing. Chapman and Hall/CRC (2015)
3. Gustafson, J.L.: A radical approach to computation with real numbers. Supercomput. Front. Innov. **3**(2), 38–53 (2016)
4. Gustafson, J.L., Yonemoto, I.T.: Beating floating point at its own game: posit arithmetic. Supercomput. Front. Innov. **4**(2), 71–86 (2017)
5. Johnson, J.: Rethinking floating point for deep learning. CoRR, vol. abs/1811.01721 (2018). http://arxiv.org/abs/1811.01721
6. Conforti, M., Cornuéjols, G., Zambelli, G.: Integer Programming. Graduate Texts in Mathematics, Springer, Cham (2014). https://doi.org/10.1007/978-3-319-11008-0

Hybrid SORN Hardware Accelerator for Support Vector Machines

Nils Hülsmeier[1]([✉])[iD], Moritz Bärthel[1][iD], Jochen Rust[2][iD], and Steffen Paul[1][iD]

[1] Institute of Electrodynamics and Microelectronics (ITEM.me),
University of Bremen, Bremen, Germany
{huelsmeier,baerthel,steffen.paul}@me.uni-bremen.de
[2] DSI Aerospace Technologie GmbH, Bremen, Germany
jochen.rust@dsi-as.de

Abstract. This paper presents a new approach for support vector filtering to accelerate the training process of support vector machines (SVMs). It is based on the Sets-of-Real-Numbers (SORN) number format, which provides low complex and ultra fast computing. SORNs are an interval based binary number format, showing promising results for complex arithmetic operations, e.g. multiplication or fused multiply-add. To apply SORNs to high dimensional vector arithmetic, a combination of SORN arithmetic and fixed-point adder trees is used. This Hybrid SORN approach combines the advantages of SORNs, concerning reduction of computational costs and time, and fixed point adders in terms of precision. A Hybrid SORN support vector filtering architecture is implemented on an FPGA board with Zynq 7000 XC7Z100 SoC and evaluated for the MNIST dataset. It can be considered as hardware accelerator, reducing the training time by factor 1.38 for one-versus-rest and 2.65 for one-versus-one SVM implementation.

Keywords: SORN · Hybrid SORN · support vector machine · hardware accelerator · FPGA · MNIST · machine learning

1 Introduction and Related Work

Support vector machines (SVMs) have proven to be powerful classifiers and useful regression tools [13]. Their high computational costs during training and the success of convolutional neural networks, however, is the reason that SVMs are rarely used in modern image processing. While the cascade SVM already reduces the computational costs significantly, the training is still complex and time consuming. Therefore, more radical approaches are necessary to improve the SVM even more.

The authors acknowledge the financial support by the Federal Ministry of Education and Research of Germany in the project "Open6GHub" (grant number: 16KISK016).

J. Gustafson et al. (Eds.): CoNGA 2023, LNCS 13851, pp. 77–87, 2023.
https://doi.org/10.1007/978-3-031-32180-1_5

The usage of alternative hardware architectures or number formats requiring less resources are options to decrease computational costs and latency, respectively. Various binary number formats are applied in machine learning algorithms, using different resolutions and value ranges (s. Fig. 1). Besides the widely used floating point standard IEEE-754 and fixed point representations (FxD), also new approaches exist, e.g. the posit format or brain floating point (Bfloat) [14]. While posits, Bfloats and floating point numbers cover real numbers and are mostly used in computers, FxD covers rational numbers and is used for customized hardware architectures (s. Fig 1). The SORN representation is a binary number format, representing the real numbers using a low resolution of intervals and exact values. It allows ultra fast and low complex computing, while the interval arithmetic provides correct results. However, SORN adders cause interval growths that reduce the accuracy, resulting in non-significant results. To counteract this behavior, the Hybrid SORN approach was presented, which combines SORN and FxD format to apply SORN-based arithmetic to high dimensional vector arithmetic [1].

SORNs can be used to provide low complex implementations of algorithms, e.g. k-Nearest Neighbor in [1] or edge detection for image processing in [8]. Furthermore, SORNs are well suited to reduce the complexity of optimization problems by excluding wrong solutions in advance. In [6] and [9] they are used as preprocessor for MIMO symbol detection and a sphere decoder, respectively. Also the proof of concept of a SORN-based cascade SVM was presented in [5]. It shows a Matlab implementation of the traditional cascade SVM, using the SORN format to reduce the complexity during the training.

In contrast to [5], in this work the Hybrid SORN approach is used for support vector (SV) filtering and is implemented on FPGA. An architecture for SV filtering that differs from the traditional cascade SVM is used and the acceleration of this approach is evaluated. The new approach presented in this work shows better filter performance at lower complexity than the previous publication.

2   Support Vector Machines

The SVM is a supervised machine learning algorithm, proven to be an effective classifier for a wide range of tasks [13]. SVMs are binary classifiers, separating two classes by inserting an optimal hyperplane that can be determined based on its SVs [2]. Therefore, the decision function for any vector $\mathbf{x}$ becomes

$$f(\mathbf{x}) = \mathbf{w} \cdot \mathbf{x} + b, \tag{1}$$

where the hyperplane is defined by $f(x) = 0$ and classes are determined by the sign of Eq. (1) [2]. The SVs are those vectors of the training dataset that fulfill $f(\mathbf{x}) = \pm 1$. The optimal hyperplane maximizes the margin between the classes and minimizes the number of errors, leading to the dual optimization problem

$$\min_{w,b,\xi} \frac{\|\mathbf{w}\|^2}{2} + C \sum_{i=1}^{N} \xi_i, \tag{2}$$

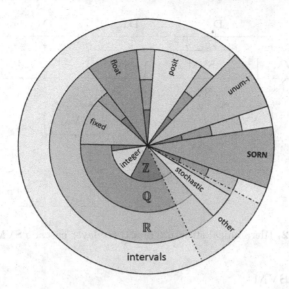

Fig. 1. Overview of different number formats and their value range.

subject to the constraint

$$y_i \left(\mathbf{x}_i \cdot \mathbf{w} + b \right) \geq 1 - \xi_i, \ \xi_i \geq 0, \tag{3}$$

with training data $\mathbf{x}$, labels $\mathbf{y} \in \{-1, 1\}$ and errors ξ_i. This optimization problem can be solved by Lagrangian multipliers, resulting in

$$\max_{\mathbf{\Lambda}} -\frac{1}{2} \mathbf{\Lambda D \Lambda} + \mathbf{\Lambda}^T \mathbf{1} \tag{4}$$

subject to the constraints

$$0 \leq \alpha_i \leq C, \ \mathbf{y}^T \mathbf{\Lambda} = 0, \tag{5}$$

where $\mathbf{\Lambda} = (\alpha_1, ..., \alpha_N)^T$ are the Lagrange multipliers and $D_{i,j} = y_i y_j \mathbf{x}_i \cdot \mathbf{x}_j$. Equation (4) can be solved by various iterative optimization algorithms, e.g. gradient descent [12]. The solution respecting $\mathbf{\Lambda}$ provides the hyperplane $\mathbf{w} = \sum_{i=1}^{N} \alpha_i y_i \mathbf{x}_i$ [2]. For non-linear classification, a Kernel $K(\mathbf{x}_i, \mathbf{x}_j) = \phi(\mathbf{x}_i) \cdot \phi(\mathbf{x}_j)$ can be used to map the input data into a high-dimensional feature space. Then, the input becomes $D_{i,j} = y_i y_j K(\mathbf{x}_i \cdot \mathbf{x}_j)$.

Since SVMs are binary classifiers, two options to exploit multiclass classification exist. For $N > 2$ classes one SVM can be trained to classify this specific class, resulting in N SVMs, each classifying one class. This method is called one-versus-rest and requires the complete training dataset for each single class SVM. Another method is one-versus-one training. It separates the dataset into subsets of two classes, considering each possible combination of two classes in the dataset. Hence, one-versus-one training results in more different SVMs compared to one-versus-rest, but on significantly smaller datasets.

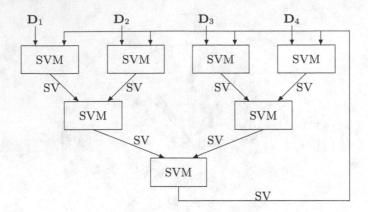

Fig. 2. Hierarchical structure of a three layer cascade SVM.

2.1 Cascade SVM

Since the complexity of the quadratic optimization problem (see Eq. (4)) increases exponentially for an increasing number of training vectors, SVMs require a long time period for training. Therefore, the cascade SVM was introduced to allow parallel SVM training [3]. Since $\alpha_i = 0$ for non-SVs, they can be easily detected in the optimal Λ. To reduce the dimension of the optimization problem (see Eq. (4)), the concept of cascade SVM is to split the training dataset into subsets, where for each subset a low dimensional SVM is used to remove the non-SVs from the dataset (see Fig. 2). The resulting SVs after each stage are combined and fed into the next stage. This process can be repeated for various iterations until the desired reduction of the training dataset is achieved.

3   Hybrid SORN Arithmetic

The SORNs are a binary number representation developed from Unum type-II, using a combination of open intervals and fixed values to represent real numbers (see Fig. 1) [4]. In detail, a SORN number is defined by a datatype $\mathcal{D}$, consisting of specific intervals/values, e.g. $\mathcal{D} = \{\, 0 \; (0, 0.5] \; (0.5, 1] \,\}$ covers the value range between 0 and 1 with two intervals and one exact value. In binary representation each interval is represented by one bit. If a value or an interval is included in the result, the respective bit is high, otherwise the bit is low, resulting in a 3 bit representation for this example. Since no standardization, as for example for IEEE floating point exists for SORN, the datatype can be highly adapted to specific applications, including the options to include infinity and negative values in linear, logarithmic or inconsistent distributions. Arithmetic operations are processed with pre-computed lookup tables (LUTs) consisting of simple Boolean logic, defined by the datatype [6,7].

Since SORN arithmetic utilizes interval arithmetic, additions with a non zero value always result in an interval extension. For high dimensional vector

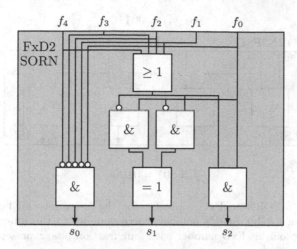

Fig. 3. Logic of a FxD to SORN converter for an incoming five-bit FxD number with no integer bits, converted into a three-bit SORN datatype.

arithmetic, simple operations, e.g. a scalar product, can result in wide intervals, for example $[-\infty, \infty]$ in a worst case scenario. Those results are not meaningful for interpretation and further computations, respectively. Therefore, the Hybrid SORN approach is used in this work, which is a combination of SORN arithmetic and FxD adder trees.

3.1 Conversions

The necessary conversions for Hybrid SORN arithmetic from SORN to FxD representation and vice-versa can be processed using simple Boolean logic (s. Fig. 3 + Fig. 4). Figure 3 shows the logic tree of a FxD to SORN converter for a five bit FxD number and a three bit SORN number. The FxD number has no integer bits and is converted into the previous introduced example SORN datatype $\mathcal{D} = \{\, 0 \ (0, 0.5] \ (0.5, 1] \,\}$. The logical operations depend on the interval bounds of the SORN datatype. Therefore, the required logic increases for larger and more complex SORN datatypes, while the FxD datatype has a small impact on the demand for logical operations. For the presented SORN datatype, e.g. a 16 bit FxD datatype with no integer bits would only increase the number of NAND gate inputs to represent the exact zero (s_0) and the number of inputs of the OR gate (see Fig. 3).

For the back conversion both interval bounds of the SORN result are converted into a reduced length FxD format separately. The resulting FxD width depends on the SORN datatype. In Fig. 4 the combinational logic for a SORN to FxD converter for the lower interval bound is shown. The incoming five bit SORN number s encodes the datatype $\mathcal{D} = \{0 \ (0, 0.125] \ (0.125, 0.25] \ (0.25, 0.5] \ (0.5, 1]\}$. Hence, $s = 00110$ is equivalent to the interval $(0.125, 0.5]$. The presented logic converts SORN bits s_i directly to FxD bits f_i, resulting in a FxD number f

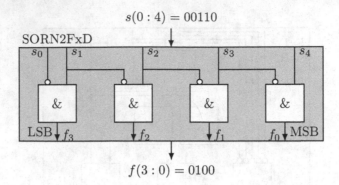

Fig. 4. Logic of a SORN to FxD converter for the lower interval bounds with an example incoming five-bit SORN number, corresponding to the interval $(0.125, 0.5]$ and the resulting four-bit FxD number with four fraction bits, representing the lower interval bound 0.125.

of four bit wordlength. For this datatype, the FxD representation for the lower interval bound has no integer bits, therefore the result corresponds to 0.125 as lower interval bound. The upper interval bound of the SORN number can be converted into the FxD format using a similar combinational logic with small modifications regarding the internal connections of incoming SORN bits and resulting FxD bits. For this datatype, the FxD representation for the upper interval bound has also four bits wordlength but one integer bit and three fraction bits. The back conversion is implemented with small LUTs, the result FxD width depends on the SORN datatype.

Depending on the application the Hybrid SORN approach is used for, either one or both interval bounds can be summed up. For datatypes that include negative numbers, it is also conceivable to consider the interval bounds respecting their absolute value. For example when adding up the intervals [−1, −0.5] and [0.5, 1], −1 and 1 would be considered as upper bound and −0.5 and 0.5 as lower bound. If only one interval bound is considered for further computations, this avoids overrating of positive or negative values, respectively.

4   Hybrid SORN Support Vector Filtering

The Hybrid SORN SV filtering process reduces the training dataset by identifying the SVs. Its underlying concept is similar to the cascade SVM (see Sect. 2.1). First, the training data set is split into subsets to filter the SVs from each subset, followed by a flat SVM training based on the reduced dataset. In contrast to a traditional cascade SVM, the Hybrid SORN approach only uses one stage. The low resolution of the datatype combined with ultra fast arithmetic operations (s. Sect. 3) allows to determine which Λ maximizes Eq. (4) for each subset k. Due to the low resolution the number of possible Λ_k is limited and all options for Λ_k can be tested to find the optimum. During the filter process, seeking the

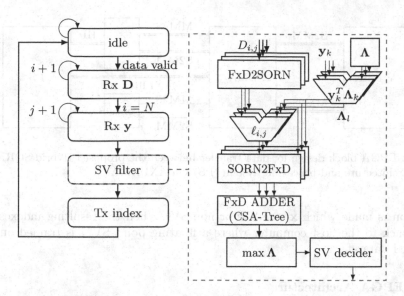

Fig. 5. Hardware architecture of Hybrid SORN SVM, implemented as FSM with Hybrid SORN processing unit.

optimal Λ with high precision is not necessary, since it is crucial to detect which argument α_i of Λ_k is zero to decide whether $\mathbf{x}_i$ is an SV. In detail, only two values of α_i are of interest, zero if $\mathbf{x}_i$ is a non-SV and $0 < \alpha_i \leq C$ if $\mathbf{x}_i$ is an SV. This results in 2^S possible combinations of Λ, where S is the subset length. The maximum subset length is chosen to $S = 8$. Therefore, 255 combinations of Λ_k have to be considered, assuming that all α_i in a subset equal zero are no suitable result.

In Fig. 5 the architecture of the Hybrid SORN SVM is shown. It is implemented as finite state machine (FSM). After receiving a subset of training data (Fig. 5: Rx $\mathbf{D}$) and labels (5: Rx $\mathbf{y}$) the Hybrid SORN SV filtering process starts. First, the Λ that fulfill the constraint (s. Eq. (5)) are evaluated, using a SORN ALU. For a symmetric datatype, instead of a SORN multiplier, the α_i can be flipped for $y_i = -1$. In this ALU, a SORN adder is used to determine the scalar product, followed by a verification which Λ_k fulfills the constraint. Since the options for Λ are constant for each SORN datatype $\mathcal{D}$, they can be stored on the FPGA. The remaining Λ_l are fed into a second SORN ALU, together with the inputs $D_{i,j}$, which are converted into SORN. This ALU calculates the products

$$\ell_{i,j} = \alpha_i D_{i,j} \alpha_j \tag{6}$$

for all subsets Λ_l. The resulting $\ell_{i,j}$ are converted and added up in a FxD adder tree, consisting of CSA adders. The maximum of the resulting sums provides the information which Λ_s maximizes Eq. (4). Based on the evaluated Λ_k the

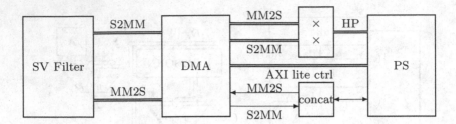

Fig. 6. FPGA block design for data transfer between the proposed Hybrid SORN SV filter architecture and processing system (PS) via AXI DMA.

decision is made which $\mathbf{x}_i$ are SVs or non-SVs. Then the resulting indexes are sent back to the host computer where a floating point SVM is trained on the reduced dataset.

4.1   FPGA Architecture

To transfer the training subsets from host computer to FPGA, an AXI Direct Memory Access (AXI DMA) Xilinx IP-Core is used. The block design is shown in Fig. 6. The DMA provides data transfer between the RAM of the on board Zynq processing system (PS) and the user defined logic. Here, the SV Filter block contains the Hybrid SORN SV filter architecture, presented in Fig. 5, combined with multiple IP-Cores provided by Xilinx. The bus structure uses independent memory-mapped to stream (MM2S) and stream to memory-mapped (S2MM) channels, consisting of AXI4-Stream buses [10]. For receiving the subsets, PS is master and the logic is slave, for writing the resulting indexes to the RAM the logic is master and the PS is slave.

5   Results

In this section the result regarding classification accuracy, training time and utilization of hardware resources are evaluated. The Hybrid SORN SV filter was implemented for the datatype

$$\mathcal{D} = \{[-1, -0.75) \ [-0.75, -0.5) \ [-0.5, -0.25) \ [-0.25, 0) \ 0$$
$$(0, 0.25] \ (0.25, 0.5] \ (0.5, 0.75] \ (0.75, 1]\}.$$

Therefore, inputs are normalized to one $0 \leq \mathbf{D}_k \leq 1$. The FxD number, resulting from the SORN2FxD converter is quantized by one integer and three fraction bits, while the FxD representation for inputs $\mathbf{D}_k$ is quantized with 16 bit. The results are evaluated for the MNIST dataset, consisting of 70,000 28×28 pixel grayscale images [11]. The training dataset comprises 60,000 images, the test dataset includes 10,000 images.

Table 1 presents the classification results and the computation time for the Hybrid SORN SV filter on FPGA, combined with a floating point SVM,

Table 1. Classification results for Hybrid SORN SV filter, compared with a floating point SVM.

Implementation	Float		this work (Hybrid SORN)	
Method	ovr	ovo	ovr	ovo
Classification error	**0.0208**	0.0326	0.0616	0.0411
Training time (CPU) [s]	244.68	243.18	176.47	**90.88**
Training time (FPGA+CPU) [s]	244.68	243.18	177.421	**91.736**

compared with an all floating point SVM in software. For both floating point SVMs the SVM classifier from scikit-learn library for python with 64 bit precision is used [15]. It was executed on a PC with 16 GB RAM and Intel i5 4570 CPU with four kernels. The SVMs use RBF kernel and the parameter $C = 1$. The performance is evaluated for one-versus-rest (ovr) and one-versus-one (ovo), respectively.

It can be seen that the floating point SVM shows a higher classification error of 3.26% and a 1.5 s faster training time for the ovo method, compared to ovr method. This implementation is considered as reference. The Hybrid SORN implementations show a higher classification error of 6.16% for ovr and 4.11% for ovo on MNIST classification. The ovo Hybrid SORN SV filter showing lower classification error compared to ovr can be explained by the small subsetsize of $S = 8$. For ovr SV filtering this results in many subsets comprising of only one class, which can cause no filtering performance and wrong SV filtering, respectively.

The higher classification error of Hybrid SORN implementation, compared with the floating point SVM can be explained by SVs that are detected as non-SVs and removed from the training dataset. A reason for a wrong SV detection could be the coarse resolution of the SORN datatype, especially the distinction between zero and non-zero values of Lagrange multipliers α_i. Another explanation is the small subsets size of the training data, which can affect the accuracy of the global optimization.

Although the low resolution of SORNs causes a lower classification accuracy, it also allows fast computing. Therefore, the computation time of the SVM implementations show a significant reduction of computational costs. For ovr, the training time is 1.38 times faster and for ovo 2.65 times faster than floating point including the filter latency. Although these accelerating factors are likely lower than GPU based hardware accelerators, it has to be considered that the proposed architecture can be combined with any other hardware accelerator. Most hardware accelerators exploit parallelization to reduce the training time. The Hybrid SORN SV filter instead reduces the training dataset, exploiting low-complex arithmetic operations of the SORN number format. The latency of the design is constant, but the acceleration, resulting from the reduction of the training dataset, is an improvement that can also be expected for combinations with other architectures.

Table 2. Synthesis results of Hybrid SORN SV filter on XC7Z100.

	FPGA Setup	Logic
Frequency	200 MHz	
Latency	1.585 µs	1.32 µs
Power	2.911 W	
LUT	165869	162047
FF	158224	152833
BRAM	2	0
DSP	0	0

Table 2 shows the synthesis results for the Hybrid SORN SV filter on an FPGA board with Zynq 7000 processor and XC7Z100 SoC. While the left column of Table 2 shows the resource utilization for the entire FPGA setup, including DMA, Zynq processing system and the design, the right column shows the utilization of the Hybrid SORN SV filter only. For a fair comparison of utilization of hardware resources, an equivalent FxD cascade SVM consisting of one stage and 8×8 subsets should be used, respectively. Unfortunately, a FxD SVM is not able to filter a relevant amount of non-SVs from 8×8 subsets, which makes a fair comparison impossible. Furthermore, the dataset and the chosen FPGA board have a large impact on the synthesis results.

The architecture operates at 200 MHz with a latency of 1.585 µs, including 0.253 µs for data transfer. The utilization of LUTs is high compared to other resources, which can be explained by the amount of Λ that are stored on the board. However, the architecture requires no DSPs at all.

6   Conclusion

In this work a new SV filtering method was presented. It uses the Hybrid SORN approach to detect non-SVs in a training dataset to reduce the computational costs during SVM training and accelerate the training process. It provides an acceleration of factor 1.38 for ovr SVM training and factor 2.65 for ovo SVM training compared to floating point, for MNIST dataset. Although the classification error of the Hybrid SORN implementation is increased compared to floating point implementation, the potential acceleration and the ability to filter SVs from small subsets makes Hybrid SORN SV filter a suitable choice. Furthermore, the concept of the Hybrid SORN SV filter architecture allows combinations with existing hardware accelerators e.g. GPUs.

For future research, the evaluation of different, application specific datasets as well as distributed architectures for on-chip training would be of interest.

References

1. Hülsmeier, N., Bärthel, M., Karsthof, L., Rust, J., Paul, S.: Hybrid SORN Implementation of k-nearest neighbor algorithm on FPGA. In: 2022 20th IEEE Interregional NEWCAS Conference (NEWCAS), Quebec, Canada (2022)
2. Cortes, C., Vapnik, V.: Support vector networks. Mach. Learn. **20**, 273–297 (1995)
3. Graf, H.P., Cosatto, E., Bottou, L., Dourdanovic, I., Vapnik, V.: Parallel support vector machines: the cascade SVM. Proc. Adv. Neural Inf. Process. Syst. 521–528 (2004)
4. Gustafson, J.: A radical approach to computation with real numbers. Supercomput. Front. Innov. **3**(2) (2016)
5. Hülsmeier, N., Bärthel, M., Rust, J., Paul, S.: SORN-based cascade support vector machine. In: 28th European Signal Processing Conference (EUSIPCO), Amsterdam, Netherlands (2021)
6. Bärthel, M., Seidel, P., Rust, J., Paul, S.: SORN arithmetic for MIMO symbol detection - exploration of the type-2 Unum format. In: 2019 17th IEEE International New Circuits and Systems Conference (NEWCAS), Munich, Germany (2019)
7. Bärthel, M., Rust, J., Paul, S.: Application-specific analysis of different SORN datatypes for Unum type-2-based arithmetic. In: 2020 IEEE International Symposium on Circuits and Systems (ISCAS), Sevilla, Spain (2020)
8. Bärthel, M., Hülsmeier, N., Rust, J., Paul, S.: On the implementation of edge detection algorithms with SORN arithmetic. In: Gustafson, J., Dimitrov, V. (eds.) Next Generation Arithmetic. CoNGA 2022. LNCS, vol. 13253, pp. 1–13. Springer, Cham (2022). https://doi.org/10.1007/978-3-031-09779-9_1
9. Bärthel, M., Knobbe, S., Rust, J., Paul, S.: Hardware implementation of a latency-reduced sphere decoder with SORN preprocessing. IEEE Access **9**, 91387–91401 (2021)
10. AXI Dma v7.1 LogiCORE IP Product Guide Vivado Design Suite, Xilinx, July 2019. https://www.xilinx.com/support/documentation/ip_documentation/axi_dma/v7_1/pg021_axi_dma.pdf. Accessed 27 Nov 2022
11. LeCun, Y., Cortes, C., Burges, C.: MNIST handwritten digit database, ATT Labs, vol. 2 (2010). http://yann.lecun.com/exdb/mnist. Accessed 10 Mar 2021
12. Wang, Q., Li, P., Kim, Y.: A parallel digital VLSI architecture for integrated support vector machine training and classification. In: IEEE Integration on Very Large Scale Integration (VLSI) Systems, vol. 23, no. 8 (2015)
13. Afifi, S., GholamHosseini, H., Sinha, R.: FPGA implementations of SVM classifiers: a review. SN Comput. Sci. **1**(133) (2020)
14. Romanov, A., et al.: Analysis of posit and Bfloat arithmetic of real numbers for machine learning. IEEE Access **9**, 82318–82324 (2021)
15. Pedregosa, F., Varoquaux, G., Gramfort, A., Prettenhofer, P.: Scikit-learn: machine learning in python. J. Mach. Learn. Res. **12**, 2825–2830 (2011)

PHAc: Posit Hardware Accelerator for Efficient Arithmetic Logic Operations

Diksha Shekhawat[1,2]($\boxtimes$) (iD), Jugal Gandhi[1,2] (iD), M. Santosh[1,2] (iD),
and Jai Gopal Pandey[1,2] (iD)

[1] Academy of Scientific and Innovative Research (AcSIR), CSIR-HRDC Campus,
Ghaziabad, Uttar Pradesh, India
[2] CSIR - Central Electronics Engineering Research Institute (CEERI),
Pilani 333031, Rajasthan, India
{diksha,jugalacsir,msantosh,jai}@ceeri.res.in

Abstract. Arithmetic accelerators are always in demand for fast computations and logic operations. Here, posit arithmetic plays an important role; it outperforms the traditional IEEE-754 floating-point in terms of accuracy and dynamic range. This paper proposes efficient sequential architectures for the posit adder/subtractor and multiplier that work according to the desired bit size of operands. Here, 32-bit architectures with different exponent sizes (*ES*) have been designed with a control unit. FPGA implementations of these architectures have been performed on the Xilinx Virtex-7 xc7vx330t-3ffg1157 and the Zynq UltraScale + MPSoC ZCU102 device. In comparison with the existing work, it is observed that the datapath delay is lowered by 64.64% for the 32-bit adder and 52.66% for the 32-bit multiplier on the Xilinx Virtex-7 FPGA device. Furthermore, the area-delay (AD) product is reduced by 52.69% and 69.30% for the 32-bit posit adder and multiplier, respectively. In addition, the proposed design has reduced dynamic power than the existing architectures.

Keywords: Posit · IEEE-754 · FPGA · Computer arithmetic · Hardware accelerator

1 Introduction

Performing floating-point (FP) arithmetic operations on traditional microprocessors leads to slow and sometimes inaccurate results. Since the 1980s, almost all computers have used the IEEE-754 standard for floating-point arithmetic to represent real numbers [1]. Embedding intelligence is an aspect of modern technological devices that facilitates quick calculation and connection. Most systems use high-computational image and signal processing applications that seek faster hardware engines. Some essential criteria for these engines are high throughput, high data rate, quick execution, and minimal resource consumption. Here, fixed-point arithmetic can be suited for hardware implementations due to its simplicity of integer-based arithmetic. However, they are not used in high-precision

J. Gustafson et al. (Eds.): CoNGA 2023, LNCS 13851, pp. 88–100, 2023.
https://doi.org/10.1007/978-3-031-32180-1_6

arithmetic. Here floating-point arithmetic is well-suited due to its large dynamic range. However, hardware resources and power consumption are the limiting factors of floating-point arithmetic. Thus, there is a need for computer arithmetic that can provide accuracy closer to floating-point and simplicity of operations similar to fixed-point arithmetic [2].

A possible substitute for the IEEE-754 floating-point numbers (floats) is proposed in [3]. It is a new data type that is known as a posit. It can be used as a direct replacement for the floating-point data type. The posit arithmetic falls under the universal number (*unum*), and unlike other *unums*, they do not require interval arithmetic or variable-size operands. Like floats, they round out if an answer is inexact. Type-III *unum*, also known as posit, is more closely related to FP representation than Type-I and Type-II *unum* [4]. Since Type-I requires extra variable-length management and Type-II *unum* requires look-up tables for most operations, whereas Type-II *unum* are less suited to fused operations [5]. In contrast to floats, posit provides many compelling advantages that include a larger dynamic range, higher accuracy, bit-wise identical results across systems, better closure, simpler hardware, and simpler exception handling. Apart from these, posits that never underflow to zero or overflow to infinity, and "Not-a-Number" (NaN) indicates an action instead of a bit pattern [3]. In addition, posit arithmetic consumes low hardware resources [6]. They provide a good dynamic range/accuracy trade-off, operate with fewer exceptions, and have tapering precision. This indicates that very large and very small numbers are less precise than those close to ± 1. Fused operations are a feature of the posit standard that may be used to compute multiple multiplications, and accumulations without intermediate rounding [7].

The overall effective exponent value in posit is influenced by an additional field of regime bits [8]. The size of the regime bits changes over time, resulting in a change in the exponent and mantissa component placements. Due to these run-time variations, the posit offers a variety of choices for dynamic range, and mantissa precision bits [9]. An m-bit posit adder/multiplier, where $m < n$, can be used instead of an n-bit floating-point adder/multiplier. According to experiments, this also stands without compromising accuracy or range, since the posit adder and multiplier have remarkable advantages in area and energy footprint over the IEEE-754 [10].

This paper aims at hardware implementations of posit arithmetic and its FPGA implementation. FPGA implementations are done on Xilinx Virtex-7 xc7vx330t-3ffg1157 and Zynq UltraScale+ MPSoC ZCU102 device. The key contributions of this work can be stated as follows:

- Proposed hardware architecture of posit adder/subtractor and multiplier with a control unit.
- We use observable methods for the delay, area-delay (AD) product, and dynamic power calculations that provide better results compared to the state-of-the-art with N and varied values of *ES*.

The rest of the paper is arranged as follows: Sect. 2 provides background and related work. The posit adder/subtractor and multiplier methodologies are presented in Sect. 3. Implementation results, evaluation, and comparisons with state-of-the-art architectures are provided in Sect. 4. Finally, Sect. 5 provides the conclusion.

2   Background and Related Work

Approximate or inexact computing is a paradigm that provides the trade-off between energy and processing time for output accuracy [11]. An approximation can only be used for non-crucial data. For finite calculations, precision may have a significant impact on arithmetic processes. Performing accurate computations and precision effects from implementing fixed points in FPGA can result in a degraded response in the control system [12]. Floating-point numbers are slower than fixed-point representations, but they can handle a larger range of numbers [13]. In the comparison of approximate, fixed-point, floating-point, and posit arithmetic is shown in Table 1.

Table 1. A comparison of approximate computing, fixed-point, floating-point arithmetic, and posit [14].

S.No.	Metrics	Approximate Computing	Fixed-Point Arithmetic	Floating-Point Arithmetic	Posit Arithmetic
1.	Interval arithmetic	No	No	Required	Not required
2.	Operands	Fixed	Fixed	Variable size	Variable size
3.	Dynamic range	Lower	Lower	Better	Higher
4.	Accuracy	Lower	Lower	Lower	Higher
5.	Closure	Least	Least	Better	Best
6.	Hardware	Complex	Complex	Complex	Simpler
7.	Exception handling	Least	Least	Better	Best
8.	Overflow	–	Positive	Infinity	No
9.	Underflow	–	Negative	Zero	No
10.	Power usage	Higher	Higher	Higher	Lower
11	Not-a-Number	–	–	Bit pattern	An action

The nearly endless amount of study that has been done on IEEE-754 since its origin in the 1980s has led to the efficient IEEE-754 designs that we have today. In comparison, posit is a manifestation of Type-II *unums* numbers. There have been some software and hardware implementations of posit since its conception. Some parameterised posit arithmetic generators have been presented in [9,10,15], and [16]. An overview of the IEEE-754 floating point standards [17] and posit [3] formats is given below.

Jaiswal et al. [15] presented a recently introduced *unums* system known as the posit system as the basis for open-source hardware termed as PACoGen. It's implementation is done using Verilog HDL techniques, which are subsequently integrated into FPGA and ASIC platforms. Jaiswal et al. [18] presented a hardware solution that generates adders and subtractors for the Type-III *unum* hypothesis. The primary goal of this study is to build a free and open-source customized Verilog HDL generator for the above-mentioned computation. Gustafson et al. [19] primarily compare both posit number systems with the IEEE 754 floating-point standard. It was a theory paper that compared IEEE-754 with posit arithmetic. By performing arithmetic operations on the hardware framework of an FPGA, Hou et al. [20] compared the IEEE-754 system and the posit, as well as their performance results in terms of accuracy and dynamic range, determining that the posit achieved considerable performance and effectiveness. Xiao et al. [21] have proposed hardware for the proposed posit adder/subtractor, multiplication, division, and square root functions, which has been proposed by Xiao et al. [21]. In this, an indefinite posit format created that uses the least amount of space on circuits for hardware implementations. In order to do this, the author substituted an alternate add-and-subtract approach for the Newton-Raphson method while performing division and square root operations, respectively. Each of these functions was then further realised using an FPGA framework.

Malik et al. [22] have performed floating-point divider and multiplier inverse techniques on FPGA. The primary goal of the study is to increase throughput. The author used 32-bit single-precision floats in his implementation. When used in a CPU, real numbers, which are a superset of integer numbers, offer particular difficulties [23]. Cococcioni et al. [24] have combined RISC-V open architecture with posit arithmetic to effectively enable posit functionality within a RISC-V core without altering the behavior of other components. They provided a RISC-V instruction set architecture (ISA) modification that performs the conversion between 8 or 16-bit posits and 32-bit IEEE-754 floats or fixed-point representations. Sharma et al. [25] presented arithmetic empiricism; they present a comprehensive, general-purpose processor-based architecture. Floating-point and posit data types can coexist in applications running on CLARINET, allowing researchers to use it as a platform to gauge the impact of posit arithmetic in real-world floating-point applications.

2.1 The IEEE-754 Standard

The IEEE-754 standard is one of the most widely used floating-point formats. It has a number of hardware and software implementations. The standard defines double-precision and single-precision floating-point formats, which are used in a majority of embedded applications involving numerical computations with a wide dynamic range [17]. The IEEE-754 format consists of three fields: a sign bit, an exponent bit, and fraction bits. The sign bit, which is the most important bit, specifies whether the input operand is positive or negative.

$$val = (-1)^{Sign} \times 2^{(Exp-Bias)} \times 1.fraction \tag{1}$$

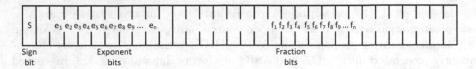

Fig. 1. The IEEE-754 format.

The significand or mantissa is another name for the fraction bits [26]. The floating-point number format is shown in Fig. 1. Thus, a value in the IEEE-754 number is calculated using Eq. (1).

2.2   Posit Format

Posit construction uses three interpolation rules to calculate values between 0 to $\pm\infty$ given in [3]. Posit can be placed on a circle and share the idea of a real projection on a circle like Type-II *unums*, but distinct design decisions allow the posit operation to be implemented without using a look-up table [27]. The negative and positive infinity of the projective reals meet at the top, unlike the real number line, which wraps the line around a circle.

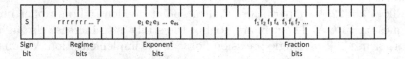

Fig. 2. Posit format.

$$P = (Sign)[Regime \times Exponent \times Mantissa] \qquad (2)$$

Detailed information on the posit number system has been provided in [3,28]. Posit format has just one zero, which is expressed by all bits having a '0' value, and only one Infinity, which is expressed by all bits having a '0' value except the sign bit. Additionally, posit assumes all values are normalised numbers because it ignores the subnormal or denormal representation. The posit comprises four components: a sign, a regime, an exponent, and a mantissa. The perception of an N-bit posit depends on the exponent size. An N-bit posit is interpreted by its exponent size. In comparison to the floating-point norm, posit has an additional field called regime bits. The sign bit is either '0' or '1', indicating if the number is positive or negative, the same as in the floating point. The sequence of identical bits that follow the sign bit and end with the counter bit represents the value of the regime bits. The length of this sequence of identical bits is represented by the value k, which is positive if these bits are '1' and negative if they are '0'. The value of the regime is computed using Eqs. (3) and (4).

$$Regime = useed^k \qquad (3)$$

where
$$used = 2^{2^{es}} \qquad (4)$$

The format of the posit is shown in Fig. 2. If any bit remains after the sign and regime bits, the next field is a complement for the exponent bits, and the fraction bits come after the exponent bits. Overall posit (P) is calculated as shown in Eq. (2).

3   Posit Arithmetic Controller Design Methodology

This section proffers a detailed posit arithmetic generator approach for addition/subtraction and multiplication operations. The extraction of posit data, arithmetic processing, posit building, rounding, and final processing are all provided in this section. The proposed posit adder/subtractor and multiplier with control unit are shown in Fig. 3. The algorithms and architectures for the adder/subtractor and multiplier of the posit are given in [9,10,15], and [14].

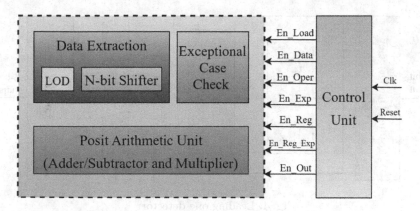

Fig. 3. Posit arithmetic unit with the controller.

3.1   Posit Adder/Subtractor

This module functions primarily as a similar floating-point adder/subtractor arithmetic unit. At this point, the computation of the exponent, the regime value, and the core operation of mantissa addition/subtraction is performed. An approach for the posit adder generator is as follows:

3.1.1   Exceptional Case Check

Before posit data extraction, the special cases need to be examined first, which are $\pm\infty$ and 0. Several IEEE-754 float exceptions are consolidated into two examples of posit arithmetic. If all the bits are zero in input operands, it is a zero posit representation, and if all bits are zero in input operands, except the sign bit leads to an infinity posit representation. $\pm\infty$ and 0 are reciprocals of each other; therefore, dividing any non-zero number by zero does not result in an error; it simply returns infinity.

3.1.2   Data Extraction

Posit data extraction includes the extraction of sign, regime, exponent, and mantissa bits from the input operands. It consists of a leading-one detector (LOD)/leading-zero detector (LZD) and a left shifter, which is based on the barrel shifter. LOD can be used for both purposes if the input of zero sequences is 1's complemented. LOD decodes the run length (RL) of the regime in inputs. The architecture of LOD is shown in Fig. 4. After this, the left shifter shifts the input by the run length and evicts the regime bits. As a result, the exponent is moved to the extreme left and then extracts the exponent bits of size ES from the most significant bit (MSB) of the input posit strings, and the rest of the bits are taken as fraction bits.

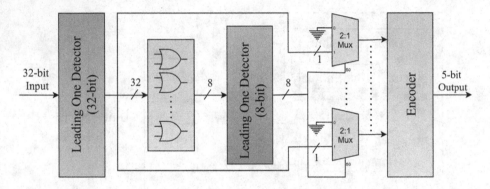

Fig. 4. Leading one detector.

3.1.3   Addition/Subtraction Arithmetic

After data extraction, addition/ subtraction arithmetic is performed. The absolute arithmetic procedure is governed by an XOR operation between the two sign bits. The sign, regime, exponent, and mantissa's large and small values are calculated depending on both input values and used to add or subtract the mantissa operands. A decimal alignment of mantissa operands is necessary to perform mantissa arithmetic. For this, the smaller mantissa is right-shifted by the difference between the total values of the large and small exponents. Now, the addition/subtraction of the large mantissa and the right-shifted small mantissa is performed. To normalise the mantissa addition, the mantissa addition is shifted to the left by one bit. However, in the case of effective mantissa subtraction, if the values of the large mantissa and the small mantissa, which are shifted by the total exponent value, have relatively similar values, normalisation of the mantissa is needed because the value of mantissa addition may lose some MSB bits. This necessitates a LOD operation after arithmetic processing as well as additional left shifting. Following the preceding steps, the final regime value and exponent are computed.

3.1.4 Final Output Processing

In this section, packing, rounding, and final processing of the posit has been done. Data are constructed using a $2 \times N + 3$ GRS bit data structure. A series of the complemented sign bits from the output of the normalised exponent make up the MSB N-bits. Additionally, because the regime ending bit is contrary to the regime sequence bits, the regime sequence ending bit, which is kept immediately following the N-bit regime sequence, is the same sign-bit. The desired regime sequence would be a sequence of complemented sign bits of the normalised exponent. Its purpose was to set up the desired regime sequence since a regime is made up of a sequence of '1' for a positive sequence and a sequence of '0' for a negative sequence. The mantissa is placed after the final exponent output ES-bits in the following N-1 bits, and three guarding (G), rounding (R), and sticking (S) bits are appended to the packed regime, exponent, and mantissa data in the left side bit (LSB) for rounding. By right-shifting the previously created packed data by the final regime output value, the required composition of the posit is obtained. Following the aforementioned processing, rounding is done. Only one rounding method, round-to-nearest-even, is mentioned in the posit format. The sticky bit will also include the shifted final regime bits at the LSB for rounding considerations.

3.2 Posit Multiplier

The posit multiplier arithmetic first checks for exceptional cases; after that, data extraction is done, analogous to posit adder arithmetic. The first two steps, exceptional cases check and data extraction is identical to the posit adder/subtractor arithmetic. After these two steps, multiplier arithmetic is done. After multiplier arithmetic, the final processing is done, which is the same as in posit adder/subtractor arithmetic.

3.2.1 Multiplication Arithmetic

After completion of the first two steps, multiplier arithmetic has been done. A 1-bit XOR function between the input sign bits is required to compute the sign bit. The combined exponent is calculated and consists of both regimes, exponents, and overflow values. Then, the normalised exponent is computed. The output MSB of mantissa multiplication is inspected for any mantissa multiplication overflow. For adequate normalisation, the mantissa is left shifted by one bit for the multiplication overflow of the mantissa, and the final exponent computation is incremented by one. The bit width, which is the result of the mantissa multiplication and is the total of the individual mantissa widths, can be obtained without the requirement to place an additional 3-bit at the end of the result. Then, *ES*-bits of the final exponent and the final regime length bits are calculated from a combined exponent and a normalised exponent. After this operation, the final packing and rounding process is done, similar to the posit adder/subtractor arithmetic.

3.3   Control Unit

In the proposed design, the controller is designed in a pipelined manner to allow the different components of the adder/subtractor and multiplier architecture. By this approach, the control unit can enable the component that is needed by the control signals that are required to be initiated at a particular moment. The control unit, as shown in Fig. 3, has seven control signals. The En_Load signal is used to load data into the hardware accelerator, and the exceptional cases are verified for both inputs. After this, the data extraction component is enabled by the En_Data signal, and the data is extracted from the inputs. Then, the En_Oper signal enables the core addition/subtraction or multiplication operations to be performed. The En_Exp and En_Reg signals are used to compute the total/normalised exponent and regime components. After this, the regime and exponent components are combined using the En_Reg_Exp control signal, and then the final processing of output is done. Then, the final output is computed using the En_Out signal.

4   Implementation Results and Evaluation

Posit adders and multipliers have been successfully implemented on Xilinx Virtex-7 xc7vx330t-3ffg1157 and Zynq UltraScale+ MPSoC ZCU102 for a range of *ES* values.

Table 2. LUT utilization of 32-bit posit adder/subtractor and multiplier with different values *ES* on the Virtex-7 device.

S.No.	Bit Pattern	Posit Adder		Posit Multiplier		
		LUTs	Flip-Flops	LUTs	Flip-Flops	DSPs
1.	(32,1)	1587	291	449	119	4
2.	(32,2)	1611	130	448	120	4
3.	(32,3)	1634	135	444	121	4
4.	(32,4)	1577	297	438	122	4
5.	(32,5)	1585	299	456	123	4
6	(32,6)	1263	312	446	124	4

Table 3. LUT utilization of 32-bit posit adder/subtractor and multiplier with different values *ES* on Zynq UltraScale+ MPSoC ZCU102 device.

S.No.	Bit Pattern	Posit Adder		Posit Multiplier		
		LUTs	Flip-Flops	LUTs	Flip-Flops	DSPs
1.	(32,1)	1641	291	427	119	4
2.	(32,2)	1633	230	423	120	4
3.	(32,3)	1647	235	429	121	4
4.	(32,4)	1623	297	429	122	4
5.	(32,5)	1629	299	427	123	4
6	(32,6)	1540	312	430	124	4

Table 4. Datapath delay (ns) for 32-bit adder/subtractor with different values of *ES* on the Virtex-7 device.

S.No.	Bit Pattern	Posit Adder		Posit Multiplier	
		Proposed	[15]	Proposed	[15]
1.	(31,1)	7.534	19.150	9.310	19.076
2.	(31,2)	6.896	19.984	9.310	18.921
3	(31,3)	6.389	19.752	8.453	19.203

Table 5. Area-delay product (AD) for 32-bit adder/subtractor with different values of *ES* on the Virtex-7 device.

S.No.	Bit Pattern	Posit Adder		Posit Multiplier	
		Proposed	[15]	Proposed	[15]
1.	(32,1)	11956.45	23190.65	4180.19	12742.77
2.	(32,2)	11109.46	25480.00	4170.88	12866.28
3	(32,3)	10439.62	22155.00	3753.12	13826.20

Table 6. Area-delay product (AD) for the 32-bit adder/subtractor with different values of *ES* on the Zynq UltraScale + MPSoC ZCU102 device.

S.No.	Bit Pattern	Posit Adder		Posit Multiplier	
		Delay (ns)	AD	Delay (ns)	AD
1.	(32,1)	9.398	15422.11	7.006	2991.56
2.	(32,2)	9.132	14912.55	7.322	3097.20
3	(32,3)	9.181	15121.10	7.134	3060.48

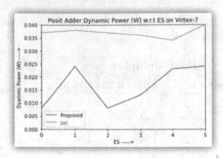

(a) Dynamic power of posit adder.

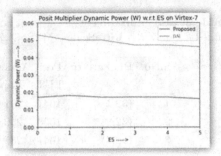

(b) Dynamic power of posit multiplier.

Fig. 5. Power implementation results on Virtex-7 FPGA device.

The proposed work shows the use of LUTs, flip-flops, and DSPs for the posit adder and multiplier for Virtex-7 and Zynq ZCU102 in Table 2 and Table 3, respectively. In Virtex-7 FPGA, the proposed architecture of the 32-bit adder utilizes 0.75% of LUTs and the 32-bit multiplier utilizes 0.21% of LUTs. Similarly, the proposed architecture in Zynq ZCU102 uses 0.59% LUTs and the 32-bit multiplier uses 0.15% LUTs.

Compared to [15], the proposed architecture requires 64.64% lower datapath delays for 32-bit posit adders and 52.66% lower datapath delays for 32-bit posit multipliers, respectively, as shown in Table 4. Furthermore, the area-delay product is improved by 52.69% for the 32-bit posit adder and 69.30% for the 32-bit posit multiplier, as shown in Table 5. The datapath delay and the area-delay product are given in Table 6. Furthermore, the proposed work has a lower dynamic power than the existing architecture, as shown in Fig. 5. It can be observed that the proposed architectures have comparable lower dynamic power, area-delay product, and datapath delay.

5   Conclusion

A hardware accelerator for adders/subtractors and multipliers of 32-bit word size (N) and different exponent sizes (*ES*) with posit arithmetic has been presented. They have been implemented on the Xilinx Virtex-7 xc7vx330t-3ffg1157 and Zynq UltraScale+ MPSoC ZCU102 device FPGA device. The proposed posit adder/subtractor and multiplier architecture have better dynamic power than existing architectures. Compared to existing architectures, the presented work has improved the datapath of 64.64% for 32-bit adders and 52.66% for 32-bit multipliers on the Virtex-7 FPGA device. Furthermore, it reduces the area-delay product by 52.69% and 69.30% for 32-bit posit adders and multipliers.

Acknowledgement. This work has been carried out at Integrated Circuits and Systems Group, CSIR - Central Eléctronics Engineering Research Institute (CEERI), Pilani, Rajasthan, India. We extend our sincere gratitude to the Director, CSIR-CEERI, Pilani, India, for providing the required resources to carry out this research work.

References

1. IEEE standard for floating-point arithmetic, IEEE Std 754–2019 (Revision of IEEE 754–2008), pp. 1–84 (2019)
2. van Dam, L.: Enabling high performance posit arithmetic applications using hardware acceleration (2018)
3. Gustafson, J.L., Yonemoto, I.T.: Beating floating point at its own game: posit arithmetic. Supercomput. Front. Innov. **4**(2), 71–86 (2017)
4. Sravya, A.M., Swetha, N., Panigrahy, A.K.: Hardware posit numeration system primarily based on arithmetic operations. In: 2022 3rd International Conference for Emerging Technology (INCET), pp. 1–8 (2022)
5. Gustafson, J.L.: The End of Error: Unum Computing. Chapman and Hall/CRC, Boca Raton (2017)
6. Buoncristiani, N., Shah, S., Donofrio, D., Shalf, J.: Evaluating the numerical stability of posit arithmetic. In: 2020 IEEE International Parallel and Distributed Processing Symposium (IPDPS), (New Orleans, LA, USA, USA), pp. 612–621. IEEE, 18–22 May 2020
7. Mallasén, D., Murillo, R., Del Barrio, A.A., Botella, G., Piñuel, L., Prieto-Matias, M.: PERCIVAL: open-source posit RISC-V core with quire capability. IEEE Trans. Emerg. Top. Comput. **10**(3), 1241–1252 (2022)
8. van Dam, L., Peltenburg, J., Al-Ars, Z., Hofstee, H.P.: An accelerator for posit arithmetic targeting posit level 1 blas routines and pair-hmm. In: Proceedings of the Conference for Next Generation Arithmetic 2019, CoNGA 2019, (New York, NY, USA), Association for Computing Machinery (2019)
9. Jaiswal, M.K., So, H.K.-H.: Architecture generator for type-3 unum posit adder/subtractor. In: 2018 IEEE International Symposium on Circuits and Systems (ISCAS), (Florence, Italy), pp. 1–5. IEEE, 27–13 May 2018
10. Chaurasiya, R., et al.: Parameterized posit arithmetic hardware generator. In: 2018 IEEE 36th International Conference on Computer Design (ICCD), (Orlando, FL, USA, USA), pp. 334–341. IEEE, 7–10 October 2018
11. Barua, H.B., Mondal, K.C.: Approximate computing: a survey of recent trends-bringing greenness to computing and communication. J. Inst. Eng. (India) Ser. B **100**(6), 619–626 (2019)
12. Martín-Hernando, Y., Rodríguez-Ramos, L.F., Garcia-Talavera, M.R.: Fixed-point vs. floating-point arithmetic comparison for adaptive optics real-time control computation. In: Adaptive Optics Systems, vol. 7015, p. 70152Z (2008). International Society for Optics and Photonics
13. Sasidharan, A., Nagarajan, P.: VHDL implementation of IEEE 754 floating point unit. In: International Conference on Information Communication and Embedded Systems (ICICES2014), pp. 1–5 (2014)
14. Shekhawat, D., Jangir, A., Pandey, J.G.: A hardware generator for posit arithmetic and its FPGA prototyping. In: 2021 25th International Symposium on VLSI Design and Test (VDAT), pp. 1–6. IEEE (2021)

15. Jaiswal, M.K., So, H.K.-H.: PACoGen: a hardware posit arithmetic core generator. IEEE Access **7**, 74586–74601 (2019)
16. Jaiswal, M.K., So, H.K.H.: Universal number posit arithmetic generator on FPGA. In: 2018 Design, Automation & Test in Europe Conference & Exhibition (DATE), (Dresden, Germany), pp. 1159–1162. IEEE, 19–23 March 2018
17. Kahan, W.: IEEE standard 754 for binary floating-point arithmetic. Lect. Notes Status IEEE **754**(94720–1776), 11 (1996)
18. Jaiswal, M.K., So, H.K.-H.: Architecture generator for type-3 Unum posit adder/subtractor. In: 2018 IEEE International Symposium on Circuits and Systems (ISCAS), pp. 1–5 (2018)
19. Gustafson, J.L., Yonemoto, I.T.: Beating floating point at its own game: posit arithmetic. Supercomput. Front. Innov. Int. J. **4**, 71–86 (2017)
20. Hou, J., Zhu, Y., Du, S., Song, S.: Enhancing accuracy and dynamic range of scientific data analytics by implementing posit arithmetic on FPGA. J. Signal Process. Syst. **91**, 1137–1148 (2019)
21. Xiao, F., Liang, F., Wu, B., Liang, J., Cheng, S., Zhang, G.: Posit arithmetic hardware implementations with the minimum cost divider and squareroot. Electronics **9**(10), 1622 (2020)
22. Malík, P.: High throughput floating-point dividers implemented in FPGA. In: 2015 IEEE 18th International Symposium on Design and Diagnostics of Electronic Circuits & Systems, pp. 291–294 (2015)
23. Mallasén, D., Murillo, R., Del Barrio, A.A., Botella, G., Piñuel, L., Prieto-Matias, M.: Customizing the CVA6 RISC-V core to integrate posit and quire instructions. In: 2022 37th Conference on Design of Circuits and Integrated Circuits (DCIS), pp. 01–06. IEEE (2022)
24. Cococcioni, M., Rossi, F., Ruffaldi, E., Saponara, S.: A lightweight posit processing unit for RISC-V processors in deep neural network applications. IEEE Trans. Emerg. Top. Comput. **10**(4), 1898–1908 (2022)
25. Sharma, N.N., et al.: CLARINET: a quire-enabled RISC-V-based framework for posit arithmetic empiricism. J. Syst. Archit. **135**, 102801 (2023)
26. Lafage, V.: Revisiting what every computer scientist should know about floating-point arithmetic, arXiv preprint arXiv:2012.02492 (2020)
27. Cococcioni, M., Ruffaldi, E., Saponara, S.: Exploiting posit arithmetic for deep neural networks in autonomous driving applications. In: 2018 International Conference of Electrical and Electronic Technologies for Automotive, pp. 1–6. IEEE (2018)
28. Gustafson, J.L.: Posit arithmetic. Mathematica Notebook describing the posit number system, vol. 30 (2017)

Fused Three-Input SORN Arithmetic

Moritz Bärthel[1,2]([✉])([iD]), Chen Yuxing[2], Nils Hülsmeier[1,2]([iD]), Jochen Rust[3]([iD]),
and Steffen Paul[1,2]([iD])

[1] Institute of Electrodynamics and Microelectronics (ITEM.me), Bermen, Germany
{baerthel,huelsmeier,steffen.paul}@me.uni-bremen.de
[2] University of Bremen, Bremen, Germany
[3] DSI Aerospace Technologie GmbH, Bremen, Germany
jochen.rust@dsi-as.de

Abstract. The Sets-of-Real-Numbers (SORN) format for digital arithmetic and signal processing represents real numbers with small sets of exact values and intervals, enabling low-complex and fast computing of arithmetic operations. The format derives from the universal numbers (unum) and has already proven to be a valuable alternative to legacy formats like fixed point or floating point.

The main challenge of SORN arithmetic is degenerating accuracy due to increasing intervals widths, which is tackled in this work with the proposal of fused SORN arithmetic for the three-input operations addition, multiplication and multiply-add, as well as the three-input hypot function. Evaluations on accuracy and hardware performance for different SORN datatypes show that accuracy improvements of up to 60% can be achieved, along with moderate to high hardware complexity increases. In some cases even improvements for both accuracy and hardware performance can be achieved.

Keywords: SORN · unum · computer arithmetic · fused multiply-add

1 Introduction and Related Work

Computer arithmetic and digital signal processing architectures are mostly based on the well-established number formats fixed point and IEEE-745 floating point. In recent years, however, alternative number formats for representing real values in digital systems are an emerging topic, in order to address current design challenges such as energy efficiency and high performance computing. This development is mainly driven by the requirements of specific applications such as machine learning, where variations of the existing floating point formats are evaluated [9], as well as new approaches such as the posit format [13].

Another new approach for a digital number representation is the unum type-II-based Sets-of-Real-Numbers (SORN) format [6]. SORNs are an interval-based

The authors acknowledge the financial support by the Federal Ministry of Education and Research of Germany in the project "Open6GHub" (grant number: 16KISK016).

low-precision representation, where a bit vector is used to specify values from a predefined set of intervals that perfectly tile the real number line. Unlike traditional interval arithmetic, where both interval bounds are represented with a separate fixed or floating point value [10], a single SORN bit represents a complete interval, which strongly reduces the resulting hardware complexity of the corresponding arithmetic operations. These operations are performed using precomputed SORN lookup tables (LUTs). The setup of SORN representation and arithmetic enables fast computing with low complexity, at the expense of low precision, compared to legacy number formats like fixed point or floating point.

Due to this low precision, SORN arithmetic is not general-purpose. However, SORNs can be used effectively either as a replacement for threshold-based algorithms, or in preprocessing modules for complex optimization algorithms. Possible applications for SORN arithmetic are sphere decoding for MIMO communication [3], edge detection in image processing [2], or classification algorithms for machine learning [8].

The biggest challenges in the design of SORN arithmetic operations are on one hand the complexity of the LUTs which increases exponentially with the number of bits used for a SORN datatype, and on the other hand the accuracy[1] of the results which degenerates with increasing datapath length, due to increasing interval widths. Approaches to tackle these challenges are adaptions of the SORN datatype [1] and the introduction of fused arithmetic, i.e. the combination of multiple arithmetic operations in one SORN LUT, as evaluated for single- and two-input SORN operations in [4]. Fused arithmetic is a well-known approach for legacy formats like floating point. The fused multiply-add (FMA) or multiply-accumulate operation is even included in the IEEE-754 standard for floating point [11].

In this work fused arithmetic is evaluated for three-input SORN addition, multiplication, and multiply-add operations, as well as for the three-input hypot function $\sqrt{x^2 + y^2 + z^2}$. Section 2 describes the principles of the SORN number format and its LUT-based arithmetic, and introduces the three-input fused arithmetic operations. These operations are evaluated in Sect. 3 and Sect. 4, in terms of output accuracy and hardware complexity, compared to non-fused equivalent architectures. The work is concluded in Sect. 5.

2   Type-II Unums and SORNs

The type-II unums derive from the original type-I unum format, which is a floating point representation with variable exponent and mantissa widths and an uncertainty bit. This so-called ubit indicates an open interval whenever a value would have been rounded [7]. This leads to a representation of the reals using exact values and open intervals in between. Type-II unums adapt this ubit approach and represent the reals with small sets of intervals and exacts, the

---

[1] The term *accuracy* within the context of interval-based SORN arithmetic is discussed in Sect. 3.1.

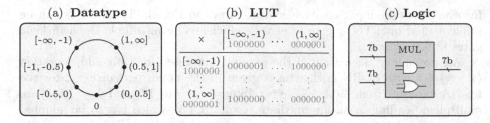

Fig. 1. The SORN arithmetic design flow includes (a) defining the datatype, (b) setting up the arithmetic LUTs, and (c) implementing the LUTs with Boolean logic.

Sets-of-Real-Numbers. The different values/intervals within this SORN representation can be varied, or even adapted towards less or no exact values and half-open intervals [1]. Such a representation, in the following also called SORN datatype, is shown in Fig. 1a. The given datatype consists of 7 elements, includes the values zero and infinity, and provides a $\log_2$-based value distribution with half-open intervals. Further datatypes with different bitwidths and $\log_2$ or linear distributions, which are used in this work, are given in Table 1.

2.1 SORN Arithmetic

The main idea of SORN arithmetic is to encode the given datatype into a bit string, where every bit encodes the presence or absence of the respective value/interval. Interval unions are represented with consecutive bits. With this binary representation, a simple way of implementing arithmetic operations can be achieved. Every operation is encoded into a LUT that includes the result

Table 1. Different SORN datatype configurations utilizing linear and log-based interval distributions.

label	config
lin-7-A	$[-\infty, -3)$ $[-3, -1.5)$ $[-1.5, 0)$ 0 $(0, 1.5]$ $(1.5, 3]$ $(3, \infty]$
lin-7-B	$[-\infty, -100)$ $[-100, -50)$ $[-50, 0)$ 0 $(0, 50]$ $(50, 100]$ $(100, \infty]$
log-7-A	$[-\infty, -1)$ $[-1, -0.5)$ $[-0.5, 0)$ 0 $(0, 0.5]$ $(0.5, 1]$ $(1, \infty]$
log-7-B	$[-\infty, -64)$ $[-64, -32)$ $[-32, 0)$ 0 $(0, 32]$ $(32, 64]$ $(64, \infty]$
lin-9-A	$[-\infty, -1)$ ... $[-1/3, 0)$ 0 $(0, 1/3]$ $(1/3, 2/3]$ $(2/3, 1]$ $(1, \infty]$
lin-9-B	$[-\infty, -120)$ ... $[-40, 0)$ 0 $(0, 40]$ $(40, 80]$ $(80, 120]$ $(120, \infty]$
log-9-A	$[-\infty, -2)$ ... $[-0.5, 0)$ 0 $(0, 0.5]$ $(0.5, 1]$ $(1, 2]$ $(2, \infty]$
log-9-B	$[-\infty, -128)$ ... $[-32, 0)$ 0 $(0, 32]$ $(32, 64]$ $(64, 128]$ $(128, \infty]$
lin-11-A	$[-\infty, -1)$ ... $[-0.25, 0)$ 0 $(0, 0.25]$ $(0.25, 0.5]$ $(0.5, 0.75]$ $(0.75, 1]$ $(1, \infty]$
lin-11-B	$[-\infty, -200)$ ... $[-50, 0)$ 0 $(0, 50]$ $(50, 100]$ $(100, 150]$ $(150, 200]$ $(200, \infty]$
log-11-A	$[-\infty, -2)$ ... $[-0.25, 0)$ 0 $(0, 0.25]$ $(0.25, 0.5]$ $(0.5, 1]$ $(1, 2]$ $(2, \infty]$
log-11-B	$[-\infty, -256)$ ... $[-32, 0)$ 0 $(0, 32]$ $(32, 64]$ $(64, 128]$ $(128, 256]$ $(256, \infty]$

for every possible input combination, as shown in Fig. 1b. These LUTs can be implemented on RTL or gate level very efficiently using simple Boolean logic gates [2,6,8] (Fig. 1c).

An exemplary calculation of the regular, non-fused multiply-add operation $(x \times y) + z$ with SORN arithmetic is given in the upper part of Fig. 2 for the lin-7-A datatype from Table 1. The two intervals $x = (0, 1.5]$ and $y = (1.5, 3]$ are multiplied, leading to an intermediate result $(0, 4.5]$, which has to be adapted to the given datatype, and is therefore converted to $(0, \infty]$. This intermediate result is then added with $z = [-3, -1.5)$ leading to the result $[-3, \infty]$.

2.2   Fused SORN Operations

The given example for a non-fused multiply-add operation indicates the main challenge for SORN arithmetic in complex datapaths, which is decreasing accuracy caused by increasing output interval widths. The output of the given example contains 6 one-bits out of 7 bit total word length, which indicates a drastic loss of information from the input to the output. Additionally, the output contains an infinity interval which impedes further calculations with this value.

Both of these problems can be tackled with the so-called fused arithmetic, where the multiply-add operation is encoded directly into a three-dimensional SORN LUT. This approach removes the intermediate rounding step and leads to lower output widths and less infinity intervals. For the given example in Fig. 2, the intermediate rounding step $(0, 4.5] \to (0, \infty]$ is avoided, leading to an output value $[-3, 3]$, which reduces the output width by 1 and contains no infinity value.

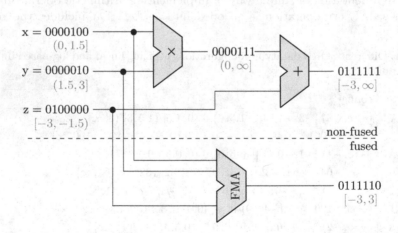

Fig. 2. SORN arithmetic example for non-fused and fused multiply-add for the lin-7-A datatype.

3   Fused Addition, Multiplication and Multiply-Add

In order to evaluate the proposed approach of fused SORN arithmetic, the RTL implementations of both the non-fused and fused versions for three-input addition, multiplication, and multiply-add are compared in this section. All three operations were implemented for the 12 datatypes given in Table 1, both as non-fused and fused architecture, as depicted in Fig. 2. In the following the accuracy and hardware performance results of all implemented designs are discussed.

3.1   Accuracy

For traditional, non-interval fixed point or floating point arithmetic, the term *accuracy* is used as a measure for the distance of a computed result to the actual correct value, obtained with infinite precision. The accuracy of single-valued digital arithmetic is affected by rounding, under- and overflow, and limited by the precision of the applied number format [5]. For interval arithmetic, the term *accuracy* can be interpreted slightly different. Since the correct result of a calculation is encompassed by an interval, the accuracy indicates the distance of the interval bounds to the correct result, which can be measured by the width or diameter of the interval. Another term for *accuracy* in this context is *overestimation* [12].

The accuracy of a SORN value can be measured by the width of the represented interval, which is equivalent to the number of consecutive one-bits in a binary SORN value. The best case is a one-hot binary value representing the smallest possible interval width, depending on the chosen datatype. A SORN value with all-one bits represents the interval $[-\infty, \infty]$ and does not provide any valuable information. In Fig. 3 the mean output widths in bit of the implemented three-input operations are given as a measure for the output accuracy. The mean is obtained from simulations over all possible one-hot input values for a given SORN datatype without infinity-intervals. The reduction of the output width for the respective fused operation over its corresponding non-fused version is given in %.

The first observation from the presented results is that all fused designs show at least an equal, but in most cases a reduced mean output width, compared to the non-fused equivalents. The addition operation shows the smallest gains, multiplication the highest. Except for multiplication, the reduction scales with the utilized datatype size; the more bits are used, the higher the improvement. Another observation is that for all operations that include at least one multiplication, the datatypes utilizing larger values (lin/log-B) show a much higher reduction than those with a higher resolution between 0 and 1 (lin/log-A). This can be explained with avoided infinity intervals due to fused operations, which do not appear when multiplying values between 0 and 1. A difference between linear and logarithmic distribution is only visible for the addition, here the log-based datatypes show a slightly higher reduction. In general, it can be stated that fused multiplication with up to 28.8% reduction and fused multiply-add

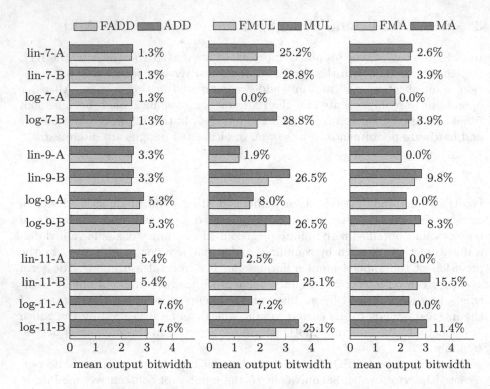

Fig. 3. Mean output bitwidths for non-fused and fused three-input addition, multiplication and multiply-add, evaluated for one-hot input values, with output bitwidth reduction for fused operations in %.

with up to 15.5% show valuable reductions of the mean output widths, while the reduction for fused addition with up to 7.6% is rather moderate.

3.2 FPGA Synthesis

In order to evaluate the hardware performance of the implemented operations for an FPGA platform, all designs were synthesized for a ZYNQ-7 ZC702 Evaluation Board from Xilinx for a frequency of $f = 150$ MHz. Since the designs are composed of logic gates only, no DSPs or BRAM modules from the FPGA are used. The utilized LUTs as a measure of the required area are given in Fig. 4, along with the respective path delay for every design. The power consumption of the implemented designs is negligible compared to the power consumed by the entire FPGA, therefore no significant differences among the fused and non-fused modules are visible and the power consumption is not displayed.

As expected, the three-dimensional SORN LUTs for the fused operations show a higher complexity than the non-fused combination of two-dimensional SORN LUTs. This is true for every evaluated operation and SORN datatype. However, significant differences between the operations and datatypes are visible.

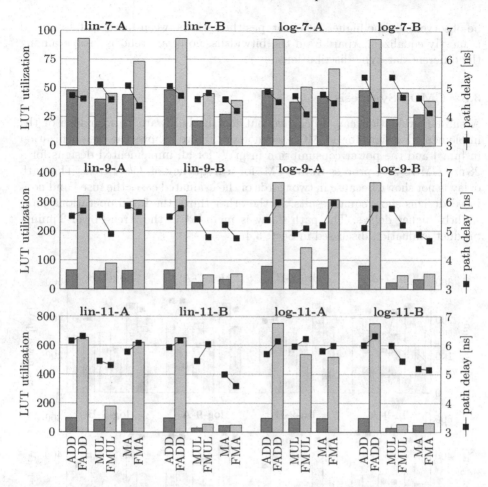

Fig. 4. FPGA Synthesis results for non-fused and fused three-input addition, multiplication and multiply-add, for a ZYNQ-7 ZC702 Evaluation Board (xc7z020clg484-1) with $f = 150$ MHz.

While for the addition operation the fused design always requires at least double and at most eight times the area of the non-fused design, for multiplication and multiply-add in some cases a much smaller area increase can be observed. Especially for the fused multiply-add operation the area increase is small, compared to the other operations. For the lin-11-B dataype, the FMA operation utilizes only 4.3% more LUTs than the non-fused design while achieving a 15.5% better accuracy (see Sect. 3.1).

The critical path delay of every design is also shown in Fig. 4. The results show that the path delay is not necessarily related to the required LUTs, some fused modules with higher area utilization than their non-fused equivalents still show a significantly lower path delay. Especially for the 7b datatypes this behavior can

108   M. Bärthel et al.

be observed, for the higher bit datatypes the ratio between fused and non-fused
is mostly equalized. Apart from the bitwidths, no clear trend is visible among
the different datatype distributions.

3.3 CMOS Synthesis

A similar evaluation can be carried out for the hardware performance of the
implemented designs for a CMOS technology. Figure 5 shows the area utilization
in [µm²] and the power consumption in [µW] for all implemented designs for a
28 nm CMOS SOI process from STM, for a frequency of $f = 1$ GHz. The path
delay is not shown because in two thirds of the evaluated cases the fused and non-
fused designs show equal results. In the other third, the fused operations show
slightly higher delays. The path delay is included in the Area-Power-Timing-
product evaluation discussed in Sect. 3.4.

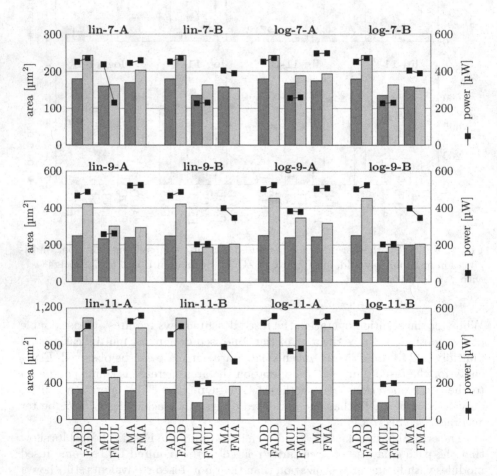

Fig. 5. Synthesis results for non-fused and fused three-input addition, multiplication
and multiply-add, for 28 nm CMOS with $f = 1$ GHz.

The area results from Fig. 5 show a trend similar to the FPGA results from Sect. 3.2: the addition operations shows the highest area increase, while for multiplication and multiply-add the area increase of the fused designs is much smaller for most of the cases. For FMA and the lin/log-7-B datatypes even a small reduction of the area can be achieved. In general, the area increase for the fused designs in CMOS is much smaller than for the FPGA evaluation. For the addition operation, the mean area increase over the 12 different datatypes is 101%, for multiplication 43%, and for multiply-add 51%.

The power consumption is up to 6% higher for most of the fused designs, compared to their non-fused equivalents. However, for the lin/log-B datatypes the FMA operation achieves a lower power consumption (12% reduction on average), as well as the fused multiplication for the lin-7-A and log-9-A datatypes (47% and 1% reduction, respectively).

3.4 Accuracy vs. Complexity

Since the hardware performance of the fused three-input operations is mostly worse, compared to non-fused, whereas the accuracy results are mostly better for the fused designs, a joint evaluation is helpful in order to rate the trade-off between both measures. Therefore an accuracy ratio r_{acc} is introduced, which compares the mean output width of fused and non-fused designs for every operation and datatype, based on the results presented in Sect. 3.1:

$$r_{acc} = \frac{\text{fused mean out width}}{\text{non-fused mean out width}} \tag{1}$$

For the hardware performance, the Area-Power-Timing-product (APT-product) given in $[\mu m^2 \times \mu W \times ns]$ is used as a combined measure, based on the CMOS results from Sect. 3.3. The APT-product ratio r_{APT} compares the hardware performance of fused vs. non-fused:

$$r_{APT} = \frac{\text{fused APT } [\mu m^2 \times \mu W \times ns]}{\text{non-fused APT } [\mu m^2 \times \mu W \times ns]} \tag{2}$$

Both ratios are plotted against each other in Fig. 6. A ratio < 1 represents an improvement for the fused over the non-fused design for the respective measure. The line for balanced ratios $r_{acc} + r_{APT} = 2$ represents cases where the percentage degradation of one measure is compensated by the other.

About two thirds of the evaluated fused and non-fused pairs neither achieve an improved APT-product, nor balanced ratios, especially the designs utilizing 11b datatypes and those implementing the addition operation. For multiplication and multiply-add, however, for in total nine of the different datatype-operation combinations utilizing mostly lin/log-7/9-B datatypes, constellations better than balanced ratios or even with both ratios < 1 can be achieved. Four FMA and one fused multiplication operation achieve an improvement for both accuracy and hardware complexity. Four fused multiplication architectures can compensate the increased APT-product by an improved accuracy. On top of that, two

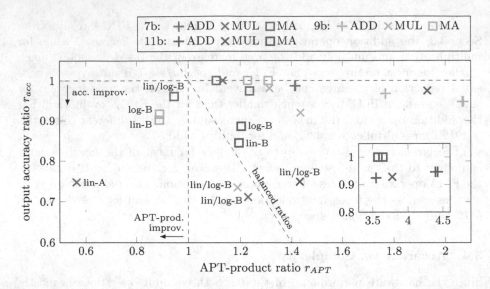

Fig. 6. Output accuracy ratio r_{acc} vs. APT-product ratio r_{APT} for fused three-input addition, multiplication and multiply-add. A ratio < 1 indicates an improvement for the fused design over the non-fused. Balanced ratios are achieved with $r_{acc} + r_{APT} = 2$.

11b multiply-add cases and two 11b multiplication cases are close to the balanced ratio line and might be worth considering in order to utilize the improved accuracy.

4   Fused 2D and 3D Hypot Function

In order to consider more complex operations and the combination of fusing single-input and two- or three-input functions, in this section the three-input hypot function

$$\text{hypot}(x, y, z) = \sqrt{x^2 + y^2 + z^2} \tag{3}$$

is evaluated. The hypot function is used for calculating three-dimensional euclidean distances and is included as a subroutine in programming languages like C++ or Python, in order to avoid intermediate under- and overflows. The hypot function with two inputs is also part of the IEEE-754 standard [11].

The block diagrams for the implementations of the non-fused, 2D and 3D fused hypot versions are shown in Fig. 7. For the 2D version the single-input functions square and square root are fused into the SORN additions with two inputs, resulting in two-input SORN operations blocks. For the 3D version all operations are combined in one three-input block. As for the previously evaluated fused operations from Sect. 3, the three designs from Fig. 7 were implemented for all 12 SORN datatypes given in Table 1 and synthesized for a 28 nm CMOS SOI process from STM, for a frequency of $f = 1$ GHz.

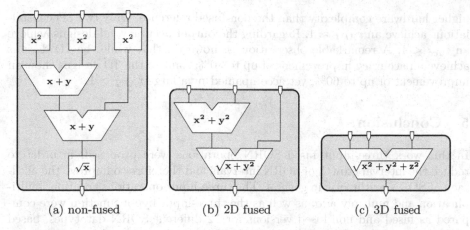

(a) non-fused   (b) 2D fused   (c) 3D fused

Fig. 7. Block diagrams for the three-input hypot function as non-fused, 2D and 3D fused designs.

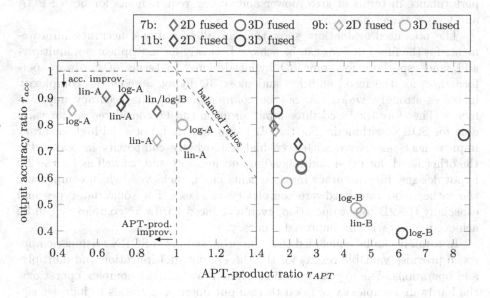

Fig. 8. Output accuracy ratio r_{acc} vs. APT-product ratio r_{APT} for 2D-fused and 3D-fused three-input hypot function. A ratio < 1 indicates an improvement for the fused design over the non-fused. Balanced ratios are achieved with $r_{acc} + r_{APT} = 2$.

According to the accuracy and APT-product ratios introduced in Sect. 3.4, Fig. 8 shows the results for the mean output width and hardware performance of the 2D and 3D fused hypot implementations, compared against the non-fused design. The two subplots separate the r_{APT}-axis into parts with different resolutions. The main observation for the hypot evaluation is that only 2D designs achieve an $r_{APT} < 1$, whereas the 3D designs mainly show a much higher hardware complexity than the non-fused reference. Only two 3D constellations achieve an $r_{APT} \approx 1$. Regarding the output accuracy, all designs achieve an $r_{acc} < 1$. A remarkable observation is, however, that while the 2D designs achieve an accuracy improvement of up to 30%, some of the 3D designs show an improvement of up to 60%, yet accompanied by a large $r_{APT} > 1$.

5 Conclusion

In this work three-input fused SORN operations were proposed, in order to reduce the interval growth of SORN intervals and therefore to improve the accuracy of SORN arithmetic in general. The three-input operations addition, multiplication and multiply-add, as well as the three-input hypot function were compared as fused and non-fused versions for 12 different SORN datatypes, based on RTL implementations of the respective designs. The utilized evaluation metrics are 1.) accuracy in terms of output SORN interval width, and 2.) hardware performance in terms of area, power and timing requirements for both FPGA and CMOS target platforms.

The presented evaluations show that for all operations, accuracy improvements for the fused designs can be achieved, mostly for multiplication, multiply-add, and especially for some 3D hypot designs. In terms of hardware performance, for the fused addition and most 3D hypot designs the complexity increases strongly, which can not be compensated by the accuracy improvements. Therefore the fused three-input addition can be considered as not valuable for SORN arithmetic. For the 3D hypot function, potential high accuracy improvements are payed with even higher hardware complexity increases. On the other hand, for fused multiplication and multiply-add, as well as for the 2D hypot designs, high accuracy improvements can be achieved, which compensate the rather moderate hardware complexity increases. For some datatypes and especially the 2D hypot operation, even a reduced hardware complexity can be achieved, along with an improved accuracy.

In total, it can be concluded that the proposed fused SORN arithmetic approach provides valuable results for the three-input multiplication and multiply-add operations. The hypot evaluations show that for more complex operations, the hardware complexity of fused three-input operations trends to increase significantly and has to be weighed against the likewise potentially high accuracy improvements. For future work this trend needs to be further evaluated with more complex three-input functions and more complex SORN datapaths in general.

References

1. Bärthel, M., Rust, J., Paul, S.: Application-specific analysis of different SORN datatypes for unum type-2-based arithmetic. In: 2020 IEEE International Symposium on Circuits and Systems (ISCAS), pp. 1–5 (2020). https://doi.org/10.1109/ISCAS45731.2020.9181182

2. Bärthel, M., Hülsmeier, N., Rust, J., Paul, S.: On the implementation of edge detection algorithms with SORN arithmetic. In: Conference on Next Generation Arithmetic, pp. 1–13. Springer (2022). https://doi.org/10.1007/978-3-031-09779-9_1

3. Bärthel, M., Knobbe, S., Rust, J., Paul, S.: Hardware implementation of a latency-reduced sphere decoder with SORN preprocessing. IEEE Access **9**, 91387–91401 (2021). https://doi.org/10.1109/ACCESS.2021.3091778

4. Bärthel, M., Rust, J., Gustafson, J., Paul, S.: Improving the precision of SORN arithmetic by introducing fused operations. In: 2022 IEEE International Symposium on Circuits and Systems (ISCAS), pp. 258–262 (2022). https://doi.org/10.1109/ISCAS48785.2022.9937595

5. Goldberg, D.: What every computer scientist should know about floating-point arithmetic. ACM Comput. Surveys (CSUR) **23**(1), 5–48 (1991)

6. Gustafson, J.L.: A radical approach to computation with real numbers. Supercomput. Front. Innovations **3**(2), 38–53 (2016). https://doi.org/10.14529/jsfi160203

7. Gustafson, J.L.: The End of Error: Unum Computing. CRC Press, Boca Raton (2015)

8. Hülsmeier, N., Bärthel, M., Karsthof, L., Rust, J., Paul, S.: Hybrid SORN implementation of k-nearest neighbor algorithm on FPGA. In: 2022 20th IEEE Interregional NEWCAS Conference (NEWCAS), pp. 163–167 (2022). https://doi.org/10.1109/NEWCAS52662.2022.9841985

9. Johnson, J.: Rethinking floating point for deep learning (2018). https://doi.org/10.48550/ARXIV.1811.01721

10. Kirchner, R., Kulisch, U.W.: Hardware support for interval arithmetic. Reliable Comput. **12**(3), 225–237 (2006). https://doi.org/10.1007/s11155-006-7220-9

11. Microprocessor Standards Committee of the IEEE Computer Society: IEEE standard for floating-point arithmetic. IEEE Std 754-2008, 1–70 (2008). https://doi.org/10.1109/IEEESTD.2008.4610935

12. Rump, S.M.: Verification methods: rigorous results using floating-point arithmetic. Acta Numer **19**, 287–449 (2010). https://doi.org/10.1145/1837934.1837937

13. Zolfagharinejad, M., Kamal, M., Afzali-Khusha, A., Pedram, M.: Posit process element for using in energy-efficient DNN accelerators. IEEE Trans. Very Large Scale Integr. (VLSI) Syst. **30**(6), 844–848 (2022). https://doi.org/10.1109/TVLSI.2022.3165510

Towards a Better 16-Bit Number Representation for Training Neural Networks

Himeshi De Silva[1]([✉]), Hongshi Tan[2], Nhut-Minh Ho[2], John L. Gustafson[3], and Weng-Fai Wong[2]

[1] Institute for Infocomm Research, A*STAR, Singapore, Singapore
himeshi_de_silva@i2r.a-star.edu.sg
[2] National University of Singapore, Singapore, Singapore
{tanhs,minhhn,wongwf}@comp.nus.edu.sg
[3] Arizona State University, Tempe, USA
jlgusta6@asu.edu

Abstract. Error resilience in neural networks has allowed for the adoption of low-precision floating-point representations for mixed-precision training to improve efficiency. Although the IEEE 754 standard had long defined a 16-bit float representation, several other alternatives targeting mixed-precision training have also emerged. However, their varying numerical properties and differing hardware characteristics, among other things, make them more or less suitable for the task. Therefore, there is no clear choice of a 16-bit floating-point representation for neural network training that is commonly accepted. In this work, we evaluate all 16-bit float variants and upcoming *posit*™ number representations proposed for neural network training on a set of Convolutional Neural Networks (CNNs) and other benchmarks to compare their suitability. Posits generally achieve better results, indicating that their non-uniform accuracy distribution is more conducive for the training task. Our analysis suggests that instead of having the same accuracy for all weight values, as is the case with floats, having greater accuracy for the more commonly occurring weights with larger magnitude improves the training results, thereby challenging previously held assumptions while bringing new insight into the dynamic range and precision requirements. We also evaluate the efficiency on hardware for mixed-precision training based on FPGA implementations. Finally, we propose the use of statistics based on the distribution of network weight values as a heuristic for selecting the number representation to be used.

Keywords: Neural Networks · 16-bit Floating-point · Half-precision · Posit

1 Introduction

Owing to the size of datasets and the complexity of models used for learning at present, training a large neural network can easily require days or weeks even on

J. Gustafson et al. (Eds.): CoNGA 2023, LNCS 13851, pp. 114–133, 2023.
https://doi.org/10.1007/978-3-031-32180-1_8

modern GPUs. Because 16-bit data types halve the required memory and bandwidth demands of 32-bit floating-point and therefore can significantly improve performance and energy efficiency, IEEE 754 standard "half-precision" floats (IEEE16) and several other 16-bit floating-point variations have been proposed for deep learning. However, each of these formats have significantly different properties giving them varying degrees of suitability for training neural networks. Figure 1 shows the *relative decimal accuracy* (RDA) (defined in Sect. 7) between consecutive number pairs for 16-bit float formats (all published variations) and posit formats studied in this work, which we collectively refer to as FP16. The width of a graph shows the dynamic range while the height shows the RDA distribution in that range, for each format. The different accuracy distributions of the number representations lead to varying success in neural network training, as demonstrated by the test loss for a representative benchmark in Fig. 2. To overcome accuracy degradation, researchers have had to rely on custom accuracy saving techniques. However, the exact accuracy degradation behavior of each FP16 format and the generality of each technique is not known. While mixed-precision training with IEEE16 has reported 2–4.5× speedup, mechanisms used to improve training accuracy also increases training overhead [19]. Therefore, there is no clear consensus as to what the optimal 16-bit float representation is for training or what characteristics of a number format lead to better training results.

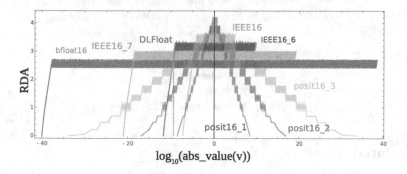

Fig. 1. RDA - FP16

CNNs have been studied and adopted widely for tasks such as image classification. Here, we test all FP16 number formats previously proposed for CNNs (as well as new ones), under *identical conditions*, to assess their relative capabilities for CNN training benchmarks of varying sizes. We also do the same for newer language translation models to test the versatility of the formats. In this paper we will:

- Demonstrate empirically that for a 16-bit IEEE-type float format, the optimal number of exponent bits producing the best results is 6.
- Show that posits produce better accuracy results, which suggests that their non-uniform accuracy distribution is more suitable for training.

- Analyze the accuracy for a selected benchmark to show that having more accuracy for commonly occurring weights with larger magnitude is key. Because all previously studied 16-bit float formats have uniform accuracy distributions (Fig. 1), this idea has not been presented previously.
- Propose a new accuracy saving technique for neural network training that adds no overhead, which is that of shifting the peak RDA of posits based on the distribution of weight values.
- Evaluate the FP16 formats in terms of hardware costs for conversion and accuracy under different rounding modes to gain a more holistic and practical understanding of their capabilities in mixed-precision training.

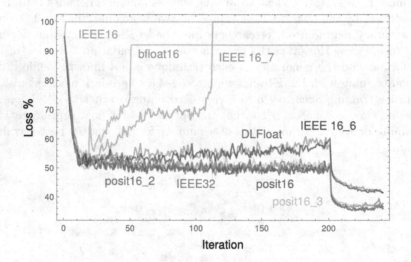

Fig. 2. Test loss - FP16

2   Related Work

The IEEE 754 standard [3] provides all details related to floating-point data types that are implemented on most systems. Its "half-precision" format, IEEE16, specifies 5 exponent bits. To achieve training results comparable to IEEE32 using IEEE16 representations for weights, activations and gradients, several accuracy saving mechanisms need to be employed. They include maintaining copies of master weights in IEEE32 for weight update, loss scaling (not required for CNNs) and accumulating IEEE16 vector dot products into IEEE32 values [17]. Mixed-precision training with bfloat16 requires the same techniques except for loss scaling [2]. Another FP16 format, DLFloat, has a 6-bit exponent and aims to simplify the hardware for floating-point computations [1]. When it is used in training, weights, biases, activations, errors and weight updates are represented in DLfloat, with fused-multiply-add instructions used to perform the matrix multiplications and convolution operations at 16-bit precision.

A reduced-precision dot product algorithm which initially accumulates smaller chunks of a long dot product and then accumulates their partial sums hierarchically coupled with stochastic floating-point rounding has been used to reduce the representation of weights, activations and gradients to an 8-bit float format. The accumulations for forward and backward passes occur in a 16-bit float with a 6-bit exponent and so does the regularization, momentum computation and weight update—which uses a master copy of the weights at 16-bit precision [24]. Another attempt at reducing the representation to 8-bit float format for weights, activations, errors and gradients uses techniques such as quantization, stochastic rounding, loss scaling, IEEE32 computations and accumulations and maintaining master weight copies in IEEE16 [16].

A hybrid exponent size scheme has been proposed to enable 8-bit floats to work across a broader range of networks and models. This scheme stores weights and activations with a 4-bit exponent while tensors in the backward pass are stored with a 5-bit exponent. The very low number of bits of significance requires loss scaling with multiple scaling factors, and conversion across different formats along with other optimizations [22]. Recently, ultra-low (4-bit) precision combined with other techniques have been proposed for training [23]. These training schemes require either enhanced versions of 16-bit accuracy-saving techniques or even more complex mechanisms that add overhead. Because all of them still make use of 16-bit or 32-bit floats, assessing the various 16-bit formats and their capabilities is still useful even when using such 8-bit representations.

Taking a cue from neural network inference, floats with precision as low as a single bit have been tested for training [25]. Similarly, 16-bit (and smaller) fixed-point representations have also been studied for training DNNs [4,6,12]. However, these either work only on small training examples or require mechanisms such as dynamic scaling, shared exponents, specialized instructions for high precision steps, or other complex accuracy management schemes and improvements to match IEEE32 accuracy. For example, the Flexpoint format actually has a 16-bit significand with separate exponent bits. Our own experiments with fixed-point did not produce useful results even for the smallest benchmarks, thus we are excluding it from discussion.

Although posits have been explored briefly for training and inference [7, 8,15], it has not been evaluated or compared against other formats extensively. Moreover, as we will demonstrate, layer-wise scaling is not necessary for training with 16-bit posits.

3   16-Bit Float and Posit Formats

3.1   IEEE 754 Standard Type Float Formats

An IEEE float contains three fields: a 1-bit sign S, a w-bit biased exponent E, and a $(t = p - 1)$-bit trailing significand field digit string $T = d_1 d_2...d_{p-1}$; the leading significand bit, d_0, is implicitly encoded in E. The value v inferred from this representation is given by Eq. 1. The default rounding mode as defined by the Standard is round-to-nearest-even (RNE).

$$v = \begin{cases} \text{NaN (Not a Number)} & \text{if } E = 2^w - 1, T \neq 0 \\ (-1)^S \times (+\infty) & \text{if } E = 2^w - 1, T = 0 \\ (-1)^S \times 2^{1-emax} \times \\ \quad (0 + 2^{1-p} \times T) & \text{if } E = 0, T \neq 0 \\ 0 & \text{if } E = 0, T = 0 \\ (-1)^S \times 2^{E-bias} \times \\ \quad (1 + 2^{1-p} \times T) & \text{all other cases} \end{cases} \tag{1}$$

Since 2008, the Standard defines a 16-bit *binary16* format, commonly referred to as "half-precision" and here referred to as IEEE16, for which $w = 5, t = 10$. The value v of an IEEE16 float can be inferred by substituting these values along with $p = 11$, $emax = 15$, $bias = 15$, in Eq. 1.

The *bfloat16* format is supported in the deep learning framework Tensorflow. According to information available, the bfloat16 format is used for storing activations and gradients in memory for mixed-precision training. While there is no official standard for this format, a bfloat16 number is similar to an IEEE 754 floating-point data with a 1-bit sign, $w = 8$ and $t = 7$ [11]. Therefore the value v of a bfloat16 representation can be derived by substituting these values along with $p = 8$, $emax = 127$, $bias = 127$, in Eq. 1.

We also designed an IEEE-style 16-bit format that has a 6-bit exponent and 9-bit fraction and a format with a 7-bit exponent and 8-bit fraction. In our work, we will refer to these formats as IEEE16_6 and IEEE16_7 respectively. The IEEE16_6 format is similar to DLFloat in Sect. 3.2 except that IEEE16_6 supports the default rounding and all exceptions of the IEEE 754 Standard, including subnormals. The value, v of a IEEE16_6 representation can be derived by substituting values $w = 6$, $p = 10$, $emax = 31$, $bias = 31$, in Eq. 1. The value v of a IEEE16_7 representation can be derived by substituting values $w = 7$, $p = 9$, $emax = 63$, $bias = 63$, in Eq. 1.

3.2 DLFloat

DLFloat is a representation similar to IEEE16_6 [1]. However, to simplify the hardware design for DLFloat, it does not support subnormals (i.e. when $E = 0$). Instead, when $E = 0$, v is treated like a normal float with a bias of 31. Other differences are that there is a single representation for infinities and NaN, the sign of zero is ignored, and the only rounding mode for DLFloat is round to nearest, up (RNU).

3.3 Posit

A *posit* number, as described in its Standard [20], is defined by four fields as shown in Fig. 3(a) and has recently shown promise in CNN training [15,18]. To decode a posit value, one must know the total width of the posit, *nbits* (16, in this case), and the width *es* of the exponent field E. We test *es* values of 1, 2 and 3 referred to as posit16_1, posit16_2 and posit16_3. Other posit environment variables of interest are *maxpos*, the largest real value expressible as a posit and its reciprocal *minpos*, the smallest nonzero value expressible as a posit.

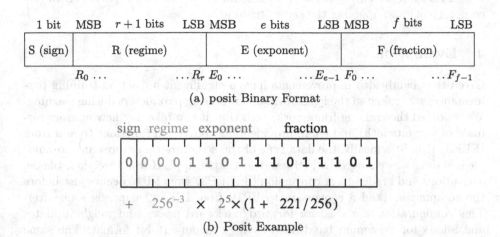

(a) posit Binary Format

(b) Posit Example

Fig. 3. General Posit Format and 16-bit Posit Example

$$v = \begin{cases} 0 & \text{if } p = 00\cdots 0 \\ \text{Not-a-Real (NaR)} & \text{if } p = 10\cdots 0 \\ (1 - 3S + F)\times \\ \quad 2^{(-1)^S (R\times 2^{es}+E+S)} & \text{otherwise} \end{cases} \qquad (2)$$

The four fields of the posit are a 1-bit sign S, regime R consisting of r bits identical to R_0 terminated by $1 - R_0$ ($r + 1$ bits total length) or by reaching the end of the posit (r bits total length), exponent E represented by e exponent bits, terminated by a maximum of es or the end of the posit, and fraction F represented by f fraction bits terminated by the end of the posit. The value of R is $-r$ if R_0 is 0, and $r-1$ if R_0 is 1. E is es bits wide, with 0 bit padding in the least significant bits if the exponent field has fewer than es bits because of the regime length. F represents an unsigned integer divided by 2^f. The representation (S, R, E, F) of the posit p represents the value v which is inferred from the fields by Eq. 2 (The equation gives the binary representation of p in the first two cases). The equation for v looks quite different from that for standard floats because posits are based on 2's complement representation whereas floats are based on sign-magnitude representation. Not-a-Real (NaR) condenses all exception values into a single case.

Rounding for a real value x to a posit is given by the following rules; If x is exactly expressible as a posit, it is unchanged. If $|x| > maxpos$, x is rounded to $sign(x) \times maxpos$. If $0 < |x| < minpos$, x is rounded to $sign(x) \times minpos$. For all other values RNE is used. To further understand the decoding of a posit number consider the example in Fig. 3(b). Here $nbits = 16$, $es = 3$. The value of the posit can be derived from Eq. 2. A more intuitive decoding that works for positive values is to raise $2^{2^{es}}$ to the power of R and multiply it by 2^E and $1 + F$. Posits representing negative values can be decoded by negating them (2's complement) and applying the same technique.

4   Evaluation

Given that bandwidth improvements have a significant impact on training performance, we evaluated the FP16 formats for storing parameters during learning. We modified the training framework, such that it can take any new number format (of any bitwidth) and train, provided the conversion functions to and from IEEE32 [10]. Specifically, the data type of the structure that stores and communicates data was changed to FP16 and so that it applied to all weights, biases, activations and gradients. A conversion to IEEE32 from FP16 occurs just before the computation and a conversion to FP16 from IEEE32 happens soon after. This configuration was used for forward/backward passes and weight updates and allows for maximum bandwidth savings for any 16-bit format. The same setup was used both for training and validation.

Our goal with these experiments was to observe how each format will perform in training on its own to identify format characteristics that are most suitable for training. Therefore, we did not use precision enhancement techniques such as maintaining a master copy of weights. *The original IEEE32 hyperparameters (i.e. batch size, training epochs, learning rates, momentum, weight decay) were unchanged for the FP16 experiments*. This approach is consistent with current literature. For reproducibility, we fixed the random seed and did not use cuDNN. Tests were conducted using publicly available models. To minimize conversion overhead between the formats and FP32, we also implemented some BLAS routines. CNN datasets used are MNIST, FASHION-MNIST, CIFAR10, CIFAR100 [13], and ILSVRC 2012 [21]; the networks used are LeNet, cuda-convnet, NIN [14], SqueezeNet [9], and AlexNet. All are publicly available, or provided with the deep learning framework.

5   Results

Table 1 shows a summary of the CNN benchmark configurations that were used for our experiments and accuracy results in the fourth block of rows for each FP16 format. The results indicate that although all of the formats perform well for the smallest models and datasets, some formats begin to struggle as the benchmark complexity increases. The IEEE-type format that delivers the best accuracy across networks is IEEE16_6. DLFloat shows similar performance although slightly inferior to IEEE16_6 possibly due to the absence of subnormals. This clearly shows that the best configuration of bits for an IEEE 754 type format for CNN training is possibly IEEE16_6 with 6 bits of exponent and 9 bits of fraction. The posit representations, especially posit16_2, perform considerably better than any other format across all networks. It is closely followed by posit16_3 in

Table 1. Benchmark configuration, accuracy, BLEU score

Model	LeNet	LeNet	convnet	NIN	Squeeze -Net	Alex -Net	Res -Net18	Trans. Base	Trans. Base
Dataset	MNIST	FMNIST	CIFAR 10	CIFAR 100	Image -Net	Image -Net	Image -Net	30K	IWSLT 14
Batch Size	64	64	100	128	32	256	32	128	128
Iterations	10K	10K	60K	120	170	450	800	2270	30780
IEEE32	98.70%	89.10%	78.70%	56.06%	56.40%	57.04%	67.88%	35.42	23.54
bfloat16	98.24%	89.08%	76.02%	0.96%	0.32%	52.40%	61.88%	35.18	21.68
DLFloat	98.66%	89.38%	77.96%	45.48%	54.24%	46.56%	69.12%	35.49	9.43
IEEE16	98.70%	89.22%	73.02%	NaN	0.00%	53.08%	NaN	0	Error
IEEE16_6	98.72%	89.60%	78.56%	46.28%	54.72%	46.84%	68.00%	35.59	12.6
IEEE16_7	98.46%	89.54%	78.74%	NaN	0.24%	9.96%	67.52%	35.16	9.46
posit16_1	98.72%	89.38%	9.76%	54.92%	50.80%	50.68%	0.00%	34.31	9.45
posit16_2	98.78%	89.36%	77.74%	53.92%	56.80%	53.60%	67.64%	35.18	24.97
posit16_3	98.66%	89.30%	79.72%	53.74%	56.48%	53.16%	67.60%	35.06	24.32

many cases and posit16_1 in some cases (for example NIN/CIFAR100), despite posit16_1's limited dynamic range.

Table 2 gives the dynamic ranges of all formats. Note that posit16_1's dynamic range is smaller than all of the other formats except for IEEE16. Even in that case, it is only marginally greater for values of smaller magnitude. However, formats with greater dynamic range such as bfloat16 do not perform as well. This suggests that limited dynamic range is not the sole reason for the failure of a format as it is often attributed to in the case of IEEE16. However, IEEE16 shows better performance than other float types in the case of AlexNet/Imagenet, which highlights the challenges of developing a format that can perform well across a wide range of networks and datasets.

Because neural networks are increasingly being used in application areas such as language translation, we also tested these formats on the Transformer Base Model for language translation from German to English. The last two columns of Table 1 shows the BLEU score results from these experiments. All formats perform well for the 30K dataset. However, for the IWSLT-14 dataset posit16_2 manages to perform as well as IEEE32, demonstrating again the versatility of the posit formats.

Aside from accuracy, the FP16 formats also differ in their rounding modes. Posits use saturation rounding (see Sect. 3.3) for values beyond their dynamic range while floats underflow to 0 or overflow to infinity. We experimented with changing the rounding mode to saturation rounding for float formats, as well as to underflow to 0 and overflow to infinity for posits, and performed the training. Saturation rounding severely affected the accuracy of all the float formats. Due to its larger dynamic range, underflows in posit16_3 are rare and therefore its results remained unchanged. posit16_2's results remained the same or improved except in the case of Squeezenet. posit16_1 showed the most dramatic changes in some cases due to its smaller dynamic range. This suggests that having the posit distribution's accuracy in the appropriate range of the learnt parameters is more important than the choice of whether they saturate or underflow.

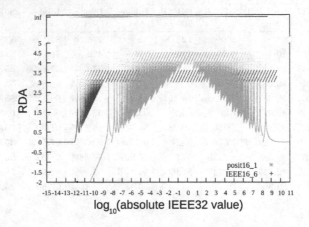

Fig. 4. RDA w.r.t IEEE32 of IEEE16_6 vs posit16_1

Maintaining a copy the weights at a higher precision (referred to as "master" weights) for weight updates is a technique used to improve the accuracy for training with float formats [2,17]. It works by updating 32-bit weights with 16-bit gradients and then converting them to 16-bit weights for use in the forward and backward phases of the training. We implemented this technique for the NIN/CIFAR100 benchmark and IEEE16 and bfloat16 formats. The NaN result for IEEE16 did not change as the cause for it was activations overflowing to infinity that were then being multiplied by zero. For bfloat16 the accuracy improved to 47.86%. Given that this technique requires 3× more memory for weights and that there are other formats that perform better without it, the technique only adds additional work and is redundant.

6   Hardware Implications

All 16-bit floating point formats provide the same savings in memory consumption. However, any performance gain they bring about is dampened by costs associated with converting between the format and IEEE32 as well as their implementation on hardware when employed in mixed-precision training. To understand these hardware associated costs we implemented the conversion routines on an FPGA platform. Table 3 presents these results on a Xilinx U250 Alveo Data Center Accelerator Card with synthesis done in Vivado 2018.2. Looking at the depth, i.e., the number of cycles required for one conversion, bfloat16 is the most efficient because it only involves rounding and right shifting to convert an IEEE32 value to a bfloat16 value, and a left shift of a bfloat16 by 16 bits to get

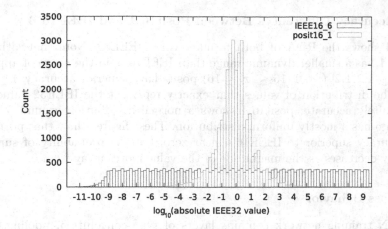

Fig. 5. Distribution of Infinitely Accurate Numbers of IEEE16_6 vs posit16_1

to the IEEE32 value. DLFloats, which eliminate subnormals as well as simplify rounding, follows bfloat16. Owing to the variable length regime R, the posit formats have a slightly higher depth than these two formats. Among the posit formats there is only a slight difference in depths. However, the IEEE 754 style formats are the most expensive for conversion owing to the more complicated conversion logic (subnormals, rounding modes, etc.).

7   Accuracy Analysis

Given the numerous differences between the floating-point formats, we set out to identify which of their characteristics are responsible for better accuracy. Due to the many complexities of the training process, we selected the NIN/CIFAR100 benchmark for the analysis as it is the simplest with discerning accuracy results. To further make our analysis concise, we picked the best performing posit and float formats, which are posit16_1 and IEEE16_6 respectively. For both formats, we sampled activations, weights, biases and gradients during training and analyzed each value's RDA as compared to the RDA of its corresponding value when training with IEEE32. In effect, we treat the IEEE32 value as the precise value. The RDA between an exact value x and its approximated value $\hat{x}$ is obtained from the following equation [5];

$$RDA(x, \hat{x}) = \log_{10}(|x|/|x - \hat{x}|)$$

We measure the RDA when $x \neq 0$. When $x = \hat{x}$, the RDA is ∞. Because we treat the IEEE32 values as the reference, we measure how accurate each of these formats are when representing IEEE32 values.

7.1 Accuracy Differences Between Posit16_1 and IEEE16_6

Figure 4 shows the RDA of both formats w.r.t. IEEE32. Note that although posit16_1 has a smaller dynamic range than IEEE16_6, in the range of approximately $[-1.2, 1.2]$ (i.e. $1/16 \leq |x| \leq 16$) posits have superior accuracy. Figure 5 shows the distribution of values that exactly represent the IEEE32 value, i.e. are infinitely accurate; posit16_1 shows a normal distribution around 0 while IEEE16_6 has a mostly uniform distribution. These figures show that posit16_1 has accuracy superior to IEEE16_6 near zero, but the probability of superior accuracy decreases as the magnitude of the value moves away from 0.

7.2 Loss Behavior

The NIN training network contains layers of type convolution, pooling, relu, dropout and softmax (with loss) at one end. It trains for a total of 120K iterations. Figure 6 gives the training loss from the softmax with loss function E for the two formats (and IEEE32). Posit16_1's loss closely follows that of IEEE32 while IEEE16_6's loss actually increases despite still converging. Therefore, we start the analysis by looking at the end of the network which is the loss activation and gradient values at the last layer. Figures 7 and 8 show these activations and gradients respectively near the end of training. The median loss activation accuracy in the case of posit16_1 is greater than that of IEEE16_6 despite most of the values falling outside of posit16_1's optimal accuracy range. Even in the case of gradients, the median value of posit16_1 is still slightly better even though the gradients have more values of even smaller magnitude. Note that in both these graphs, posit16_1's accuracy for smaller values is substantially lower as compared to that of IEEE16_6, due to its limited dynamic range, suggesting that the accuracy of the values with smaller magnitude has a lesser impact on the training accuracy.

7.3 Effect on Weights

The accuracy of loss gradients is affected by the weights and vice-versa. Therefore, we shift our attention to the weight layer before the loss (convolution layer *cccp6*) in the network. Figure 9 plots the accuracy of weight gradients in this layer at the end of the training. These weight gradient values are computed from the loss gradients and similarly although most values lie outside the optimal posit accuracy range, posits still retain accuracy similar to IEEE16_6 for weight gradients too. However, looking at the accuracy of weights at the end of the training in Fig. 10, posits clearly have better median accuracy. Figure 11 shows the distribution of the weight values in this layer at the end of training. In combination with Figs. 4 and 10 it is clear that a greater proportion of weight values which are also larger in magnitude fall inside posit16_1's optimal accuracy range. The accuracy of weights in all other layers in the network also showed similar behavior resulting in all of them having higher median accuracy for posits when compared to IEEE16_6.

7.4 Posit Accuracy in Training

The accuracy of learned weights has a significant impact on the training process as all other values (i.e. activations, gradients, loss) are computed from them. Therefore, the higher posit accuracy for weights most likely transcends to other values such as gradients which often may not fall into the posit optimal accuracy range, as seen from Figs. 7, 8 and 9. This in turn results in improved overall training accuracy for posits. It is also worthwhile to note that the range of the weight values stabilizes early on in the training, in this case within the first 500 iterations. This also helps to lessen the potential impact of deficiencies in accuracy at the beginning of the training.

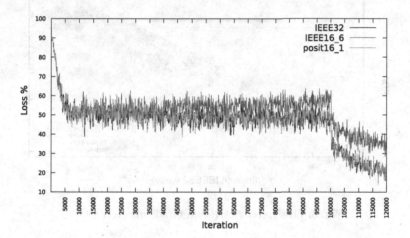

Fig. 6. NIN/CIFAR100 Training Loss

In this benchmark, the weight values are less than 1 in magnitude. Therefore, the posit accuracy distribution gives more accuracy to the weight values with larger magnitude and less accuracy to the smaller ones. This in turn gives larger activations more accuracy, which has a cascading effect through the network. The larger weights are also less effected by the errors in the small gradient values, as is evident in the plots. Moreover, the larger the gradient value, the more accuracy it will have in the case of posits. We believe that the same principle, which is to improve the accuracy of weight values by giving them more accuracy in the representation, is behind the idea of maintaining a master copy

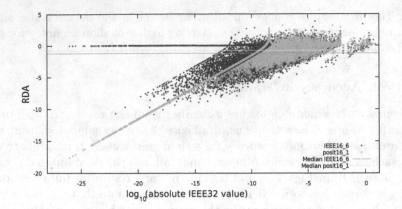

Fig. 7. Loss Layer Activations Accuracy

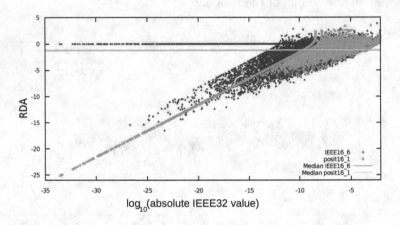

Fig. 8. Loss Layer Activation Gradients Accuracy

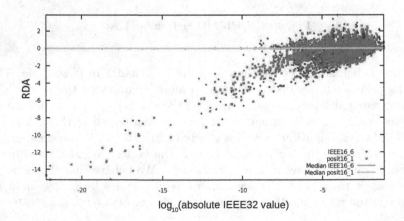

Fig. 9. Accuracy - Weight Gradients

Table 2. Exponent and dynamic ranges of the formats

Format	Min. Exp. (Normal)	Max. Exp.	Min. Value (Normal)	Max. Val
IEEE32	-149 (-126)	127	1.4×10^{-45} (1.8×10^{-38})	3.4×10^{38}
bfloat16	-133 (-126)	127	9.2×10^{-41} (1.8×10^{-38})	3.4×10^{38}
DLFloat	-31	32	2.3×10^{-10}	8.6×10^{9}
IEEE16	-24 (-14)	15	6.0×10^{-8} (6.1×10^{-5})	6.6×10^{4}
IEEE16_6	-39 (-30)	31	1.8×10^{-12} (9.3×10^{-10})	4.3×10^{9}
IEEE16_7	-70 (-62)	63	8.5×10^{-22} (2.2×10^{-19})	1.8×10^{19}
posit16_1	-28	28	3.7×10^{-9}	2.7×10^{8}
posit16_2	-56	56	1.4×10^{-17}	7.2×10^{16}
posit16_3	-112	112	1.9×10^{-34}	5.2×10^{33}

of weights at higher precision in CNN training. However, our analysis suggests that greater accuracy is needed mostly for the larger magnitude weights that are more prevalent during training.

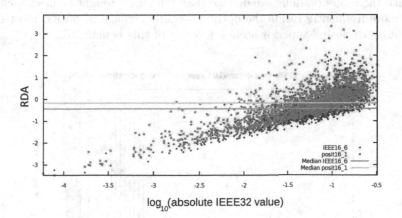

Fig. 10. Accuracy - Weights

This hypothesis also rings true for other benchmarks that were tested. Figures 12 and 13 show the corresponding weight distributions and accuracy at the third quartile for the best performing float and posit formats at the end of

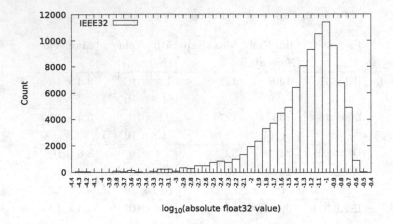

Fig. 11. Weight Histogram in layer *cccp6*

training for the SqueezeNet/ImageNet and AlexNet/ImageNet benchmarks. We selected the third quartile in this case to show the accuracy close to the peak of the weight distribution. Note that in these cases too, posits retain superior accuracy for weights, although in the case with AlexNet/ImageNet when the peak of the weight distribution (i.e. the highest frequency of weights) is more centered, the difference is less pronounced. In such cases, the weight values tend to fall outside of the optimal accuracy range of posits, and float formats with uniform accuracy distributions such as IEEE16 can achieve comparable training results.

With these observations, we deduce that the larger weight values which also occur more frequently inside the optimal accuracy range of posits, most likely contributes to posits' superior accuracy result of this benchmark.

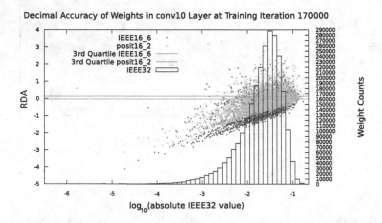

Fig. 12. Accuracy - Weights (SqueezeNet)

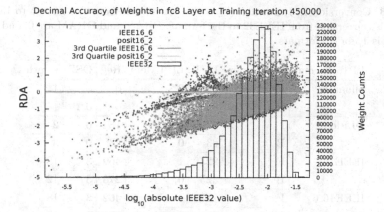

Fig. 13. Accuracy - Weights (AlexNet)

8 Shifting the Accuracy Peak

Based on our analysis, the accuracy peak of posits can be shifted into the desirable range of the large magnitude and high frequency weights to improve training accuracy. This technique can only be applied with posits, since float formats have uniform accuracy distributions (Fig. 1) and no peak. Therefore, posits have the versatility to combat both dynamic range and precision issues in training while float formats can only overcome dynamic range problems. Because the bias for shifting can be determined offline after training a few iterations, this technique adds no additional overhead except for shifting the weights.

The peak of posit16_1's accuracy lies in the range $[1/4, 4]$ ($[-0.6, 0.6]$ in Fig. 4). Figure 11 shows the value distribution of the layer *cccp6* where the larger weights begin around -0.6 on the x-axis. Based on this, we scaled posit16_1 by $1/4$ to shift its peak accuracy by $\log_{10}(1/4) \approx -0.6$. This improves the CIFAR/NIN accuracy to 55.58%, and increased the median value of weights of the layer from -0.1790 to -0.0747. Using the same technique we were able to drastically improve cuda-convnet/CIFAR10's accuracy for posit16_1 to 79.28% by using a bias of $1/64$. Figure 14 shows the IEEE32 weights (which we consider to be the actual weight value) and the difference in the accuracy of the posit weights in the last layer at the end of the training before and after the accuracy peak is shifted for this benchmark.

In our experience, because not all weight layers can be analyzed to figure out a bias value, the last weight layer of the network, which is also closest to the loss, can be used as a heuristic for this purpose. The distribution of the significant weights, once identified, can explain the differences of the posit results with different *es* values and also help pick which posit format and bias to use for training. For example, the larger the range of the distribution of values, the higher the *es* value that shows better performance for it. The bias can be identified based on the values of the weights close to the peaks and calculating the distance from it to the accuracy peak. Other posit studies for training have

Table 3. Conversion in Hardware. 'F' is the conversion from the format to IEEE32, and 'B' is conversion from IEEE32 to the format. BRAM and DRAM are 0, and Initial Interval is 1, for all formats.

FP16 Format	Conversion	LUT	LUTMem	Reg	DSP	Depth
bfloat16	F	0	0	0	0	1
	B	3	0	0	0	1
DLFloat	F	27	0	18	0	2
	B	63	0	43	0	3
IEEE16	F	223	1	469	3	18
	B	325	0	278	3	12
IEEE16_6	F	217	1	462	3	18
	B	331	0	277	3	12
IEEE16_7	F	216	1	457	3	18
	B	341	0	278	3	12
posit16_1	F	115	0	84	0	3
	B	703	0	318	0	5
posit16_2	F	112	0	83	0	3
	B	723	0	316	0	5
posit16_3	F	118	0	84	0	3
	B	596	0	314	0	5

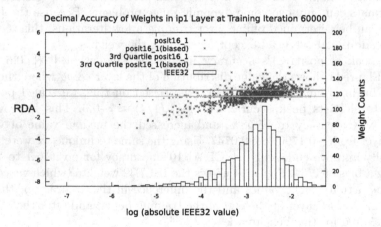

Fig. 14. Accuracy before and after shifting the accuracy peak - cuda-convnet/CIFAR10

suggested user layer-wise scaling, a technique also used with floats, to improve accuracy for low-precision training [15]. This can be costly because the scale needs to be calculated throughout the training for each type of parameter in each layer. Instead, our results indicate that for 16-bit posit training, looking at the weight distribution to calculate a bias and other posit parameters can suffice thus creating minimum overhead.

9 Discussion and Conclusion

Traditional FP16 formats studied so far for CNN training all have uniform accuracy distributions and differ mostly on their bit configuration. There is no consensus in the community as to which bit configuration is optimal. This has led to various silo works studying the effectiveness of each format and developing techniques to mitigate their individual shortcomings. However, there is no clear evidence for why those formats are the best for training versus other formats. While it is difficult to generalize numerical behavior for all neural networks, we believe our work provides useful insights through uniform (controlled) experiments. In summary:

- The IEEE 754 standard 16-bit format is inferior for out-of-the-box training of neural networks compared to the other float types.
- Non-uniform accuracy formats such as posits provide broader versatility for neural network training.
- We showed that analyzing the dynamic range and precision as they relate to the distribution of the weights is a useful indicator for selecting the FP16 format to use.
- We showed that the shifting the accuracy peak of posits leads to better results.

Although newer FP16 formats should still work in tandem with other improvements such as efficient training techniques and hyper parameter optimization, our goal in this work was to isolate the contribution of each format. Thus, we provided an unbiased evaluation of all existing 16-bit formats for training CNNs on a set of benchmarks of varying size in terms of accuracy and hardware performance. With our analysis we deduced that the superior accuracy of posits was due to the non-uniform error distribution which allows larger weights to have more accuracy. With this insight, we proposed an accuracy saving technique that shifts the peak posit accuracy into the desirable range. Best of all, it has no additional overhead. In this work we advocate for the design of 16-bit formats based on understanding the accuracy requirements of neural network training. We hope that it will guide the exploration of innovative non-traditional 16-bit, or even shorter, formats.

References

1. Agrawal, A., et al.: DLFloat: a 16-bit floating point format designed for deep learning training and inference. In: 2019 IEEE 26th Symposium on Computer Arithmetic (ARITH), pp. 92–95. IEEE (2019)
2. Burgess, N., Milanovic, J., Stephens, N., Monachopoulos, K., Mansell, D.: BFloat16 processing for neural networks. In: 2019 IEEE 26th Symposium on Computer Arithmetic (ARITH), pp. 88–91. IEEE (2019)
3. IMS Committee: IEEE Standard for Floating-Point Arithmetic. IEEE Std. 754-2019 (2019)
4. Das, D., et al.: Mixed precision training of convolutional neural networks using integer operations. arXiv preprint arXiv:1802.00930 (2018)

5. De Silva, H., Gustafson, J.L., Wong, W.F.: Making Strassen matrix multiplication safe. In: 2018 IEEE 25th International Conference on High Performance Computing (HiPC), pp. 173–182. IEEE (2018)

6. Gupta, S., Agrawal, A., Gopalakrishnan, K., Narayanan, P.: Deep learning with limited numerical precision. In: International Conference on Machine Learning, pp. 1737–1746 (2015)

7. Ho, N.M., De Silva, H., Gustafson, J.L., Wong, W.F.: Qtorch+: next generation arithmetic for Pytorch machine learning. In: Gustafson, J., Dimitrov, V. (eds.) CoNGA 2022. LNCS, pp. 31–49. Springer, Heidelberg (2022). https://doi.org/10.1007/978-3-031-09779-9_3

8. Ho, N.M., Nguyen, D.T., De Silva, H., Gustafson, J.L., Wong, W.F., Chang, I.J.: Posit arithmetic for the training and deployment of generative adversarial networks. In: 2021 Design, Automation & Test in Europe Conference & Exhibition (DATE), pp. 1350–1355. IEEE (2021)

9. Iandola, F.N., Han, S., Moskewicz, M.W., Ashraf, K., Dally, W.J., Keutzer, K.: SqueezeNet: AlexNet-level accuracy with 50x fewer parameters and <0.5 mb model size. arXiv preprint arXiv:1602.07360 (2016)

10. Jia, Y., et al.: Caffe: convolutional architecture for fast feature embedding. In: Proceedings of the 22nd ACM International Conference on Multimedia, pp. 675–678. ACM (2014)

11. Kalamkar, D., et al.: A study of bfloat16 for deep learning training. arXiv preprint arXiv:1905.12322 (2019)

12. Köster, U., et al.: Flexpoint: an adaptive numerical format for efficient training of deep neural networks. In: Advances in Neural Information Processing Systems, pp. 1742–1752 (2017)

13. Krizhevsky, A., Hinton, G., et al.: Learning multiple layers of features from tiny images. Citeseer (2009)

14. Lin, M., Chen, Q., Yan, S.: Network in network. arXiv preprint arXiv:1312.4400 (2013)

15. Lu, J., et al.: Training deep neural networks using posit number system. arXiv preprint arXiv:1909.03831 (2019)

16. Mellempudi, N., Srinivasan, S., Das, D., Kaul, B.: Mixed precision training with 8-bit floating point. arXiv preprint arXiv:1905.12334 (2019)

17. Micikevicius, P., et al.: Mixed precision training. arXiv preprint arXiv:1710.03740 (2017)

18. Murillo, R., Del Barrio, A.A., Botella, G.: Deep PeNSieve: a deep learning framework based on the posit number system. Digit. Signal Process. 102762 (2020)

19. Nvidia: Training mixed precision user guide (2020). https://docs.nvidia.com/deeplearning/sdk/pdf/Training-Mixed-Precision-User-Guide.pdf. Accessed 07 Mar 2020

20. Posit standard documentation (2022). https://posithub.org/docs/posit_standard-2.pdf. Accessed 07 Jan 2023

21. Russakovsky, O., et al.: ImageNet large scale visual recognition challenge. Int. J. Comput. Vis. 115(3), 211–252 (2015)

22. Sun, X., et al.: Hybrid 8-bit floating point (HFP8) training and inference for deep neural networks. In: Advances in Neural Information Processing Systems, pp. 4901–4910 (2019)

23. Sun, X., et al.: Ultra-low precision 4-bit training of deep neural networks. In: Advances in Neural Information Processing Systems, vol. 33 (2020)

24. Wang, N., Choi, J., Brand, D., Chen, C.Y., Gopalakrishnan, K.: Training deep neural networks with 8-bit floating point numbers. In: Advances in Neural Information Processing Systems, pp. 7675–7684 (2018)
25. Zhou, S., Wu, Y., Ni, Z., Zhou, X., Wen, H., Zou, Y.: DoReFa-net: training low bitwidth convolutional neural networks with low bitwidth gradients. arXiv preprint arXiv:1606.06160 (2016)

Improving the Stability of Kalman Filters with Posit Arithmetic

Ponsuganth Ilangovan P., Rohan Rayan$^{(\boxtimes)}$, and Vinay Shankar Saxena

Research and Technology Center, Bosch Global Software Technologies,
Bangalore, India
{PonkumarIlango.PonsuganthIlangovan,Rayan.Rohan,
VinayShankar.Saxena}@in.bosch.com

Abstract. Kalman filters are used pervasively in industrial and technical applications. One of the main causes of failure of the Kalman filter is the numerical instability caused by the use of finite precision arithmetic. These numerical issues can cause the filter to diverge which can be catastrophic, especially in a real-time, mission critical applications. Various Kalman filter mechanizations (mathematical variations) are proposed in the literature to minimize these effects, but these are usually problem specific and are usually less compute efficient than the conventional implementation of the filter. Theoretically all these mechanizations should lead to identical results but in practice, numerical differences arise due to the floating point representation used to perform the computations. In this work we aim to showcase the benefits of using the Posit number format over the IEEE754 floating point format (which is the most widely used floating point representation on modern computers) for stabilizing the Kalman filter. Specifically, we show that the ability to select the configuration of Posit based on the application allows us to use less compute power on the device and still maintain stability of the filter.

Keywords: Kalman Filters · Posit arithmetic · Numerical stability

1 Introduction

The use of Kalman filters is ubiquitous in industrial and technical applications. It sees widespread use in applications such as motion planning in robotics, navigation, signal processing and wireless sensor networks [1,4,7,12,16]. The Kalman filter combines measurement data with an analytical model of the system to provide an accurate estimate of the state of the system. It is basically a set of mathematical equations that provides an efficient computational means to estimate the state of a process or system, in a way that minimizes the mean of the squared error between the measurement and the actual state of the system [7]. There are two primary causes of failure of Kalman filtering, finite precision arithmetic and modeling errors [18]. In this work, we focus on the failure caused by finite precision arithmetic and the use of Posits [6] to mitigate these issues.

© The Author(s), under exclusive license to Springer Nature Switzerland AG 2023
J. Gustafson et al. (Eds.): CoNGA 2023, LNCS 13851, pp. 134–154, 2023.
https://doi.org/10.1007/978-3-031-32180-1_9

The implementation of Kalman filters on computers using finite precision arithmetic causes divergence or even instability of the filter [18]. Specifically, it is shown that the covariance forms of the Kalman filter measurement update are not reliable when implemented using single precision floating points [8]. It is also shown that the conventional implementation of the Kalman filter in terms of covariance matrices is particularly sensitive to round-off errors [10]. These issues are not just academic, but also occur for benign problems when working with single precision arithmetic [2, 8].

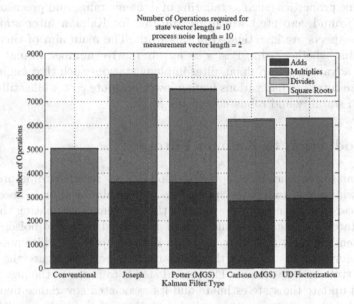

Fig. 1. Compute cost of common Kalman mechanizations [15]

Different mechanizations (mathematical variations) of the Kalman filter have been proposed to mitigate these numerical issues and claim to provide the same accuracy as covariance forms implemented in double precision [8]. But, a study comparing their numerical performance in Fig. 1 shows that in most cases the conventional filter is usually the most compute efficient implementation. This is especially significant for embedded applications where compute efficiency is very important. It is also shown that mitigation of these issues by either increasing the arithmetic precision or using a stabilized mechanization is still problem specific and requires simulation and/or experimentation [18] to find the optimal solution. It is also noted that although several decades have been spent refining these algorithms, the robustness of Kalman filters sill remains a relevant issue [9].

Some authors have also suggested that a way to mitigate the issues stemming from finite precision arithmetic (apart from using stabilized mechanizations) is to increase the precision on which the computation is performed [18]. But this solution may be infeasible to implement especially on embedded systems where compute efficiency is of utmost importance and single precision floating points are preferred to double precision [20]. Most control engineers also prefer seemingly simpler Kalman filter mechanizations for implementation and tend to dismiss instances of numerical failure [2]. In such an environment, it is essential to study means by which Kalman filter stability is maintained, while still reducing computation cost and keeping the implementation simple.

In this study we aim to evaluate a sample of the most commonly used Kalman filter mechanizations and test their numerical stability properties with the Posit number format [6]. Posit is an alternative storage format for real numbers which have specific properties (such as tailoring of dynamic range and precision, higher precision around zero etc.) which are suitable for Kalman filter stabilization and these aspects are investigated in this work. The main aim of this paper is to determine whether using Posits as an alternative number format can give numerical advantages to Kalman filter implementations such that engineers can use Kalman filter mechanizations having lower compute cost while still ensuring a degree of stability and robustness of the filter.

2 Introduction to Kalman Filters

The Kalman Filter, since its inception in 1960 [11] has seen a lot of improvements and sees widespread industrial application. The Kalman filter is an estimator for the linear-quadratic problem, which is the problem of estimating the instantaneous state of a linear dynamic system perturbed by white noise, by using measurements linearly related to the state but corrupted by white noise [10].

Concretely, the first step of the Kalman filter is to propagate the system's estimated state and covariance. The second step is to factor in the new measurements and update the state estimate and its associated covariance matrix.

Over the years, many mathematical variations of the Kalman filter, called mechanizations [2,3], have been proposed which aim to improve the stability of the filter when implemented on a computer with single precision floating points. It should be noted that all these mechanizations should theoretically produce identical results, it is only because of the underlying floating point representation that these mechanizations have varied compute and stability properties.

2.1 Classic Linear Kalman Filter

Some of the basic steps of a classic linear Kalman filter are listed below [21].

Predict Step

$$\hat{\mathbf{x}} = \mathbf{F}\mathbf{x} + \mathbf{B}\mathbf{u} \tag{1}$$

$$\hat{\mathbf{P}} = \mathbf{F}\mathbf{P}\mathbf{F}^T + \mathbf{Q} \tag{2}$$

Correct Step

$$y = z - H\hat{x} \tag{3}$$

$$K = \hat{P}H^T(H\hat{P}H^T + R)^{-1} \tag{4}$$

$$x = \hat{x} + K\hat{y} \tag{5}$$

$$P = (I - KH)\hat{P} \tag{6}$$

where,

x is the state estimate
P is the state covariance matrix
F is the state transition function
Q is the process covariance matrix
H is the measurement function
z is the measurement
y is the measurement residual
R is the measurement covariance matrix
K is the Kalman filter gain
I is the identity matrix

The classic linear filter is one of the most basic filter mechanizations but is susceptible to numerical failure. This can be caused for example in the last step of the correct step, where the inherent unsymmetrical update of the State covariance matrix (P) causes it to loose it positive definiteness. Other mechanizations are proposed which try to overcome these issues, but all of them have their own advantages and disadvantages.

It is also noted the mechanizations proposed can also be applied to extended and unscented Kalman filters since it is only the first linearization step which is different from the linear Kalman filter.

2.2 Stability of Kalman Filters

As mentioned before, one of the main reasons for stability issues in the Kalman filter is because of approximating real number arithmetic using floating points. Finding the root cause of these issues can be tricky but there has been research done which shows common modes of failure for these computations.

Some of the common failure modes are [15]:

- High value of initial state covariance matrix (P_0).
- Highly accurate measurement (R).
- Very low process noise (Q).
- If a measurement (H) is correlated to more than one state.
- Non-Symmetric update of the State covariance matrix.

It is also noted during the normal operation of the Kalman filter, the State covariance matrix P should be positive definite. When this ceases to be the case, this indicates some kind of failure in the filter.

3   Precision of Computers

An important concept when dealing with floating points is machine precision (ϵ). This is the lowest possible number when added to 1 gives a number greater than 1 when represented using finite precision arithmetic. The Posit format is depicted in [6] and the digits of precision is analyzed later with Fig. 20. Clearly, there is a tradeoff between the two formats that has to be evaluated and in the subsequent sections we perform this evaluation in the context of Kalman filter processing. For more information on Posit number formats the reader is referred to [6].

4   Posit for Kalman Filters

As discussed before in Sect. 2.2, the common failure modes boils down to the round off errors in floating point arithmetic [10]. However it is highly unlikely that round off problems occur with double precision floating points, whereas such errors can occur in applications like GPS based models, relative measurements, etc. when using single precision arithmetic [5,13]. In order to test the stability of Kalman Filters with the Posit number format, we study the behavior of these filters with a few test cases and compare them to the standard IEEE754 floating point format. Based on the configuration of Posit selected, the precision offered on certain parts of the number line is higher that that of single precision floating points. This fact can be exploited for stabilizing Kalman filter applications.

The filter is implemented in C++ and the Posit library from stillwater-sc [14] is used for the Posit emulation. We demonstrate the Kalman filter performance with Posit using two test cases, case 4.1 in which we estimate the angular states of a rotating shaft and case 4.2 in which a relative measurement is used to estimate angular states of two rotating bodies. The Kalman filter is implemented with both the conventional mechanization and the Bierman mechanization [2] where UDU factorization is done for the covariance matrix to improve stability. The notation followed for a specific Posit with total n bits and es bits for exponent size is $posit(n, es)$.

4.1   Estimating a Rotating Shaft

Here we consider a rotating shaft where we estimate its angular position and angular velocity with measurements from an extremely accurate position sensor with noise in the order of machine precision. The parameters of the filter can be varied to study the stability properties corresponding to IEEE floats and Posit.

We have our filter equations as follows,

The state variables x are the angular position (r) and angular velocity (v), the states and the state transition matrix are given as follows,

$$\mathbf{x} = [r, v]^\top \tag{7}$$

$$\mathbf{F} = \begin{bmatrix} 1 & 1 \\ 0 & 1 \end{bmatrix} \tag{8}$$

The measurement comes from an accurate position sensor where we measure the angular position (r) with measurement covariance $\mathbf{R}$, the measurement matrix $\mathbf{H}$ is given as,

$$\mathbf{H} = \begin{bmatrix} 1 & 0 \end{bmatrix} \tag{9}$$

In order to demonstrate Kalman filter failure with various floating point implementations, the parameters of the Kalman filter that we vary are the process noise $(\mathbf{Q})$, initial covariance factor (p_0) and the measurement covariance $(\mathbf{R})$.

$$\mathbf{P_0} = p_0 \mathbf{I} \tag{10}$$

The initial covariance matrix is the product of the identity matrix and the initial covariance factor as seen in the equation above.

The following table shows the parameter values and the filter performance with both the IEEE single precision and Posit number formats. ϵ is the machine precision of single precision floating point arithmetic.

Table 1. Filter parameters and results with single precision floats and Posits. Cases marked in red denotes filter failure and green denotes normal filter operation

$\mathbf{Q}$	p_0	$\mathbf{R}$	IEEE single precision	Posit
ϵ^4	1	10^{-4}	Figure [2]	Posit(32, 1) (Similar to IEEE floats)
ϵ^4	1	10^{-8}	Figure [3]	Posit(32, 1) Figure [4]
ϵ^4	2^{32}	10^3	Figure [6]	Posit(32, 1) Figure [5]
ϵ^4	2^{32}	10^3	Figure [6]	Posit(32, 4) Figure [7]

For Gaussian distributions, 99.7% of all data must fall within three standard deviations (3σ) from the mean [22]. When the state estimates from the filter violate the 3σ rule, we consider the filter to have failed. The Table 1 shows the colour-coded results for a certain set of parameters where the round-off errors push the filter to failure. With the extended precision of Posits on certain parts of the number line when compared to floats, the filter failure can be overcome if we determine the numerical operating range of the system beforehand (Figs. 3 and 4). We also notice that specific Posits are not always the better choice as we see the failure of Posit a simple case when $(\mathbf{Q}, p_0, \mathbf{R}) = (\epsilon^4, 2^{32}, 10^3)$. In this case, the numerical region around which the filter operates for the afore mentioned parameters, the precision of IEEE floats is higher than that of the selected Posit (Fig. 5 and 6). From Fig. 20 it can be seen that around 10^0, Posit(32, 1) has higher precision compared to IEEE floats but around $2^{32} \simeq 10^9$, Posit(32, 1) has lesser precision than IEEE floats.

Table 2. Filter parameters with Bierman mechanization using IEEE single precision floats and Posits. Cases marked in red denote filter failure and green denotes normal filter operation

$\mathbf{Q}$	p_0	$\mathbf{R}$	IEEE single precision	Posit
ϵ^4	1	10^{-4}	Similar to Table 1	Posit(32, 1) (Similar to IEEE floats)
ϵ^4	1	10^{-8}	Figure [5]	Posit(32, 1) Figure [9]
ϵ^4	1	10^{-8}	Figure [5]	Posit(32, 2) Figure [10]

Table 2 shows the similar tests performed with Bierman mechanization [2] of the Kalman filter in which the covariance matrix is UDU factorized in the predict step. We observe not a complete failure but a deviation from normal performance of the filter (Figs. 8, 9 and 10). This factorization of the covariance matrix can be done in the correct step also in order to improve numerical stability but doing so increases the number of operations. When the covariance matrix is factorized in both the predict and correct steps, we do not see failure for IEEE floating point for this case (Fig. 2).

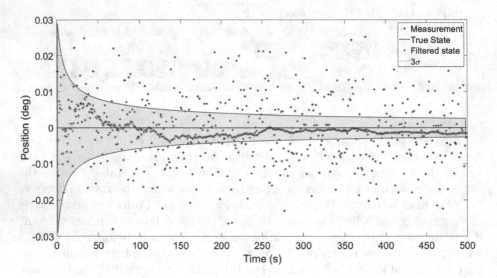

Fig. 2. Kalman filter working for case 4.1 with IEEE single precision floats, $(\mathbf{Q}, p_0, \mathbf{R}) = (\epsilon^4, 1, 10^{-4})$

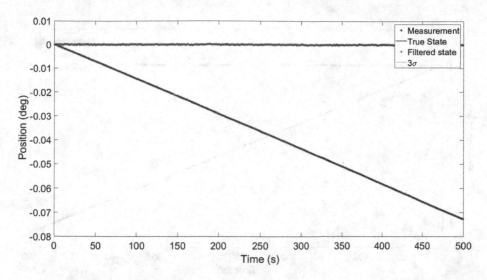

Fig. 3. Kalman filter failure for case 4.1 with IEEE single precision floats, $(\mathbf{Q}, p_0, \mathbf{R}) = (\epsilon^4, 1, 10^{-8})$

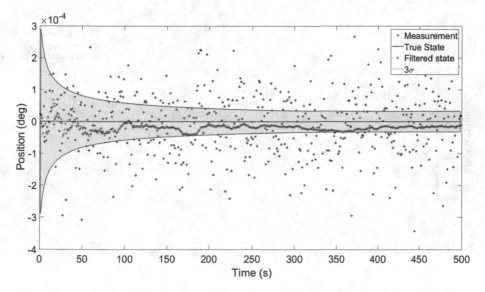

Fig. 4. Kalman filter working for case 4.1 with Posit(32, 1), $(\mathbf{Q}, p_0, \mathbf{R}) = (\epsilon^4, 1, 10^{-8})$

4.2 Two Rotating Shaft with Relative Measurement

Here we consider the estimation of the absolute position and velocity of two rotating shafts but we measure only the relative position and velocity between them. In this system, there are four state variables as shown below:

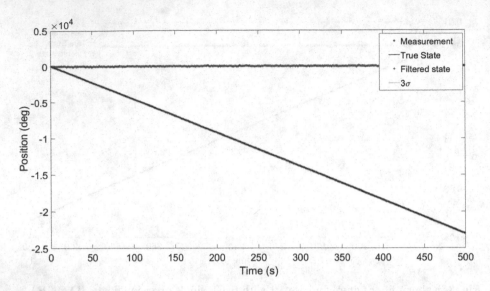

Fig. 5. Kalman filter failure for case 4.1 with Posit(32, 1), $(\mathbf{Q}, p_0, \mathbf{R}) = (\epsilon^4, 2^{32} \simeq 4.29 \times 10^9, 10^3)$

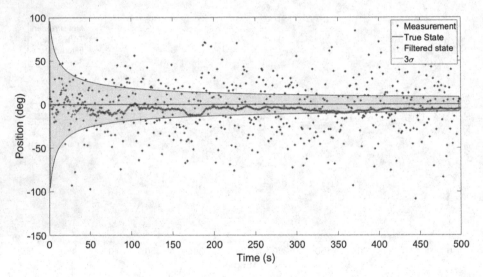

Fig. 6. Kalman filter working for case 4.1 with IEEE single precision floats, $(\mathbf{Q}, p_0, \mathbf{R}) = (\epsilon^4, 2^{32} \simeq 4.29 \times 10^9, 10^3)$

$$\mathbf{x} = [r_1, v_1, r_2, v_2]^\top \tag{11}$$

$$\mathbf{F} = \begin{bmatrix} 0 & 1 & 0 & 0 \\ 0 & 0 & 0 & 0 \\ 0 & 0 & 0 & 1 \\ 0 & 0 & 0 & 0 \end{bmatrix} \tag{12}$$

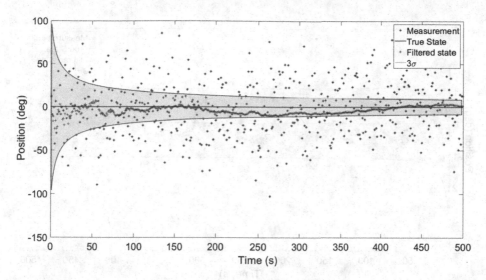

Fig. 7. Kalman filter working for case 4.1 with Posit(32, 4), $(\mathbf{Q}, p_0, \mathbf{R}) = (\epsilon^4, 2^{32} \simeq 4.29 \times 10^9, 10^3)$

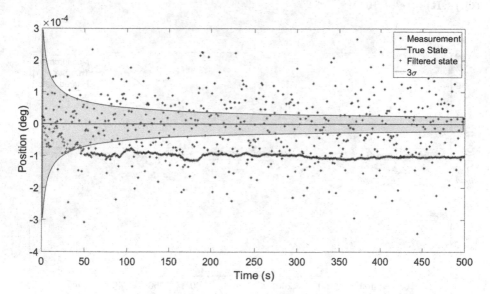

Fig. 8. Kalman filter with Bierman mechanization failure for case 4.1 with IEEE single precision floats, $(\mathbf{Q}, p_0, \mathbf{R}) = (\epsilon^4, 1, 10^{-8})$

The measurement gets worse as we measure the relative position and hence the confidence of the filter keeps on worsening, the measurement matrix ($\mathbf{H}$) is as follows,

$$\mathbf{H} = \begin{bmatrix} -1 & 0 & 1 & 0 \end{bmatrix} \tag{13}$$

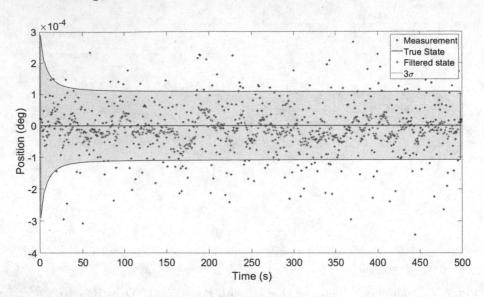

Fig. 9. Kalman filter with Bierman mechanization failure for case 4.1 with Posit (32, 1), $(\mathbf{Q}, p_0, \mathbf{R}) = (\epsilon^4, 1, 10^{-8})$

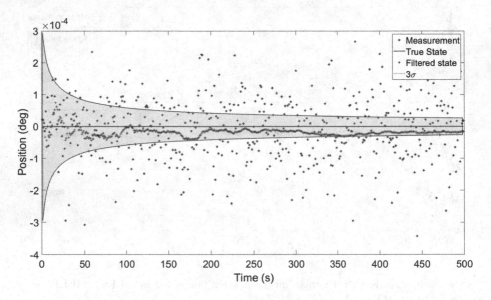

Fig. 10. Kalman filter with Bierman mechanization failure for case 4.1 with Posit (32, 2), $(\mathbf{Q}, p_0, \mathbf{R}) = (\epsilon^4, 1, 10^{-8})$

In such a setup the state covariance continues to grow unboundedly and ultimately causing ill conditioning of the state-covariance matrix and thus failure. The covariance matrix must remain symmetric positive definite during the working of the filter, when this condition is not satisfied filter lock happens. This can be studied by monitoring the eigen values of the covariance matrix or when the 3σ lines are not stable (red curve shows jagged behaviour 16), when any one of the eigen values goes to a negative value filter lock happens and subsequently the filter fails. From the plots (Figs. 11, 12, 13, 14, 15 and 16) we can see the filter behavior with double precision floating point, single precision floating point and Posit. For single precision floating points, filter lock happens in the early stages of the simulation, where the filter diverges from normal behavior, this can be seen from a comparison with double precision performance. However the same behavior was observed with Posit(32, 1). The Posit(32, 4) having a good average precision over the number line (Fig. 21) seems to sustain longer without failure, this can be seen from the error plot (Fig. 16) where the filter is at the beginning of failure due to locking but the state estimates has not diverged yet giving plausible results. On a comparison of number representation with 32 bit length Posit(32, 4) seems to perform better for this test case. The reason for this is studied in detail in 5.3. For this case with the Bierman mechanization we can see similar results and hence not shown here currently.

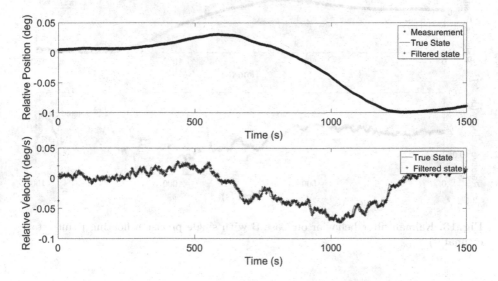

Fig. 11. Kalman filter behavior on Case B with double precision floating point (state estimates)

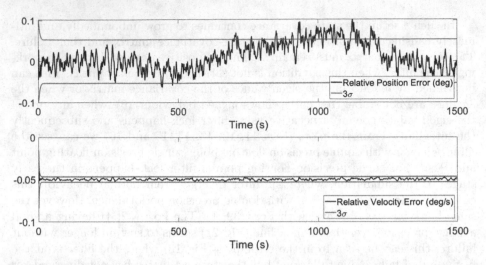

Fig. 12. Kalman filter behavior on Case B with double precision floating point (error in states)

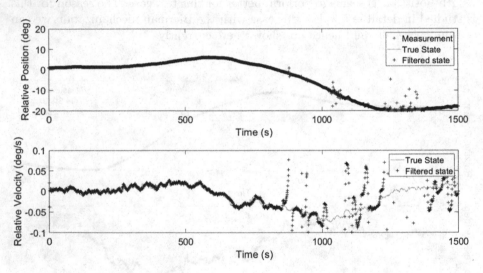

Fig. 13. Kalman filter behavior on Case B with single precision floating point (state estimates)

4.3   INS/GPS Navigation

Here we consider a Kalman filter with a navigation use case similar to [13]. The errors are modelled with equations and the system is modelled by propagating this error dynamics [19]. The states of the filter are these error states and consists of angles defined with respect to the Earth centered Earth fixed coordinate frame, this is useful in modelling aircraft dynamics and other flying bodies. By considering such a model we can see that if the GPS sensor has an accuracy of less

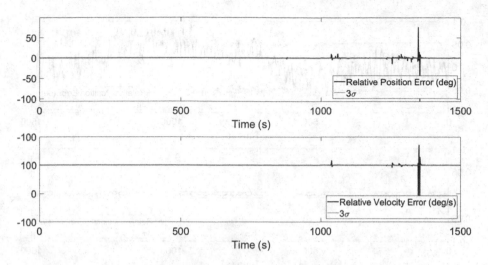

Fig. 14. Kalman filter behavior on Case B with single precision floating point (error in states)

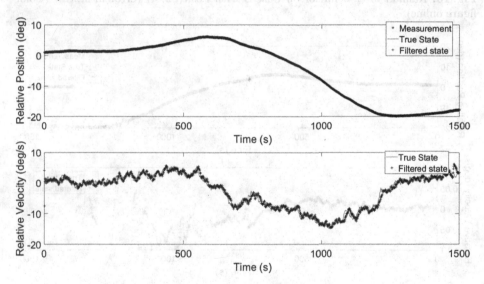

Fig. 15. Kalman filter behavior on Case B with Posit(32, 4) (state estimates)

than 10 m, then its corresponding measurement errors (in angles) corresponding to such a sensor becomes close to machine precision and hence this could cause the system to become ill-conditioned and cause the filter to fail. With any Posit configuration which has a better machine precision than single precision IEEE floats around 10^0 will be able to overcome the ill conditioning scenario for this use case.

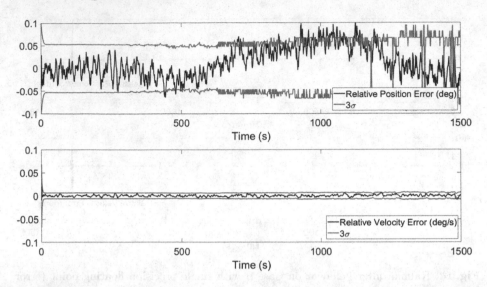

Fig. 16. Kalman filter behavior on Case B with Posit(32, 4) (error in states) (Color figure online)

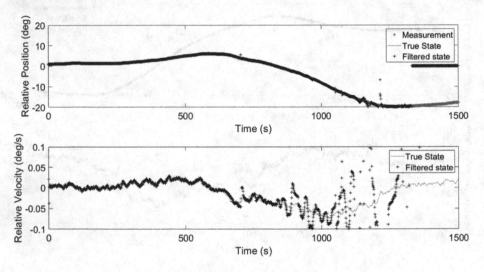

Fig. 17. Kalman filter behavior on Case B with Posit(32, 1) (state estimates)

The filter was simulated on a curved path with generated data and from the Fig. 19 it can be seen that the double precision and the Posit variant of the filter is following correct paths whereas the single precision fails to capture the correct path.

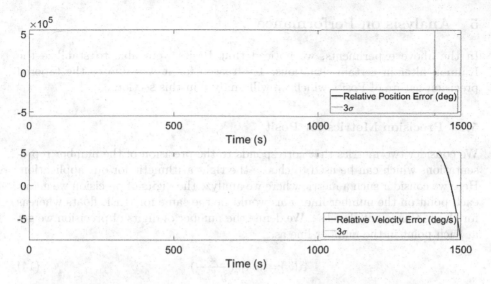

Fig. 18. Kalman filter behavior on Case B with Posit(32, 1) (error in states)

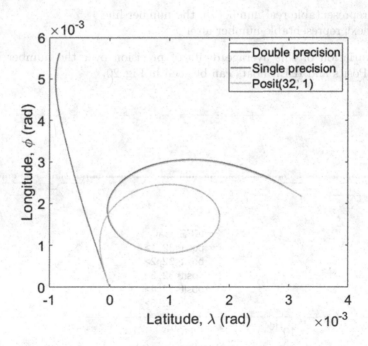

Fig. 19. Tracking of a simulated path with different arithmetic representations

5   Analysis on Performance

In the above experiments, we noticed that Posits were able to stabilize the Kalman filter in certain situations. The reason for it was due to the tapered precision nature of Posits which we will analyze in this section.

5.1   Precision Metrics for Posit

We consider two metrics that corresponds to the precision of the number representations which can be used to choose the right arithmetic for our application. Here we consider such a metric where we analyze the digits of precision we get at each point on the number line. This would be the same for IEEE floats whereas for Posits this is not the case. We define the number of digits of precision we get at each point in the number line as,

$$\alpha(x) = log_{10}(\frac{x}{y-x}) \tag{14}$$

where,

x = any representable real number on the number line
y = the next representable number after x

The variation of this average digits of precision over the number line for different Posits and IEEE floats can be seen in Fig. 20.

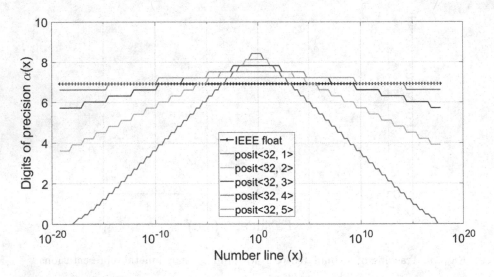

Fig. 20. Variation of digits of precision $\alpha(x)$ over number line

We can define the average precision of digits we get over the range of operation of our application for the chosen arithmetic representation as,

$$\mu = \frac{\int_{log(a)}^{log(b)} \alpha(x)dx}{\int_{log(a)}^{log(b)} dx} \tag{15}$$

where a and b are the smallest and largest numbers in the range of our application. This average precision value μ can be used as a metric to determine the suitable arithmetic for our application.

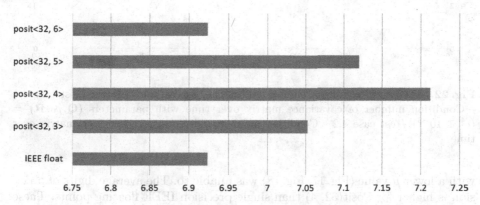

Fig. 21. Comparison of average digits of precision (μ) for IEEE single precision floats and different Posits in working range of case 4.2 ($a = 10^0, b = $ FLT_MAX in limits.h)

5.2   Analysis on Precision

In Table 1, we can see that Posit(32, 1) works well when a higher precision is required around 10^0, this corresponds to the top fully tapered region of Posit(32, 1) around 10^0 in Fig. 20. In this region the precision required is 10^{-8} (8 digits) around 1 which IEEE floating point will not be able to provide (7 digits, Fig. 20) but Posit(32, 1) can provide the required precision around 1. However in the Table 1, we can see that Posit(32, 1) fails when a precision of around 6 digits (10^3) is needed around $2^{32} \simeq 10^9$, the same can be observed from the Fig. 20 that the digits of precision for Posit(32, 1) is less than 6 digits around 10^9, and hence IEEE floating point performs better than Posit(32, 1) in this region.

Also for the test case 4.2, the covariance matrix starts with a small value and grows to a larger value, this is because the uncertainty in the system continues to grow as the system progresses, hence the floating point representation that we choose should have the good precision over the entire operating range which is a large section of the real number line. For this we can use the average digits of precision metric (μ), with this we can clearly see that how Posit(32, 4) was able to handle the test case in Sect. 4.2 (Fig. 15, Fig. 16) in the considered time interval but single precision IEEE float (Fig. 13, Fig. 14) and the posit variant

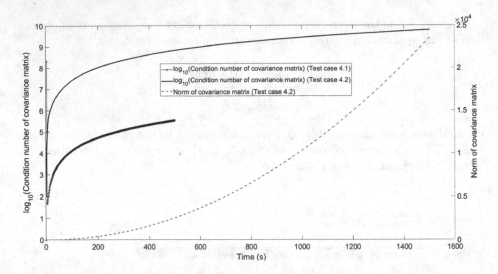

Fig. 22. Analysis of condition number and norm of covariance matrix, Test case 4.1 - Condition number of covariance matrix over time with parameters $(\mathbf{Q}, p_0, \mathbf{R}) = (\epsilon^4, 1, 10^{-8})$, Test case 4.2 - Condition number and Norm of covariance matrix over time

with a lower μ value (Fig. 17, Fig. 18) was unable to. The average digits of precision is higher for Posit(32, 4) than single precision IEEE floating points. These information about the working region of our application can be used to select the number format that would perform the best for our application.

5.3   Analysis of Condition Number

For the test case in Sect. 4.2 that we have shown before the condition number of the covariance matrix keeps on increasing and thus when the chosen number representation is not able to represent the covariance matrix properly the filter fails. Here is where we can use this information beforehand to choose our arithmetic system to work better in real-time.

By monitoring the condition number of the covariance matrix with double precision we can see some insights on the test cases. In Fig. 22 we can see the how the log_{10} of condition number of covariance matrix varies for test case 4.1 over time with the filter parameters $(\mathbf{Q}, p_0, \mathbf{R}) = (\epsilon^4, 1, 10^{-8})$.

As there is a peak initially which bounds the precision of arithmetic needed we have to choose the representation that gives the best numerical performance at that unstable number region. This choice is also between which Posits to choose as we see the dynamic precision of Posits also effect in the test results (Table 1). The plot Fig. 22 is from running the filter in double precision.

For the test case 4.2 the condition number of the covariance matrix grows to a higher value (Fig. 22) and also the norm of the covariance matrix (Fig. 22) continues to grow, we need to choose the arithmetic representation with higher precision over the whole number region. This can be decided from the average precision metric μ (Fig. 21). Hence here we see that Posit(32, 4) with larger average precision performs better (Fig. 16).

6 Conclusion

In this study we have explored some of the common failure modes in Kalman Filters and have shown that an alternate floating point representation can stabilize these operations. Specifically, we show that the Posit number format can be tailored to a specific Kalman filter application such that it performs better than single precision IEEE754 floating points. We show that selecting a Posit format having high precision near the operating range of the Kalman filter is most suitable for these applications. Also by analyzing the condition number and the norm of the covariance matrix it is possible for an application developer to select a Posit format based on the filter application which thus enables to use a less computationally demanding Kalman mechanization (Fig. 1). Also with recent advances [17], it would also be possible to switch between IEEE floating point and different Posit formats in real-time which would open the scope for a much more stable implementation of the Kalman filter depending on the filter's operating range.

7 Future Work

The Posit arithmetic standard provides an exact multiply and accumulate operator with the help of a data type called 'Quire' [6]. Quires are larger bitlength data registers that can be used to store intermediate outputs of a MAC operation in exact precision (without rounding off the results). This ability of Posits can be further utilized to improve the accuracy of the matrix multiplication operations in the Kalman filter methods discussed in this study. In our future work, we plan to explore and benchmark these improvements in accuracy. Since the Quire operations require more chip area and power, we also plan to analyze the accuracy vs power/area/speed trade-off in the case of Quire usage. Another future direction that can be explored is the design an algorithms to choose the numerically best Posit configuration dynamically based on certain markers of condition number and round off errors so that maximum stability of the Kalman filter can be ensured across the filter's operating range.

References

1. Hess, A.-K., Rantzer, A.: Distributed Kalman filter algorithms for self-localization of mobile devices. In: Proceedings of the 13th ACM International Conference on Hybrid Systems: Computation and Control (HSCC 2010). ACM, New York (2010)
2. Bierman, G., Thornton, C.: Numerical comparison of Kalman filter algorithms: orbit determination case study. Automatica **13**, 23–35 (1977)

3. D'Souza, C., Zanetti, R.: Information formulation of the UDU Kalman filter. IEEE Trans. Aerosp. Electron. Syst. **55**, 493–498 (2019). PMC6443377[pmcid]
4. Souza, É.L., Nakamura, E.F., Pazzi, R.W.: Target tracking for sensor networks: a survey. ACM Comput. Surv. Article no. 30 (2016)
5. Ford, J., Coulter, A.: Aeronautical & Maritime Research Laboratory (Australia) Filtering for precision guidance: the extended Kalman Filter/Jason J. Ford and Adrian S. Coulter (DSTO Aeronautical, 2001)
6. Gustafson, J., Yonemoto, I.: Beating floating point at its own game: posit arithmetic. Supercomput. Front. Innov.: Int. J. **4**, 71–86 (2017)
7. Welch, G., Bishop, G.: An introduction to the Kalman filter. Technical report. Chapel Hill, NC, USA (1995)
8. Gibbs, B.P.: Advanced Kalman Filtering, Least Squares and Modeling: a Practical Handbook. Wiley, Hoboken (2011)
9. Grewal, M., Kain, J.: Kalman filter implementation with improved numerical properties. IEEE Trans. Autom. Control **55**, 2058–2068 (2010)
10. Grewal, M.S., Andrews, A.P.: Kalman Filtering: Theory and Practice Using MATLAB, 4th edn. Wiley-IEEE Press (2014)
11. Kalman, R.: A new approach to linear filtering and prediction problems. J. Basic Eng. **82**, 35–45 (1960)
12. Nagarajan, K., Gans, N., Jafari, R.: Modeling human gait using a Kalman filter to measure walking distance. In: Proceedings of the 2nd Conference on Wireless Health (WH 2011). ACM, New York (2011)
13. Liu, M., Chang, G.: Numerically and statistically stable Kalman filter for INS/GNSS integration. Proc. Inst. Mech. Eng. Part G: J. Aerosp. Eng. **230**, 321–332 (2016)
14. Omtzigt, E., Gottschling, P., Seligman, M., Zorn, W.: Universal numbers library: design and implementation of a high-performance reproducible number systems library. arXiv:2012.11011 (2020)
15. Schmidt, J.: Analysis of Square-Root Kalman Filters for Angles-Only Orbital Navigation and the Effects of Sensor Accuracy on State Observability. All Graduate Theses and Dissertations (2010)
16. Thrun, S., Burgard, W., Fox, D.: Probabilistic Robotics (Intelligent Robotics and Autonomous Agents). MIT Press (2005)
17. Sharma, N., et al.: CLARINET: A RISC-V Based Framework for Posit Arithmetic Empiricism. arXiv (2020)
18. Simon, D.: Optimal State Estimation: Kalman, H Infinity, and Nonlinear Approaches. Wiley-Interscience (2006)
19. Sveinsson, A.: INS/GPS Error Analysis and Integration (2012)
20. Fico, V.M., et al.: Implementing the unscented Kalman filter on an embedded system: a lesson learnt. In: 2015 IEEE International Conference on Industrial Technology (ICIT), pp. 2010–2014 (2015)
21. Alonzo, K.: A 3D state space formulation of a navigation Kalman filter for autonomous vehicles. DTIC Document (1994)
22. Labbe, R.R., Jr.: Kalman and Bayesian Filters in Python (2020)

Evaluation of the Use of Low Precision Floating-Point Arithmetic for Applications in Radio Astronomy

Thushara Kanchana Gunaratne(✉) ⓘD

Herzberg Astronomy and Astrophysics Research Center, National Research Council Canada,
717 White Lake Road, P.O. Box 248, Kaleden, BC V0H 1K0, Canada
Thushara.Gunaratne@nrc-cnrc.gc.ca

Abstract. Conventionally, the front-end Digital Signal Processing (DSP) for applications in radio astronomy employed low-precision fixed-point arithmetic. However, the next-generation large-scale projects for radio astronomy such as the Square Kilometre Array (SKA), Atacama Large Millimeter/sub-millimeter Array (ALMA) upgrade and the proposed next-generation Very Large Array (ngVLA) have ambitious science goals that require higher sensitivities that in turn require high-precision arithmetic implementations. Also, the increasing strength, bandwidth and number of sources of Radio Frequency Interference (RFI) exacerbate the need for high-precision arithmetic. These factors lead to higher cost and power and longer design cycles for the DSP systems in radio astronomy. Meanwhile, hardware manufacturers are offering native support for low-precision floating-point number formats such as float16 and bfloat16 and variants of those. In addition to those, 'posits', a new number representation has been introduced by John Gustafson and is claiming to offer better accuracy compared to float16 under certain conditions. With these compact data formats, it is expected that signal processing systems to consume lower power and resources. For typical radio astronomical observations, the achievable sensitivity is determined by the ability to suppress RFI and the accuracy of delay correction. In the following, these two 'qualitative' aspects are studied for the front-end DSP modules of the SKA correlator and beamformer where the coefficients are represented with float16, bfloat16, variants of those formats and posit16 and compared against the current fixed-point representation.

Keywords: Digital Arithmetic · Digital Signal Processing (DSP) · bfloat16 · float16 · fixed-point · floating-point · posits · Radio Astronomy

1 Introduction

Applications in radio astronomy have immensely benefited from the advancements in Digital Signal Processing (DSP) [1]. Deployment of DSP hardware in radio astronomy started in the early 1960s with 1-bit samples/correlations [2, 3]. For the next couple of decades, the sample resolution grew to a few bits [4, 5]. During this era Radio Frequency Interface (RFI) in key frequency bands for radio astronomical observations has been quite moderate and therefore 'Multiply-Accumulate then Fourier Transform'-type XF-correlators [6–8] with two-or-three bits of resolution were sensitive enough to study relatively bright radio-sources in the sky. Nevertheless, corrections had to be applied to the 'correlation-coefficients' evaluated with such coarse quantizations [1, 4]. Meanwhile, the radio astronomers' desire to observe 'faint' sources over wider bandwidths amid the increasing strength, bandwidth and number of sources of RFI led the way to the 'Channelize then Multiply-Accumulate'-type [1], FX-correlators that offer better suppression of the in-band RFI [9–13]. Among those the TALON Frequency-Slice architecture proposed by the Herzberg Astronomy and Astrophysics (HAA) Research Center, National Research Council of Canada has been selected for the Square Kilometre Array (SKA) Mid-Telescope [12]. Further, almost identical architectures have been proposed for the correlators of the next-generation Very Large Array (ngVLA) telescope [10] and the Atacama Large Millimeter/sub-millimeter Array (ALMA) 2030 wideband sensitivity upgrade [11], respectively.

In order to achieve the required sensitivities with strong in-band RFI [14, 15] high dynamic ranges are required for wideband and sub-band signals in the Correlators and 'Beamformer[1]'. Therefore, the DSP modules for the SKA Mid Telescope SKA Mid Correlator and Beamformer (SKA Mid CBF) have been designed to process samples that are represented with the 'two's complement' number format containing 12–19 bits [17] using 'fixed-point' arithmetic [18]. Hence, the processing hardware has to facilitate wider signal paths to and from the DSP processors, large input/output data rates and large internal memory [19]. It has been estimated that the 'bit toggle rates' for Gaussian-distributed radio-astronomical signals are within the range of 25%–50%. Hence, Field Programmable Gate Arrays (FPGAs) fabricated with Complementary Metal Oxide Semiconductor (CMOS) technology operating at clock rates at hundreds of MHz, such bit-toggle rates may lead to higher power consumption [20]. All these factors aggregate to increase the power consumption in the DSP for radio astronomy where most observatories are almost always located in remote regions with few options for power. On the other hand, it is expected that extensive design efforts are needed to optimize the dynamic range of the DSP at various stages of the signal chain that would lead to longer design cycles and may result in rigid systems that may become ineffective if the conditions change due to RFI, etc.

2 Floating-Point Arithmetic

2.1 Standard Floating-Point Formats

The IEEE standard for binary floating-point arithmetic is the most commonly used floating-point format in computing devices around the world. The original standard, IEEE Standard for Binary Floating-Point Arithmetic (IEEE 754--1985) specified two types of floating-point variants; 1. The single-precision format of 32 bits and 2. The double-precision format of 64 bits, respectively and an optional extended precision format of 80 bits [21]. In 2008, this standard has been superseded by the IEEE Standard

---

[1] Beamformers combine the signals from multiple receptors in such a way to selectively enhance signals propagating from certain directions [16].

for Floating-Point Arithmetic (IEEE 754--2008) [22]. There among other revisions, two additional formats; 3. The quad-precision of 128 bits and 4. The half-precision of 16 bits were added to the standard, respectively. In 2019, minor updates have been added to the IEEE-754 format. Compared to fixed-point arithmetic, the IEEE 754 floating-point arithmetic standard offers a wider dynamic range with the same number of bits at the expense of precision for a certain range of numbers [17]. Moreover, there can be rounding errors that lead to inaccurate results. Also, the digital hardware required to implement the floating-point arithmetic operations is more complicated compared to that of fixed-point arithmetic [17].

2.2 Floating-Point Formats Supported by Major Hardware Manufactures

Due to the increasing use of Graphical Processing Units (GPUs) and FPGAs for applications in Artificial Intelligence (AI) with Deep Neural Networks (DNN), the major manufacturers such as NVIDIA for their newer range of GPUs and Intel for their Agilex series FPGAs have been offering 'native' support to the standard IEEE 754 single-precision and half-precision formats and several variants of those [23–25]. For half-precision and its variants (e.g. bfloat16 and bfloat16+), Intel Agilex Variable Precision DSP Block offers 'Fused Multiply and Accumulate' (FMA) functionality that can preserve the precision for partial sums [25]. For some of their Agilex, Stratix, Arria and Cyclone series FPGAs, Intel also offers 'Floating-Point IP Cores' that support both standard IEEE 754 double- and single- precision formats and custom 'Single-Extended Precision' format that can be configured to have a total length of 43 to 63 bits [26]. On the other hand, AMD-Xilinx offers configurable 'Floating-Point Operator' firmware blocks to facilitate both standard IEEE 754 double-, single- and half- precision formats [27, 28]. Several different versions of floating-point formats supported by Intel and AMD-Xilinx in their FPGAS and NVIDIA in its GPUs are listed in Table 1. Note that Intel's Floating-Point IP Cores and AMD-Xilinx's Floating-Point Operator firmware blocks may consume multiple 'hardened' DSP processors to implement a double- or single- precision floating-point multiplier or accumulator [26, 28].

2.3 Posits – An Emerging Number Format

In 2017, Gustafson and Yonemoto proposed 'posits' [29], a novel number format based on the 'unums' (i.e. 'Universal Numbers') [30] that was also proposed by Gustafson. Posit number system can be considered as an alternative to floating point number systems. Key features of posits include the tapered-precision, no overflow or underflow and having single representations for the zero and the infinity, respectively [29]. According to the latest standard for posit arithmetic (2022), anything that is not mathematically definable as a unique real number is specified as a 'not a real' (NaR) number [40]. This contrasts with the many 'not a number' (NaN) allocations in IEEE floating-point standard [21, 22]. It has been shown that for numerical representations containing the same number of bits, posits achieve higher precision compared to the variants of IEEE floating-point formats for a given range centering unity [31]. Hardware implementation of posit arithmetic is challenged by the variable lengths assigned to the different components of the number system [29]. Although to date, none of the major hardware manufacturers is facilitating posit arithmetic on their devices, several smaller groups have been pioneering the hardware implementation [32–34].

Table 1. The floating-point formats supported in Intel and AMD-Xilinx and NVIDIA devices

Manufacturer	Supported Formats	Details
Intel [25−26]	float32†	Standard IEEE-754 (1S : 8E : 23M)
	float16* (SNNS)	Standard IEEE-754 (1S : 5E : 10M)
	extended-float16*	Non-standard internal format (1S : 8E : 10M)
	bfloat16* (SNNS)	Non-standard (1S : 8E : 7M)
	bfloat16+* (SNNS)	Non-standard (1S : 8E : 10M)
	single-extended†	Non-standard (1S : Exp_{ES}E : Men_{ES}M) • $52 \geq Men_{ES} \geq 31$ • $Exp_{ES} \geq 11$ • $63 \geq Exp_{ES} + Men_{ES} \geq 42$
	double†	Standard IEEE-754 (1S : 11E : 52M)
AMD-Xilinx [27−28]	double╟	Standard IEEE-754 (1S : 11E : 52M)
	single╟	Standard IEEE-754 (1S : 8E : 23M)
	half╟	Standard IEEE-754 (1S : 5E : 10M)
NVIDIA [23−24]	float64 (FP64)	Standard IEEE-754 (1S : 11E : 52M)
	float32 (FP32)	Standard IEEE-754 (1S : 8E : 23M)
	tensor float32 (TF32)	Non-standard (1S : 8E : 10M)
	float16 (FP16)	Standard IEEE-754 (1S : 5E : 10M)
	bfloat16 (BF16)	Non-standard (1S : 8E : 7M)

(1S : NE : PM) indicates 1 sing-bit (S), N-exponent bits and P-mantissa (fractional) bits [22].

*Only supported in Intel's Agilex Family of FPGAs.
SNSN – Subnormal numbers are not supported.
†Supported with the Intel Floating-Point IP Cores for some Agilex, Stratix, Arria and Cyclone series FPGAs
╟Supported with Xilinx Floating-Point Operator Firmware Blocks
Note: Support for the floating-point formats in NVIDIA GPUs differs by the GPU and supported CUDA version.

3   DSP Modules Used in Typical Radio Astronomy Applications

Let's consider the example of the state of the art FX correlator (and beamformer) for the SKA Mid. As shown in Fig. 1, SKA Mid CBF facilitates four observation modes: 1. Normal- and zoom- imaging 2. Pulsar Search (PSS) Beamforming 3. Pulsar Timing (PST) Beamforming and 4. Beamforming and Calibration for Very Large Baseline

Interferometry (VLBI) [12]. It is important to note that there are signal processing modules with different configurations performing similar operations employed in the signal chains facilitating different observing modes.

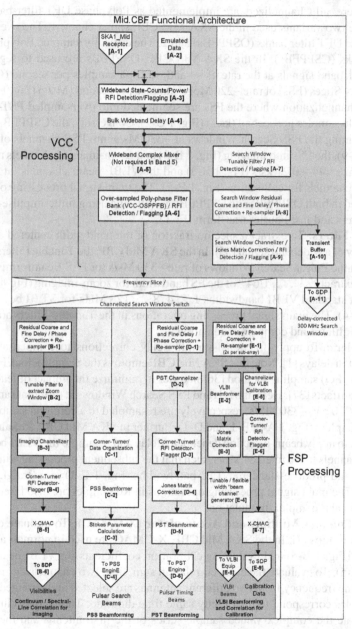

Fig. 1. The functional architecture of SKA Mid CBF showing the key signal processing modules for different observing modes (From [12] with minor modifications).

The following provides very brief introductions to the key signal processing modules of the SKA Mid CBF.

- **Channelizers:** To segment wideband signals into multiple channels of uniform bandwidth. Here, all Channelizers are implemented as Polyphase DFT filter-banks [35]. There are two variants used in the SKA Mid CBF signal chain; 1. The oversampled Polyphase DFT filter banks (OSPPFBs) and 2. The critically sampled Polyphase DFT filter-banks (CSPPFBs). In the SKA Mid CBF, OSPPFBs are used to segment the input wideband signals at the rate of ~4 and ~6 Giga samples per second (Gs/s) into Frequency Slices (FSs) of rate ~220 Mega samples per second (Ms/s) (Fig. 1 A-6) and in PST channelization where the FSs are segmented into oversampled PST-channels of ~61 kilo samples per second (ks/s) (Fig. 1 D-2). Conversely, the CSPPFBs are used in segmenting the PSS Search Windows at ~330 Ms/s into PSS channels of ~81 ks/s (Fig. 1 A-9), the FSs into imaging (Fig. 1 B-3) and zoom-imaging channels at varying rates from 13.44 – 0.21 ks/s (Fig. 1 B-3) and the VLBI 'beam-channels' at 224 Ms/s into fine-channels for calibration (Fig. 1 E-5). The main signal processing operations performed in both OSPPFBs and CSPPFBs are filtering using finite-impulse-response (FIR) filters and fast Fourier transform (FFT).
- **Tunable Filters:** To extract a specific fraction of the bandwidth centered at a given frequency of a wideband signal [35]. In the SKA Mid CBF, the Tunable Filters are used to extract the Pulsar Search Windows of rate ~330 Ms/s for PSS Beamforming (Fig. 1 A-7), to extract ½, ¼, …, $1/64^{th}$ of the FS bandwidth for zoom-imaging (Fig. 1 B-2) and to extract standard VLBI bandwidths 1, 2, 4, 8,…, 128 MHz for VLBI beamforming (Fig. 1 E-4). The main signal processing operations in the Tunable-Filters are filtering using FIR filters and complex-modulation.
- **ReSamplers:** To apply fractional-sample delay corrections to compensate for the propagation delays [1]. Note that SKA Mid CBF employs the Sample Clock Frequency Offset (SCFO) sampling method [36] in order to minimize the impact of leaked clock and RFI artifacts [37]. Here, the FSs and PSS Search Windows at different sample rates around ~220 and ~330 MS/s, respectively are resampled to a common sample rate by the ReSamplers (Fig. 1 A-8, B-1, and D-1). Further in SKA Mid CBF, ReSamplers are also used to apply beam-direction dependent delay and resample the VLBI beams into beam-channels to the rate 224 MS/s, such that the subsequent processing with Tunable Filters could produce standard VLBI bandwidths (Fig. 1 E-1) in a straight forward manner. The main signal processing operations in ReSampler are also filtering using FIR filters and complex-modulation.
- **Cross - Complex Multiply and Accumulator (X-CMAC):** To evaluate cross/auto correlation sums [1]. In the SKA Mid CBF, X-CMAC are used in normal- and zoom-imaging (Fig. 1 B-5) and evaluating calibration coefficients for VLBI beamforming (Fig. 1 E-5). To evaluate the cross correlation sum, first, two channels corresponding to the same frequency from two different antennas are selected and arranged such that the samples correspond to the exactly same time duration. Then, cross multiply and accumulate the complex-valued sample series of the first antenna and the complex conjugate of the sample-series of the second antenna. To evaluate the auto-correlation sum, repeat the steps to evaluate the cross-correlation sum with samples from the same antenna and the same channel. Additional parameters such as the 'valid-sample-count'

and 'centroid' of the integration are also calculated in X-CMAC. X-CMAC operates on 'bursting' fine-channels at ~500 Ms/s.

- **Complex-Mixer:** To shift the extracted wideband frequency segment such that the desired frequency segment falls away from the edges of the FSs (Fig. 1 A-5). The main signal processing operation in the Complex-Mixer is complex modulation.
- **Beamformers:** To selectively enhance the signals coming from weak celestial sources depending on their direction in the sky [16]. In the SKA Mid CBF, VLBI beams are formed using the *true delay-and-sum* method by scaling and combining the delay-steered VLBI beam-channels of width 224 MHz (Fig. 1 E-2). Conversely, PSS and PST beams are formed using the *phase-delay-and-sum* method where a phase-rotation is applied to narrowband channels at rates ~81 and ~61 ks/s, respectively to steer those toward desired beam direction and then scaled and combined (Fig. 1 C-5 and D-5).
- **Jones Matrix Correction:** To apply corrections for the polarization mis-matches/leakages [1]. In the SKA Mid CBF, this correction is applied as a simple matrix multiplication for the two-element vector that is consisted of the two orthogonal polarization components (Fig. 1 A-9, D-4 and E-3).
- **Corner-Turner (and RFI Detector):** To rearrange data and perform channel-wise RFI detection based on the expected power thresholds. In SKA Mid CBF, corner-turners are placed between the imaging channelizer and the X-CMAC (Fig. 1 B-4), PSS channelizer[2] and PSS Beamformer (Fig. 1 C-1), PST Channelizer and Jones Matrix Correction (Fig. 1 D-3) and VLBI channelizer and X-CMAC (Fig. 1 B-6).

4 Frequency Responses of the Channelizers, Tunable Filters and ReSamplers in SKA Mid CBF Implemented with float16, bfloat16, bfloat16+, posit16 and Similar Length Fixed-Point

The frequency responses of Channelizers and Tunable Filters are determined by the coefficients of their 'prototype' lowpass filters [35]. When these coefficients are represented with low-precision formats such as float16, bfloat16, bfloat16+, posit16 and fixed-point of similar bit-widths (e.g. 19-bits) the resulting deviation from the original values (from here on referred to as quantization errors) may lead to distortions in the frequency response. It has been observed that these distortions are more pronounced in the stop-band where the magnitude of the frequency response is very small. The stopband attenuation of the frequency responses of the Channelizers and Tunable Filters determines the suppression of interference from other celestial sources and manmade RFI [1]. One of the key requirements for the SKA Mid telescope is to achieve 1 : 1, 000, 000 dynamic range in imaging. In order to meet this requirement the total leaked power into an imaging channel should be < -60 dB. Therefore, all the Tunable Filters and Channelizers in the Imaging signal chain should suppress the 'out of channel' interference by at least 60 dB. Assuming a uniform distribution of interference power in the observed spectrum, the stopband attenuation of the frequency response for all Channelizers in the Imaging signal chain should be $\sim 60 + 10\log_{10}(N_C - 1)$ dB, where N_C is the number of channels in the channelizers, where $10\log_{10}(N_C)$ dB accounts for the leaked signal

---

[2] Search Window Channelizer.

power that 'aliased' into the channels in OSPFBs and CSPFBs [35]. As in the case of Channelizers, the stopband attenuation of all the Tunable Filters along the Imaging signal chain should be ~60 + $10\log_{10}(D)$ dB, where D is the downsampling factor of the Tunable Filter.

For the Continuum Imaging (i.e. Normal Imaging) in the SKA Mid CBF, the Imaging signal chain includes two Channelizers; 1. The VCC-OSPPFB (Fig. 1 A-6) that segments the wideband antenna signals into FSs, followed by 2. The Imaging Channelizer (Fig. 1 B-3) that segments FSs into 'fine' imaging channels. In Zoom Imaging, a configurable Tunable Filter (Fig. 1 B-2) lies between the Re-Sampler and the Imaging Channelizer.

4.1 Frequency Responses of the Prototype-Filter for the 30 Channel VCC-OSPPFB Represented with float16, bfloat16, bfloat16+, posit16 and 19-Bit Fixed-Point

In the SKA Mid CBF, there are two variants of VCC-OSPPFBs; 1. Segmenting the wideband input into 20 FSs and 2. Segmenting the wideband input into 30 FSs, respectively [37]. Between those two variants, the latter yielding 30 FSs has the most stringent requirement of 72.6 dB for stopband attenuation. For the particular design with the magnitude of unity in the passband, the maximum value and the minimum non-zero magnitude of the coefficients are 3.65e−02 and 1.21e−07, respectively. The distribution of the logarithmic magnitude of the coefficients is shown in Fig. 2. Therefore, scaling of the coefficients had to be applied to minimize the quantization errors, particularly for float16 and 19-bit fixed-point (fixed19^3) representations. For the selected scaling factors SF_F16 $= 2^{10}$, SF_B16 $= 2^{10}$, SF_B16+ $= 2^{10}$, SF_P16 $= 2^6$ and SF_X19 $= 2^4$, the magnitude responses evaluated with double, float16, bfloat16, bfloat16+, posit16 and fixed19 representations are shown in Fig. 3. Note that the magnitudes were evaluated by converting the quantized coefficients to double and scaled with the reciprocal of the scaling factors such that the magnitude responses can be easily compared visually. Conversions to float16, bfloat16 and bfloat16+ were performed using the Matlab-Executable (MEX) interface to the 'CPFloat' library [38] whereas conversions to posit16 were performed using the 'Posit Toolbox' implemented by Professor Gérard Meurant [39]. As shown in Fig. 3 the fixed19 representation achieves the closest to double (i.e. the best possible) and posit16 comes a close second with just 16 bits. The float16 and bfloat16+ representations result in almost identical magnitude transfer functions. Note that fixed19, posit16, float16 and bfloat16+ representations manage to meet the specification in stopband attenuation, whereas the bfloat16 representation fails.

4.2 Frequency Responses of the Prototype-Filter of the Imaging Channelizer Represented with float16, bfloat16, bfloat16+, posit16 and fixed19

In the SKA Mid CBF, the Imaging Channelizer segments the FSs and Zoom Windows into 16,384 overlapping channels [37]. It can be shown that the stopband attenuation should be higher than 102.1 dB in order to achieve better than 60 dB suppression of the interference. For the particular design with the magnitude of unity in the passband, the

---

^{3} The binary-point is set such that fixed19 has 18 fractional bits.

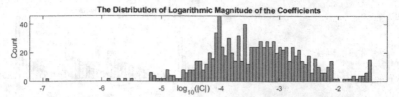

Fig. 2. The distribution of the logarithmic magnitude of the coefficients of the 30 Channel OSPPFB.

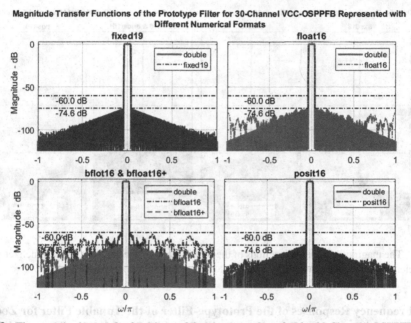

Fig. 3. The magnitude transfer functions of the prototype filter for the 30 Channel OSPPFB with coefficient represented with double, fixed19, float16, bfloat16, bfloat16+ and posit16.

maximum value and the minimum non-zero magnitude of the coefficients are 7.09e−05 and 3.15e−11, respectively. The distribution of the logarithmic magnitude of the coefficients is shown in Fig. 4. For the selected scaling factors SF_F16 = 2^{20}, SF_B16 = 2^{20}, SF_B16+ = 2^{20}, SF_P16 = 2^{12} and SF_X19 = 2^{13}, the magnitude responses evaluated with double, float16, bfloat16, bfloat16+, posit16 and fixed19 representations as in the previous section are shown in Fig. 5. Here too, the fixed19 becomes the closest to the double and posit16 comes a close second while float16 and bfloat16+ coming third with almost identical responses. The fixed19 and posit16 representations meet the requirement for the stopband attenuation for the Imaging Channelizer for the entire stopband. Meanwhile, float16 and bfloat16+ representations meet the requirement except for a few minute regions of the stopband by exceeding the limit by several dBs. As in the previous case, the bfloat16 representation fails to meet the requirement.

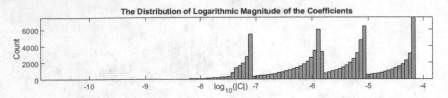

Fig. 4. The distribution of the logarithmic magnitude of the coefficients of the Imaging Channelizer.

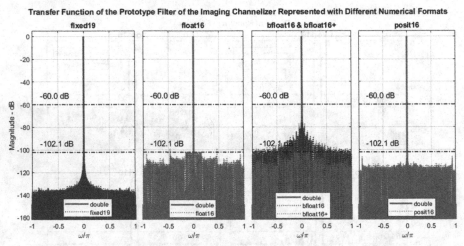

Fig. 5. The magnitude transfer functions of the prototype filter for the Imaging Channelizer with coefficient represented with double, fixed19, float16, bfloat16, bfloat16+ and posit16.

4.3 Frequency Responses of the Prototype-Filter of the Tunable Filter for Zoom Window Extraction Represented with float16, bfloat16, bfloat16 +, posit16 and fixed19

In the SKA Mid CBF, a configurable Tunable Filter is used to extract Zoom Windows of size $[\frac{1}{2}, \frac{1}{4}, .., \frac{1}{64}]$ of the FS's sample rate [37]. As mentioned previously, the most stringent stopband attenuation requirement is 78.1 dB for the case of $\frac{1}{64}$ of the FS where the down-sampling factor is the highest. For the particular design with the magnitude of unity in the passband, the maximum value of the coefficients and the minimum non-zero magnitude of the coefficients are 1.53e−02 and 1.58e−8, respectively. The distribution of logarithmic magnitude of the coefficients is shown in Fig. 6. For the selected scaling factors $SF\_F16 = 2^{16}$, $SF\_B16 = 2^{16}$, , $SF\_B16+ = 2^{16}$, $SF\_P16 = 2^8$ and $SF\_X19 = 2^6$, the magnitude responses evaluated with double, float16, bfloat16, bfloat16+, posit16 and fixed19 representations are shown in Fig. 7. As shown there the fixed19 representation achieves the closest to the double and posit16 comes a close second with just 16-bits. Here too, float16 and bfloat16+ representations seem to achieve almost identical magnitude transfer functions. Note that fixed19, posit16, float16 and bfloat16+ representations meet the specification in stopband attenuation, whereas the bfloat16 representation does not.

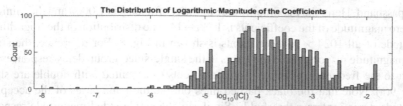

Fig. 6. The distribution of the logarithmic magnitude of the coefficients of Tunable Filter for extracting $\frac{1}{64}$ of the FS.

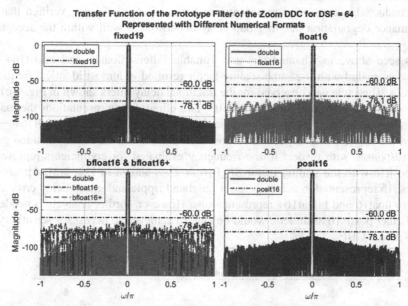

Fig. 7. The magnitude transfer function of the prototype filter for the Tunable Filter for extracting $\frac{1}{64}$ of the FS with coefficient represented with double, fixed19, float16, bfloat16, bfloat16+ and posit16.

4.4 Frequency Responses of the Fractional Delay Filter of the ReSampler Represented with float16, bfloat16, bfloat16+, posit16 and fixed19

The fractional-delay filters in the ReSamplers are of ~90% passband and therefore, the stopband attenuation is not a concern here. In fact the response beyond passband is irrelevant as the spectral components in this region are redundant and later discarded. For these fractional-delay filters the quantization of the coefficients with low-precision float16, bfloat16, bfloat16+, posit16 and fixed19 lead to both distortions of the magnitude and phase responses. In the SKA Mid CBF, the ReSampler employs a fractional delay filter bank with 1024 delay steps [37]. In order to achieve the expected sensitivities the maximum passband ripple ≤0.005 dB and the maximum error in group delay ≤0.0005 sample-period (i.e. ≤0.5 delay-step) for the central 90% of the passband. Each of the fractional delay filters is of 64 coefficients and is designed to have a magnitude of unity in the passband. Here, the maximum value of the coefficients is 1.00e0 and the minimum non-zero magnitude of the coefficients is 1.79e−14. The distribution of the 'logarithmic' magnitude of all 1024×64 coefficients is shown in Fig. 8. For reference, the single-sided magnitude responses and the errors in the single-sided group delay responses with respect to the frequency evaluated for coefficients represented with double are shown in Fig. 9(a). Note that the black dashed lines outline the boundaries of the acceptable magnitude-deviation/error thresholds. Similarly, the single-sided magnitude responses and the errors in the single-sided group delay responses with respect to the frequency evaluated for coefficients represented with fixed19 with the scaling factor SF_X19 = 1 are also shown in Fig. 9(b). As given in [37] extensive studies with simulations have been conducted with fixed19 representation for the ReSampler that verified that the performance degradation due to group delay distortions is well within the acceptable range.

As seen above in Channelizers and Tunable Filters, float16 and bfloat16+ formats when scaled with the same scaling factor resulted in almost identical frequency responses. The same was observed for the fractional delay filters shown in Fig. 9(c) and (d), respectively. Note that for both float16+ and bfloat16+ representations the magnitude and group delay responses are evaluated with scaling SF_F16 = SF_B16+ = 2^4. Finally, the single-sided magnitude responses and the errors in the single-sided group delay responses with respect to the frequency evaluated for coefficients represented with posit16 with the scaling factor SF_P16 = 2^4 is shown in Fig. 9(e). Apparently, the posit16 representation achieves lower passband ripple and group delay error compared to float16 and bfloat16+ representations. However, further analysis is needed to see whether posits16 arithmetic would be able to achieve the necessary sensitivity for the SKA Mid CBF.

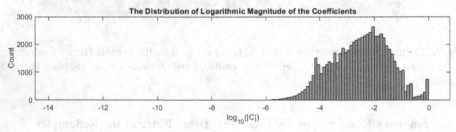

Fig. 8. The logarithmic magnitude distribution of all the coefficients of the fractional delay filter-bank in the ReSampler.

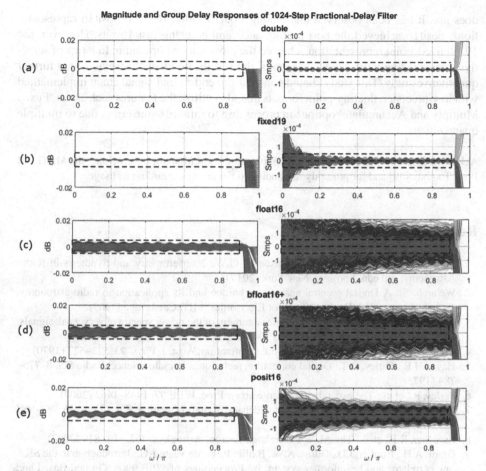

Fig. 9. (Left-column) The single-sided magnitude responses and (Right-column) The single-sided errors in the group delay responses for the 1024 fractional delay filters represented with (a) double, (b) fixed19, (c) float16, (d) bfloat16+ and (e) posit16.

5 Conclusions and Future Work

Major hardware manufacturers such as Intel, AMD-Xilinx and NVIDIA are offering native support for low-precision floating-point formats, i.e. float16, bfloat16 and variants of those in the latest FPGAs and GPUs. Although not yet supported by any of the major hardware manufacturers, the posit number system, an emerging number system, shows a lot of promise in certain areas of signal processing. Here, a preliminary qualitative study has been conducted to investigate whether these low-precision floating-point formats, namely float16, bfloat16, bfloat16+ and posit16, will be able to achieve the required suppression of RFI and sensitivity in terms of delay correction for the key signal processing modules in radio astronomy with the example of the SKA Mid CBF. In terms of the suppression of RFI along the Imaging signal chain, the results show that float16, bfloat16+ and posit16 all meet the specified requirements whereas bfloat16 does not. It has been observed that among float16, bfloat16+ and posit16 representations, posit16 achieved the best performance amidst using just 16 bits. However, the 19-bit fixed-point representation achieved the closest to the optimum. In terms of sensitivity achieved with the delay corrections, the results are inconclusive and need further quantitative study. This study should consider the end-to-end signal chain implemented with low-precision floating-point formats that also utilize the features such as the 'Fused Multiply and Accumulate' option[4] in processing to minimize the errors due to multiple quantizations.

Acknowledgments. The author is grateful to prof. Gérard Meurant for providing the MATLAB Posit Toolbox [39] and for promptly responding to the queries regarding its usage.

References

1. Thompson, A.R., Moran, J.M., Swenson-Jr, G.W.: Interferometry and Synthesis in Radio Astronomy, 3rd edn. Springer, New York (2017)
2. Weinreb, S.: A Digital spectral analysis technique and its application to radio astronomy. Technical report 412, Research Lab. for Electronics, MIT, Cambridge (1963)
3. Goldstein, R.M.: A technique for the measurement of the power spectra of very weak signals. IRE Trans. Space Electron. Telem. **8**, 170–173 (1962)
4. Cooper, B.F.C.: Correlators with two-bit quantization. Aust. J. Phys. **23**, 521–527 (1970)
5. Hagen, J.B., Farley, D.T.: Digital correlation techniques in radio science. Radio Sci. **8**, 775–784 (1973)
6. Perley, R., et al.: The expanded very large array. Proc. IEEE **97**, 1448–1462 (2009)
7. Carlson, B.R., Dewdney, P.E.: Efficient wideband digital correlation. Elect. Letts. **36**, 987–988 (2000)
8. Escoffier, R.P., et al.: The ALMA correlator. Astron. Astrophys. **462**, 801–810 (2007)
9. Grant, A.H., Bunton, J.D., Gunst, A.W., Baillie P., bij de Vaate J-G.: Introduction to the SKA low correlator and beamformer system. In: Proceedings of SPIE 9906, Ground-Based and Airborne Telescopes VI, 99062S (2016)
10. Rupen, M.P., Carlson, B., Pleasance, M.: Trident frequency slice architecture correlator/beamformer reference design for ngVLA. In: AAS, vol. 233, p. 361.06 (2019)
11. Carlson, B., Pleasance, M., Gunaratne, T., Vrcic, S.: NRC TALON frequency slice architecture correlator/beamformer (AT.CBF) for ALMA. ALMA Memo 617 (2020)
12. Pleasance, M., Carlson, B., Vrcic, S., Gunaratne, T.: TALON demonstration correlator architecture for early ska array assemblies. In: 2021 XXXIVth General Assembly and Scientific Symposium of the International Union of Radio Science (URSI GASS) (2021)
13. van der Byl, A., et al.: MeerKAT correlator-beamformer: a real-time processing back-end for astronomical observations. J. Astron. In: Telesc. Instrum. Syst. **8**(1), 011006 (2021)
14. van der Merwe, P.S., Andriambeloson, J.A.: On-site wideband spectrum measurements. Mesa Solutions (Pty) Ltd., SKA/17/12/11 - Rev1 (2018). (Restricted Access)
15. Selina, R., Ojeda, O. Y.: Headroom, dynamic range, and quantization considerations. ngVLA Electron. Memo **8** (2021)

---

[4] The 32-bit IEEE standard single precision output for float16 and bfloat16 + in Variable Precision DSP Blocks offered with Intel Agilex FPGAs [25] and 256-bit wide 'Quire' proposed for the 16-bit posits [31].

16. Trees, H.L.V.: Detection, Estimation, and Modulation Theory, Optimum Array Processing. Wiley-Interscience, New York, Chichester (2002)
17. Ercegovac, M.D., Lang, T.: Digital Arithmetic. Morgan Kaufmann Publishers (2004)
18. Gunaratne, T., Carlson, B., Comoretto, G., Rupen, M., Pleasance, M.: An end-to-end model for the correlator and beamformer of the square kilometer array mid telescope. In: Modeling, Systems Engineering, and Project Management for Astronomy IX. International Society for Optics and Photonics (2020)
19. Pleasance, M., Zhang, H., Carlson, B., Webber, R., Chalmers, D., Gunaratne, T.: High-performance hardware platform for the square kilomtre array mid correlator and beamformer. In: 2017 XXXIInd General Assembly and Scientific Symposium of the International Union of Radio Science (URSI GASS) (2017)
20. Early Power Estimators (EPE) and Power Analyzer. https://www.intel.com/content/www/us/en/support/programmable/support-resources/power/pow-powerplay.html. Accessed 01 Nov 2022
21. IEEE Standard for Binary Floating-Point Arithmetic. ANSI/IEEE Std 754-1985, pp. 1–20 (1985). https://doi.org/10.1109/IEEESTD.1985.82928
22. IEEE Standard for Floating-Point Arithmetic. IEEE Std 754-2008, pp. 1–70 (2008). https://doi.org/10.1109/IEEESTD.2008.4610935
23. NVIDIA Corporation, NVIDIA Tesla P100 GPU architecture, WP-08019-001 v01.1 (2016)
24. NVIDIA Corporation, NVIDIA A100 tensor core GPU architecture, Whitepaper v1.0 (2020)
25. Intel Corporation, Intel® Agilex™ Variable Precision DSP Blocks User Guide. 683037, V21.2. https://www.intel.com/content/www/us/en/docs/programmable/683037/21-2/variable-precision-dsp-blocks-overview.html. Accessed 01 Nov 2022
26. Intel Corporation, Floating-Point IP Cores User Guide. https://www.intel.com/content/www/us/en/docs/programmable/683750/20-1/about-floating-point-ip-cores.html. Accessed 01 Nov 2022
27. AMD-Xilinx Corporation, Floating-Point Operator. https://www.Xilinx.com/products/intellectual-property/floating_pt.html. Accessed 01 Nov 2022
28. AMD-Xilinx Corporation, Performance and Resource Utilization for Floating-point v7.1 (IP Core for Vivado Design Suite Release 2022.2). https://www.Xilinx.com/htmldocs/ip_docs/pru_files/floating-point.html. Accessed 01 Nov 2022
29. Gustafson, J.L., Yonemoto, I.: Beating floating point at its own game: posit arithmetic. Supercomput. Front. Innov.: Int. J. 4(2), 71–86 (2017)
30. Gustafson, J.L.: The End of Error: Unum Computing. Chapman and Hall/CRC, Boca Raton (2015)
31. de Dinechin, F., Forget, L., Muller, J.-M., Uguen, Y.: Posits: the good, the bad and the ugly. In: 2019 Proceedings of the Conference for Next Generation Arithmetic (CoNGA), pp. 1–10. Association for Computing Machinery, New York (2019)
32. Mallasén, D., Murillo, R., Barrio, A.A.D., Botella, G., Piñuel, L., Prieto-Matias, M.: PERCIVAL: open-source posit RISC-V core with quire capability. IEEE Trans. Emerg. Top. Comput. 10, 1241–1252 (2022)
33. Podobas, A., Matsuoka, S.: Hardware implementation of POSITs and their application in FPGAs. In: 2018 IEEE International Parallel and Distributed Processing Symposium Workshops (IPDPSW), pp. 138–145 (2018)
34. Jaiswal, M.K., So, H.K.-H.: PACoGen: a hardware posit arithmetic core generator. IEEE Access. 7, 74586–74601 (2019)
35. harris, f.j: Multirate Signal Processing for Communication Systems (Ed2). River Publishers, S.l. (2021)
36. Carlson, B., Gunaratne T.: Signal processing aspects of the sample clock frequency offset scheme for the SKA1 mid telescope array. In: 2017 XXXIInd General Assembly and Scientific Symposium of the International Union of Radio Science (URSI GASS), Montreal, QC (2017)

170   T. K. Gunaratne

37. Gunaratne, T., Carlson, B., Comoretto, G.: Novel RFI mitigation methods in the square
kilometre array 1 mid correlator beamformer. J. Astro. Inst. **8**(1) (2019)
38. Fasi, M., Mikaitis, M.: CPFloat: A C library for emulating low-precision arithmetic. MIMS
EPrint 2020.22, The University of Manchester, UK (2020)
39. Meurant, G.: Posit arithmetic matlab toolbox. https://gerard-meurant.pagesperso-orange.fr/
soft_meurant_n.html. Accessed 21 Nov 2022
40. Posit Working Group, Standard for Posit™ Arithmetic (2022). 2 Mar 2022

PLAUs: Posit Logarithmic Approximate Units to Implement Low-Cost Operations with Real Numbers

Raul Murillo[1]([✉]) [ID], David Mallasén[2] [ID], Alberto A. Del Barrio[2] [ID],
and Guillermo Botella[2] [ID]

[1] Facultad de Ciencias Físicas, Universidad Complutense de Madrid,
28040 Madrid, Spain
ramuri01@ucm.es
[2] Facultad de Informática, Universidad Complutense de Madrid, 28040 Madrid, Spain
{dmallase,abarriog,gbotella}@ucm.es

Abstract. The posit numeric format is getting more and more attention in recent years. Its tapered precision makes it especially suitable in many applications including machine learning computation. However, due to its dynamic component bit-width, the cost of implementing posit arithmetic in hardware is more expensive than its floating-point counterpart. To solve this cost problem, in this paper, approximate logarithmic designs for posit multiplication, division, and square root are proposed. It is found that approximate logarithmic units are more suitable for applications that tolerate large errors, such as machine learning algorithms, but require less power consumption.

Keywords: Approximate Computing · Posit · Multiplication · Division · Square Root

1 Introduction

From a historical perspective, and since scientific calculation has been established in computer science, the applications based on real numbers adopted the IEEE 754 *de facto* standard for floating-point [10] systems as their starting point.

Nevertheless, the drawbacks of this numerical representation open the door to many improvements. The standard is not perfect, as inherently it has several shortcomings that are not desirable, such as rounding and reproducibility issues, signed zero or excess of NaN representations [6].

Other alternatives to IEEE 754-2008 compliant arithmetic developed in the last years are the Half-Unit-Biased (HUB) format, proposed by Hormigo and

This work was supported by grant PID2021-123041OB-I00 funded by MCIN/AEI/ 10.13039/501100011033 and by "ERDF A way of making Europe", by a 2020 Leonardo Grant for Researchers and Cultural Creators, from BBVA Foundation, whose id is PR2003_20/01, and by the CM under grant S2018/TCS-4423.

J. Gustafson et al. (Eds.): CoNGA 2023, LNCS 13851, pp. 171–188, 2023.
https://doi.org/10.1007/978-3-031-32180-1_11

Villalba [9], Flexpoint [16], developed by Intel, High-Precision Anchored (HPA) numbers [1], developed by ARM, NVIDIA TensorFloat [26], Microsoft Floating Point (MSFP) [31], 8-bit Hybrid Floating Point (HFP8) [34], developed by IBM, and posit^{TM} arithmetic, which is the focus of this work. Another interesting approach tightly related to posits is the Self-Organising NUMbers (SONUMs) proposed by Klower [15], which tries to optimize the mapping of real numbers to binary patterns. In addition to these, we can talk about the *transprecision* movement [18], introduced by Benini et al., as an attempt to optimize the use of low-precision formats leveraging the applications; or the renaissance of the logarithmic format, originally proposed in the 60s-70s by authors like Mitchell [19] or Swartzlander [33], but that is catching attention again due to its good trade-off in error-tolerant applications as DNNs [12–14, 28].

As mentioned, one of the most promising contributions is the posit number system, introduced by John L. Gustafson in 2017. Since then, the posit^{TM} format has been catching fire and, besides custom designs, the literature describes the application of posits in different areas such as climate modeling [15], optical flow, [32], neural networks [21], or linear algebra [17].

The posit format offers compelling advantages over the IEEE 754 floating-point format. Under the same bit-width, posits provide a better trade-off than floats between dynamic range and decimal accuracy. What is more, it has been shown that an n-bit floating-point adder/multiplier could be safely replaced by an m-bit posit adder/multiplier where $m < n$ [2,5,11], the latter being, therefore, more efficient in terms of area and energy requirements. In contrast with floating-point, whose IEEE standard indicates the implementation of exception handling and subnormal numbers as mandatory for fully compliant circuits, posit arithmetic includes just two special cases (single 0 and $\pm\infty$), which simplifies the hardware designs. In addition, posits use a single rounding scheme (round to nearest, ties to even), solving the reproducibility issue mentioned for IEEE 754 floats, and the standard introduces the so-called *fused operations*, which allow performing computations with more than two operands (such as the dot product) without intermediate rounding, thus reducing the error of such computations. Last but not least, comparison of posit numbers can be done in the same manner as 2's complement integers, so this hardware can be reused if it is already on the CPU [17]. Posit arithmetic is currently under investigation, and there are already several studies that suggest a competitive advantage of this format in fields such as deep learning [21]. However, it is not yet clear whether IEEE floats could be completely replaced [3], mainly because posit units in literature are larger and more power-hungry than their IEEE 754 counterparts.

Previous works exploring the design and cost of posit arithmetic units [11, 20, 23] show that the multiplier is one of the most power-hungry units. In order to mitigate this problem, Murillo et al. proposed a Posit Logarithmic Approximate Multiplier (PLAM) [22] and tested it on error-tolerant applications. This work extends the idea illustrated in PLAM in order to propose Posit Logarithmic Approximate Units (PLAUs) for performing costly operations as divisions or square roots. Besides the noticeable improvements in synthesis terms, our experiments showcase that their application has no further impact on the accuracy of certain algorithms as *K-NN*. To the best of our knowledge, this is the first work proposing and testing the use of a whole set of approximate posit units.

The rest of the paper is organized as follows: Sect. 2 briefly discusses the posit format and its associated arithmetic. Section 3 describes the proposed Posit Logarithmic Approximate Units (PLAUs): multiplication, division and square root. Also, the error of approximating logarithms when performing arithmetic operations will be analytically detailed here. Section 4 deals with the results and analysis. Hardware implementation and several use cases in the computer vision domain will be shown. Finally, Sect. 5 concludes this paper.

2 Background

2.1 Posit Arithmetic

The parameters n and es are needed to define a posit number configuration: Posit$\langle n, es \rangle$. Where n is the total bit-width, and es is the maximum bit-width of the exponent. The most common pair of parameters appearing in the literature [3,21,22] have been Posit$\langle 8,0 \rangle$, Posit$\langle 16,1 \rangle$ and Posit$\langle 32,2 \rangle$. Apart from that, the latest Standard for Posit Arithmetic (2022) [7], fixes the value of es to 2 to simplify hardware design and ease conversion between different posit sizes.

The posit format only distinguishes two special cases: zero and Not a Real (NaR), which are represented as $0 \cdots 0$ and $10 \cdots 0$ respectively. The rest of the representations are composed of four fields as shown in Fig. 1:

- The sign bit s;
- The variable-length regime field r, consisting of w bits equal to the initial regime bit r_0, i.e. the bit placed before the sign, followed by $\overline{r_0}$ or the end of the posit. This field encodes a scaling factor r given by Eq. (1);
- The exponent e, consisting of at most es bits, which encodes an integer unbiased value e. If any of its bits are located after the least significant bit of the posit, that bit will have value 0;
- The variable-length fraction field f, composed of the remaining m bits. Its value $0 \leq f < 1$ is given after dividing the corresponding m-bits unsigned integer by 2^m.

$$r = \begin{cases} -w & \text{if } r_0 = 0, \\ w - 1 & \text{if } r_0 = 1. \end{cases} \tag{1}$$

When employing traditional sign and magnitude decoding, the real value X of a generic posit is given by Eq. (2). The main differences with respect to the IEEE 754 floating-point format are the existence of the regime field and the use of an unbiased exponent. It must be noted that the latest works as [24] have shown that two's complement decoding is more efficient than sign and magnitude's. In two's complement decoding, the hidden bit is considered to be 1 if the number is positive, or -2 if the number is negative, which simplifies the decoding stage of

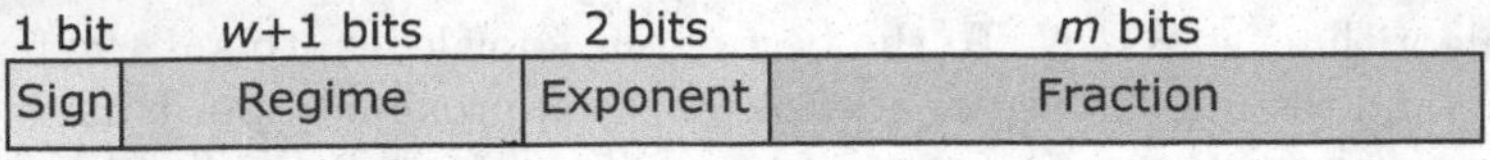

1 bit	w+1 bits	2 bits	m bits
Sign	Regime	Exponent	Fraction

Fig. 1. Posit arithmetic format.

the posit representation [8,24]. Nonetheless, in this paper we will consider sign and magnitude decoding because it is easier to apply the logarithm properties.

$$X = (-1)^s \times 2^{4r} \times 2^e \times (1 + f). \tag{2}$$

The variable-length regime field acts as a long-range dynamic exponent. Since it is a dynamic field, it can occupy more bits to represent larger numbers or leave more bits to the fraction field when looking for accuracy in the neighborhoods of ± 1. However, detecting these variable-sized fields adds some hardware overhead.

As an example, let 01101010 be the binary encoding of a Posit8, i.e. a Posit$\langle 8, 2 \rangle$ according to the latest Posit Standard. The first bit $s = 0$ indicates a positive number. The regime field 110 gives $w = 2$ and therefore $r = 1$. The next two bits 10 represent the exponent $e = 2$. Finally, the remaining $m = 2$ bits, 10, encode a fraction value of $f = 2/2^2 = 0.5$. Hence, from (2) we conclude that $01101010 \equiv (-1)^0 \times (16)^1 \times 2^2 \times (1 + 0.5) = 96$.

2.2   Related Work

From the moment posits were introduced in 2017, the research community has attempted to develop native hardware for this arithmetic. PACoGen [11] is a complete arithmetic unit that supports the four basic math operations. One of its focuses is flexibility, as it can support all combinations of bit-width and number of exponent bits. However, it has limitations for 0-bit exponents. This was solved in [20], where a VHDL generator written in C++ was used to develop posit adder/subtractor and multiplier fully-parameterized units, including 0-bit exponents. A similar approach was followed for fused multiply-accumulate (MAC) units in [23].

Regarding the division between posits, PACoGen [11] likely offers the first implementation in literature, and is based on the Newton-Raphson method. It used a lookup table (LUT) of size $2^8 \times 9$ for the initial guess of the reciprocals. In addition, this also presented a pipelined division architecture for 32-bit posits with 6 exponent bits. The work in [29] described another divider, which used a different iterative expression and provided an algorithmic way of finding the initial guess for the inverse approximation. In both works, posit numbers were decoded with a sign-magnitude scheme. A different approach for division and square root algorithms of posit numbers was studied in [35]. Utilizing two's complement decoding, the non-restoring algorithm was employed to implement the divider. This implementation required much less area than the Newton-Raphson divider from [11], but at the cost of higher latency. In the same fashion as [35], the non-restoring algorithm was also used for constructing a division/square root unit in [30].

Using approximate computing for the multiplication operation using posit arithmetic has been explored by recent works [22,25]. The first of these approaches fixed the bit-width of the fraction multiplier to 13 bits in the case of 32-bit posits. If the fraction is longer than these 13 bits, the remaining bits are truncated. To compensate for this approximation error, an iterative method with a shift-based multiplier is used. One drawback when the fraction bit-width is large is that, since there is only one degree of approximation for all computations, this case induces a high error.

The second approach proposes a logarithm-approximate multiplier for posits that leverages Mitchell's logarithm multiplication algorithm [19]. This is combined with converting the linear domain multiplication to the logarithm domain addition. The error that follows from this approximation is relatively large. However, this logarithm-based design reduces significantly the resource cost.

3   The Proposed Posit Logarithmic Approximate Units (PLAUs)

In this paper, we expand the concepts presented in [22]. In addition to the approximate multiplier shown in that work, we also propose integrating those ideas into divisions and square roots. We show that the units that implement those operations can also benefit from the reduced cost.

Firstly, it is worth noting that, in the multiplication and division operations, the computation of the sign is independent of the computation of the other fields. In addition, the square root of negative numbers results in NaR exception. Therefore, without loss of generalization, let us consider non-negative posit numbers in the following explanation.

On the other hand, in [19], Mitchell proposed an approximation in the conversion process between the linear domain and the logarithmic domain. In the logarithmic domain, operations like multiplication and division can be performed with simple addition and subtraction, respectively. As the fraction f of any posit is within range $[0, 1)$, $\log_2(1+f) \approx f$. Therefore, taking logarithms on both sides of Eq. (2), the non-negative posit number X can be approximated in the logarithmic domain as (3) shows:

$$\log_2 X = 4 \times r + e + \log_2(1+f) \approx 4 \times r + e + f. \qquad (3)$$

For notational simplicity, the scaling factors formed by the regime and the exponent can be reassembled, so that $2^{4r} \times 2^e = 2^k$. Hence, $k+f$ is the approximation of the logarithm value of X, where k and f are usually named *characteristic* and *fraction*, respectively.

We can perform arithmetic operations of converted values in the logarithmic domain and convert the result back to the linear domain by the aforementioned approximation, as detailed in [19].

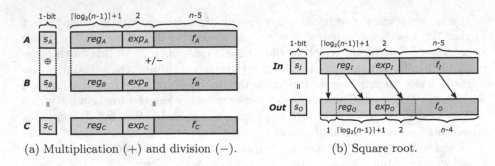

(a) Multiplication (+) and division (−).   (b) Square root.

Fig. 2. Hardware implementation for the proposed logarithm approximate posit units.

3.1 Posit Multiplication

Let us consider two posit numbers A and B in the form $(-1)^s \times 2^k \times (1+f)$. The exact result of the product of such numbers, $P = A \times B$, is given by Eq. (4). On the other hand, converting numbers to the logarithmic domain allows computing the multiplication as the addition of fixed point numbers. In such a case, the product is obtained by taking the anti-logarithm of the sum of the logarithms of both operands. However, using the approximation (3) of the logarithm eliminates the need for an anti-logarithm step to obtain the approximate product, as depicted in Eq. (5). Recall that the signs are computed independently, and to leverage logarithmic approximation the addition of fractions must be in the range $[0, 1)$, so a correction needs to be applied otherwise.

$$P_{exact} = (-1)^{s_A+s_B} \times 2^{k_A+k_B} \times (1 + f_A) \times (1 + f_B). \qquad (4)$$

$$P_{approx} = \begin{cases} (-1)^{s_A+s_B} \times 2^{k_A+k_B} \times (1 + f_A + f_B) & \text{if } f_A + f_B < 1, \\ (-1)^{s_A+s_B} \times 2^{k_A+k_B+1} \times (f_A + f_B) & \text{if } f_A + f_B \geq 1. \end{cases} \qquad (5)$$

The hardware implementation of the proposed logarithm approximate posit multiplier is shown in Fig. 2a. As can be seen, the decoded regime, exponent, and fraction can be gathered to perform addition. In this way, both conditions of Eq. (5) can be simultaneously computed in hardware. When $f_A + f_B \geq 1$, the carry bit from the resulting fraction field is directly added as a carry-in to the exponent addition, that is, the resulting scaling factor is corrected as $k_A + k_B + 1$. Note that, for such implementation, the implicit bit 1 of the fractions is not considered. More details of this approach can be found in [22].

3.2 Posit Division

From an algebraic point of view, performing the quotient of two posit numbers, $Q = A/B$, $B \neq 0$, is analogous to the multiplication process. The exact result is obtained by dividing the scale factors (subtracting the exponents) and the fractions with the implicit bit, as depicted in Eq. (6). However, performing the division of fixed point numbers in hardware is extremely costly [4]. On the other hand, the logarithm of the quotient of two quotients is equal to the difference between their logs. Using this property, the approximated quotient is given by Eq. (7).

$$Q_{exact} = (-1)^{s_A - s_B} \times 2^{k_A - k_B} \times (1 + f_A)/(1 + f_B). \tag{6}$$

$$Q_{approx} = \begin{cases} (-1)^{s_A - s_B} \times 2^{k_A - k_B} \times (1 + f_A - f_B) & \text{if } f_A - f_B \geq 0, \\ (-1)^{s_A - s_B} \times 2^{k_A - k_B - 1} \times (2 + f_A - f_B) & \text{if } f_A - f_B < 0. \end{cases} \tag{7}$$

Such an approach reduces the hardware resources and delays tremendously, since the multiple iterations needed to compute the division of fractions precisely are replaced by a single subtraction. The hardware implementation of the proposed logarithm approximate posit divider is shown in Fig. 2a. As can be seen, the only difference with respect to the multiplier is the use of subtraction instead of addition. Again, the proposed scheme allows handling both conditions of (7) simultaneously: when $f_A - f_B < 0$ the carry bit is subtracted from the subsequent fields (exponent and regime), and in such a case, adding 2 to the subtraction $f_A - f_B$ just flips the implicit fraction bit, while remains the explicit part of the fraction unchanged.

3.3   Posit Square Root

The exact root of a non-negative posit number is defined by Eq. (8). As in the case of division, computing the square root of the fixed-point fraction requires considerable hardware resources [4]. Again, the conversion into the log domain simplifies the computation of such an operation. Recall that square roots can be written as powers with exponent $1/2$, and the logarithm of a number raised to a power is the exponent times the logarithm of the base number. Therefore $\log_2(\sqrt{1+f}) \approx f/2$ yields to Eq. (9), an approximation of the square root of a posit.

$$R_{exact} = \sqrt{2^k \times (1+f)} = 2^{k/2} \times \sqrt{1+f}. \tag{8}$$

$$R_{approx} = 2^{k/2} \times (1 + f/2). \tag{9}$$

Notice that in both (8) and (9) it is necessary to divide specific values by 2. However, when implementing this in software, multiplying and dividing by powers of 2 is equivalent to shifting the binary encoding of the values. In particular, division by 2 can be implemented by shifting one bit to the right (keeping the regime sign). Therefore, the posit logarithm approximate square root can be implemented in hardware as illustrated in Fig. 2b. In fact, the least significant bit (LSB) of the fraction can be used as a rounding bit to reduce the overall error.

3.4   Approximation Error

Approximating logarithms of posit numbers introduces certain error when performing arithmetic operations. To analyze it, we consider the relative error formula, defined as (10):

$$E_{rel} = \frac{approx - exact}{exact} = \frac{approx}{exact} - 1. \tag{10}$$

Such an expression represents the error that may occur when arithmetic operations are performed according to the schemes proposed. This way, the result obtained is not only independent from the magnitude of the value, but also its sign indicates whether the approximation is an over- or an underestimation of the actual value.

Substituting (4) and (5), (6) and (7), and (8) and (9) in (10) yields:

$$E_{mul} = \begin{cases} \dfrac{1 + f_A + f_B}{(1 + f_A)(1 + f_B)} - 1 & \text{if } f_A + f_B < 1, \\[4mm] \dfrac{2(f_A + f_B)}{(1 + f_A)(1 + f_B)} - 1 & \text{if } f_A + f_B \geq 1. \end{cases} \tag{11}$$

$$E_{div} = \begin{cases} \dfrac{(1 + f_A - f_B)(1 + f_B)}{(1 + f_A)} - 1 & \text{if } f_A - f_B \geq 0, \\[4mm] \dfrac{(2 + f_A - f_B)(1 + f_B)}{2(1 + f_A)} - 1 & \text{if } f_A - f_B < 0. \end{cases} \tag{12}$$

$$E_{sqrt} = \frac{1 + f/2}{\sqrt{1 + f}} - 1. \tag{13}$$

Let us examine now the expressions (11), (12) and (13) for their maximum and minimum values. One may notice that the relative errors of approximation, E_{mul}, E_{div}, and E_{sqrt}, are functions that just depend on the fraction of the corresponding operands. It should be recalled that the fraction of any posit number f is a number between zero and one.

By computing the corresponding derivatives, one can find the critical points of the aforementioned functions. More details of these computations can be found in [19]. Figure 3 shows the contour map of E_{mul}, E_{div} as functions of the fractions f_A and f_B, as well as the E_{sqrt} given by the fraction f. The multiplication error is maximum when $f_A = f_B = 1/2$, and substituting these values in (11) gives $E_{mul} = -1/9$, or -11.1%. The maximum possible divide error will be $E_{div} = 1/8$, or 12.5%, and will occur at $f_A = 0$, $f_B = 1/2$ or $f_A = 1$, $f_B = 1/2$. The square root error is a monotonically increasing function, so its maximum, when $f = 1$, is $E_{sqrt} = 3/\sqrt{8} - 1$, or 6.06%. The minimum multiply error will

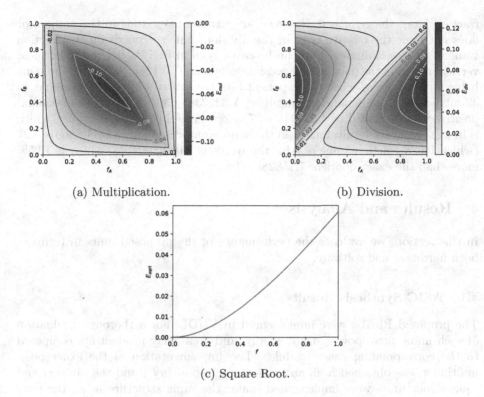

(a) Multiplication.

(b) Division.

(c) Square Root.

Fig. 3. Contour plot of the relative error between logarithmic approximate and exact posit operations.

be zero and will occur when f_A or f_B is zero or one. The minimum error for division will also be zero and will occur when f_B is zero or one, or when f_A and f_B are equal. The minimum error at square root operation will occur when the fraction is zero, and such an error will be zero as well. Of course, the fraction of any posit can never reach unity since $0 \leq f < 1$.

All in all, the largest error is 12.5% in the case of the division. Nevertheless, it must be noted that in error-tolerant applications, such as image filters or machine learning, these errors can be affordable and will impact very little on the quality of the results, as Sect. 4 will illustrate.

Finally, one may wonder how the tapered precision of posit arithmetic affects the proposed approximate computing. At first, it must be noted that extreme magnitudes in posit arithmetic have no fraction bits, which are the source of error in the proposed methods. Therefore, from the analytic point of view, no error is done when dealing with such values in the case of square root, nor multiplication (in the latter, no matter which operand has extreme magnitude, as can be seen either in Eq. (11) or Fig. 3a). The case of division is slightly different, as the error function is non-symmetric for the fractions of numerator and denominator. When the denominator value is an extreme magnitude (and therefore has no fraction bits), the error is 0. However, an extreme magnitude in the numerator does not limit the relative error of the division, but it depends on the fraction value of the denominator. This can be easily seen in Fig. 3b, where the leftmost vertical region of the map gets all possible values in $[0, 0.125]$. Naturally, the same behavior is observed when the exponent bits are shifted out. As an example, in 32-bit posits, approximately computing $1.32923e + 36 = 2^{120}$ (the maximum positive value) divided by $1.23794e + 27 = 2^{90}$, gives $1.07374e + 09 = 2^{30}$, which is in fact the exact result; but when the denominator is changed by $1.85691e+27$ (which has a fraction value of 0.5), the result is $8.05306e + 08$, which is 12.5% more than the exact quotient $7.15828e + 08$.

4   Results and Analysis

In this section, we evaluate the performance of the proposed units in terms of both hardware and software.

4.1   ASIC Synthesis Results

The proposed PLAUs were implemented in VHDL. For a thorough evaluation of such units, area, power, delay, energy, and area-delay product are compared to the corresponding exact modules. The implementation of the exact posit multiplier was obtained from an open-source repository[1], and the division and square root units were implemented under the same structure using the non-restoring algorithm. Standard cell synthesis has been performed using Synopsys Design Compiler with a 45-nm library by TSMC.

Relative to the area and power of the multiplier, it is remarkable in Fig. 4a and Fig. 4b how the approximate multiplier can synthesize correct designs up to 1150 MHz, which is more than double that of its exact 550 MHz counterpart. Additionally, we have an enhancement of around 70% for designs with a frequency range up to 450MHz, this score goes up to 80% in the 450–550 MHz range. Figure 4c shows an improvement in terms of delay of around 8.5% up to frequencies of 350 MHz; from there, it evolves the same as its exact counterpart. As Fig. 4d and Fig. 4e depict, the proposed logarithmic multipliers exhibit a ratio of energy and ADPs with an improvement of 80% up to 250 MHz, and close to 90% in areas close to the maximum frequency (around 350 MHz). Finally, Fig. 4f presents the cost of the approximate multiplier compared to the exact counterpart throughout several operating frequencies. All in all, the cost in area and ADP range from 20–30% while in power and energy between 20–13%, which is equivalent to savings of 80–87%.

Concerning the approximate divider, we show in Fig. 5a and Fig. 5b how the divider can synthesize correct designs up to 1150 MHz, which is almost eight times more than its exact equivalent (150 MHz). Apart from that, we have an improvement of around 90% for designs with a frequency range up to 150 MHz.

---

[1] https://github.com/artecs-group/Flo-Posit/tree/c737c1c.

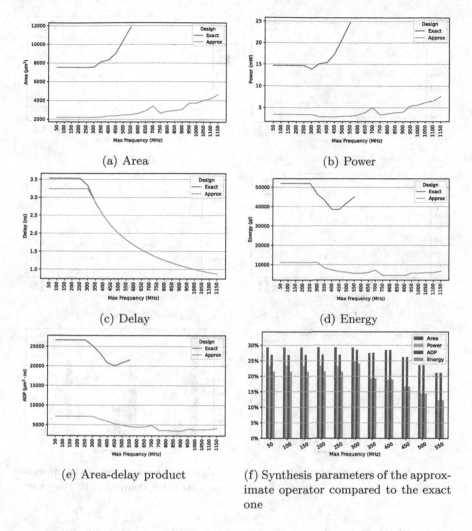

(a) Area

(b) Power

(c) Delay

(d) Energy

(e) Area-delay product

(f) Synthesis parameters of the approximate operator compared to the exact one

Fig. 4. Comparison of multiplication implementations for Posit$\langle 32, 2 \rangle$.

Figure 5c shows a refinement in terms of delay around 80% to 50% up to frequencies of 150 MHz. The proposed logarithmic dividers show an improvement of 90% up to 50 MHz, and close to 95% in areas close to the maximum working frequency of the exact design (around 150 MHz) in Fig. 5d and Fig. 5e. Finally, Fig. 5f presents the cost of the approximate divider compared to the exact counterpart at different working frequencies. The cost in area and power ranges from 29–11% and 11–09% of the exact counterparts, respectively, which represents an ADP and energy savings between 98–94% and 99–96%, respectively.

Regarding the approximate square root, on the one hand, we depict in Fig. 6a and Fig. 6b how the approximate square root can synthesize correct designs up to

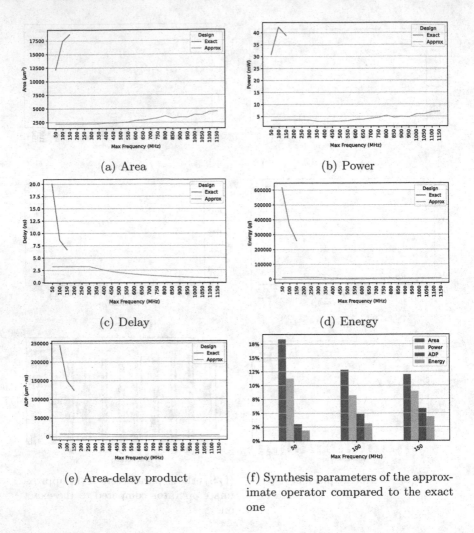

(a) Area

(b) Power

(c) Delay

(d) Energy

(e) Area-delay product

(f) Synthesis parameters of the approximate operator compared to the exact one

Fig. 5. Comparison of division implementations for Posit⟨32, 2⟩.

1150 MHz, which is almost five times more than its exact 250 MHz counterpart. On the other hand, we have an improvement between 85–90% for designs with a frequency range up to 250MHz. Figure 6c reveals an improvement in terms of delay of around 80% to 50% up to frequencies of 250 MHz. Figure 6d and Fig. 6e illustrate an energy and ADP improvement of 90% up to 50 MHz, and near to 95% in areas close to the maximum frequency (around 250 MHz). Finally, Fig. 6f presents the cost of the approximate square root compared to the exact design working at different frequencies. The cost in area and power varies from 18% to 9% and from 11% to 8% respectively. This represents a gain in ADP and energy between 98–94% and 99–96%, respectively.

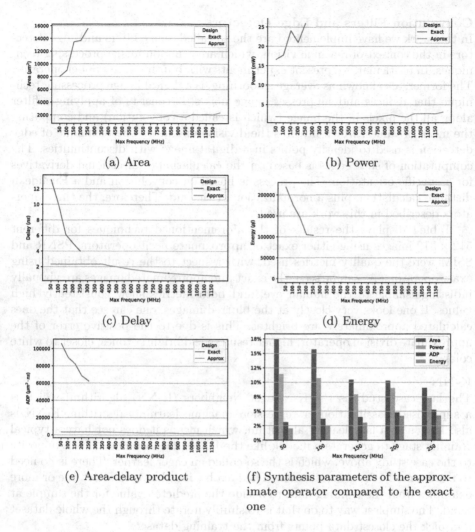

(a) Area

(b) Power

(c) Delay

(d) Energy

(e) Area-delay product

(f) Synthesis parameters of the approximate operator compared to the exact one

Fig. 6. Comparison of square root implementations for Posit⟨32, 2⟩.

4.2   Use Cases

In this section, a set of error-tolerant applications are evaluated. Some typical computer-vision and machine learning kernels will be employed to test the accuracy of the proposed PLAUs. For ease of use, these approximate operators were implemented in software using Universal library [27]. Such software modules were tested to ensure they behave like the hardware components described above.

We calculated in each use-case the pertinent error metric such as Peak Signal-to-Noise Ratio (PSNR), Structural Similarity Index Measure (SSIM), or classification accuracy.

Convolution Filters and Edge Detectors

In this work we have implemented are the so-called image filters and edge detectors in the context of machine vision, which are common image processing techniques. In particular, we present experiments with blur filter and Sobel operator. The former, also known as average smoothing, is a digital image processing technique that reduces and suppresses image noises. It consists of applying a filter along all the pixels in the image (which is called a convolution) and computing the mean of values, which involves the division operator. The technique of edge detection is used to identify points in a digital image with discontinuities. The computation of such edges is based on the calculation of directional derivatives for a specific orientation. The process is based on convolution and a Euclidean distance calculation, plus a normalization at the end. Therefore, the three operators described in this work are used.

Table 1 displays the results of the aforementioned techniques for different 512×512 images using either exact or approximate posit operators. PSNR and SSIM were the quality metrics used, with respect to the result obtained using exact operators. As can be seen, the exact and approximated images are virtually indistinguishable to the human eye, and both metrics show consistently high values. If one looks very closely at the blurred images, one can see that the ones calculated approximately are brighter. This is due to the positive error of the approximate division operator; higher results yield brighter tones, closer to white color.

K-NN

The last case study is the K-Nearest Neighbors (K-NN) algorithm, which is a supervised classification or regression machine learning algorithm. K-NN is also known as a lazy learner algorithm, which means it does not have a typical training stage to generate a model, like the DNNs, for instance. This is opposite to the case study above, which is the so-called an eager learner. There is no need to train a model for generalization. The idea behind that is to select one or more examples from the training data to decide the predicted value for the sample at hand. The simplest way to do that is to simply iterate through the whole dataset and pick the closest data points from the training dataset.

This application requires computing the Euclidean distance among points, which uses multiplication and square root operations. Therefore, we replace such operations with their corresponding approximate version.

Four well-known datasets[2] for classification are selected for this task. Each dataset is split into train and validation sets with a rate of 70–30%. We consider the optimal number of neighbors k for each case (determined by the elbow method). The total accuracy achieved by the algorithms is depicted in Table 2. Although the intermediate results are slightly different when using exact and approximate operators, the final accuracy is the same in both cases.

---

[2] Accessed from https://archive.ics.uci.edu on May 3, 2023.

Table 1. Image processing accuracy results.

	Cameraman	Lenna	Peppers	Baboon
Exact Computation				
Approximate Computation				
	PSNR: 27.6019 SSIM: 0.98217	PSNR: 29.0023 SSIM: 0.98281	PSNR: 28.2892 SSIM: 0.98318	PSNR: 28.7468 SSIM: 0.97396
Exact Computation				
Approximate Computation				
	PSNR: 51.0439 SSIM: 0.99909	PSNR: 44.5427 SSIM: 0.99629	PSNR: 45.6212 SSIM: 0.99629	PSNR: 38.2694 SSIM: 0.99503

Table 2. K-NN accuracy results.

Dataset	Instances	Attributes	Classes	k	Exact	Approx.
Iris	150	3	3	5	95.55%	95.55%
Wine	178	13	3	7	67.92%	67.92%
Glass	214	9	7	5	59.38%	59.38%
Breast Cancer	569	30	2	13	94.74%	94.74%

5   Conclusions

The posit number format is gaining attention in recent years. Its tapered precision makes it convenient and attractive in many applications such as signal processing, and machine learning, among others. Nonetheless, the main handicap of this format is the cost of the implementation of the functional units, mainly due to the existence of dynamically variable fields. The work presented here uses a logarithmic approximation paradigm within posit arithmetic to design and test operators that reach an accuracy very similar to the posit exact version and yet achieve huge savings in terms of area and power.

The three designs have been implemented to handle low-cost operations with real numbers and are the so-called Posit Logarithmic Approximate Units (PLAUs): multiplication, division, and square root. These units are competitive with respect to their exact counterparts. Multiplication exhibits an ADP and energy savings of 80–70% and 80–87% respectively. Both division and square root evince an ADP and energy savings between 98–94% and 99–96% correspondingly.

Regarding the error, fault-tolerant applications have been tested, such as K-NN, and image filters that make use of the operators presented. The results suggest a high trade-off between accuracy and efficiency with respect to their equivalent that do not use the logarithmic approximation paradigm.

References

1. Burgess, N., Goodyer, C., Hinds, C.N., Lutz, D.R.: High-precision anchored accumulators for reproducible floating-point summation. IEEE Trans. Comput. **68**(7), 967–978 (2019). https://doi.org/10.1109/TC.2018.2855729
2. Chaurasiya, R., et al.: Parameterized posit arithmetic hardware generator. In: 2018 IEEE 36th International Conference on Computer Design (ICCD), pp. 334–341. IEEE (2018). https://doi.org/10.1109/ICCD.2018.00057
3. de Dinechin, F., Forget, L., Muller, J.M., Uguen, Y.: Posits: the good, the bad and the ugly. In: Proceedings of the Conference for Next Generation Arithmetic (ACM 2019), Singapore (2019). https://doi.org/10.1145/3316279.3316285
4. Ercegovac, M.D., Lang, T.: Digital Arithmetic. Elsevier (2004). https://doi.org/10.1016/B978-1-55860-798-9.X5000-3
5. Fatemi Langroudi, S.H., Pandit, T., Kudithipudi, D.: Deep learning inference on embedded devices: fixed-point vs posit. In: 2018 1st Workshop on Energy Efficient Machine Learning and Cognitive Computing for Embedded Applications (EMC2), pp. 19–23. IEEE, Williamsburg, VA, USA (2018). https://doi.org/10.1109/EMC2.2018.00012
6. Goldberg, D.: What every computer scientist should know about floating-point arithmetic. ACM Comput. Surv. **23**(1), 5–48 (1991). https://doi.org/10.1145/103162.103163
7. Posit Working Group: Standard for posit™ arithmetic (2022). https://github.com/posit-standard/Posit-Standard-Community-Feedback
8. Guntoro, A., et al.: Next generation arithmetic for edge computing. In: 2020 Design, Automation & Test in Europe Conference & Exhibition (DATE), pp. 1357–1365 (2020). https://doi.org/10.23919/DATE48585.2020.9116196
9. Hormigo, J., Villalba, J.: New formats for computing with real-numbers under round-to-nearest. IEEE Trans. Comput. **65**(7), 2158–2168 (2016). https://doi.org/10.1109/TC.2015.2479623
10. IEEE Computer Society: IEEE standard for floating-point arithmetic. IEEE Std 754-2019 (Revision of IEEE 754-2008) **2019**, 1–84 (2019). https://doi.org/10.1109/IEEESTD.2019.8766229
11. Jaiswal, M.K., So, H.K.: PACoGen: a hardware posit arithmetic core generator. IEEE Access **7**, 74586–74601 (2019). https://doi.org/10.1109/ACCESS.2019.2920936

12. Johnson, J.: Rethinking floating point for deep learning. arXiv e-prints (2018). https://doi.org/10.48550/ARXIV.1811.01721
13. Kim, M.S., Del Barrio, A.A., Oliveira, L.T., Hermida, R., Bagherzadeh, N.: Efficient Mitchell's approximate log multipliers for convolutional neural networks. IEEE Trans. Comput. **68**(5), 660–675 (2018). https://doi.org/10.1109/TC.2018.2880742
14. Kim, M.S., Del Barrio Garcia, A.A., Kim, H., Bagherzadeh, N.: The effects of approximate multiplication on convolutional neural networks. IEEE Trans. Emerg. Top. Comput. **10**(2), 904–916 (2022). https://doi.org/10.1109/TETC.2021.3050989
15. Klöwer, M., Düben, P.D., Palmer, T.N.: Number formats, error mitigation, and scope for 16-bit arithmetics in weather and climate modeling analyzed with a shallow water model. J. Adv. Model. Earth Syst. **12**(10), e2020MS002246 (2020). https://doi.org/10.1029/2020MS002246
16. Köster, U., et al.: Flexpoint: an adaptive numerical format for efficient training of deep neural networks. In: Advances in Neural Information Processing Systems (NIPS), pp. 1742–1752. Curran Associates, Inc. (2017)
17. Mallasén, D., Murillo, R., Barrio, A.A.D., Botella, G., Piñuel, L., Prieto-Matias, M.: PERCIVAL: open-source posit RISC-V core with quire capability. In: IEEE Transactions on Emerging Topics in Computing, pp. 1–12 (2022). https://doi.org/10.1109/TETC.2022.3187199
18. Malossi, A.C.I., et al.: The transprecision computing paradigm: concept, design, and applications. In: 2018 Design, Automation Test in Europe Conference Exhibition (DATE), pp. 1105–1110 (2018). https://doi.org/10.23919/DATE.2018.8342176
19. Mitchell, J.N.: Computer multiplication and division using binary logarithms. IRE Trans. Electron. Comput. **EC-11**(4), 512–517 (1962). https://doi.org/10.1109/TEC.1962.5219391
20. Murillo, R., Del Barrio, A.A., Botella, G.: Customized posit adders and multipliers using the FloPoCo core generator. In: 2020 IEEE International Symposium on Circuits and Systems (ISCAS), pp. 1–5 (2020). https://doi.org/10.1109/ISCAS45731.2020.9180771
21. Murillo, R., Del Barrio, A.A., Botella, G.: Deep PeNSieve: a deep learning framework based on the posit number system. Digit. Signal Process. **102**, 102762 (2020). https://doi.org/10.1016/j.dsp.2020.102762
22. Murillo, R., Del Barrio Garcia, A.A., Botella, G., Kim, M.S., Kim, H., Bagherzadeh, N.: PLAM: a posit logarithm-approximate multiplier. IEEE Trans. Emerg. Topics Comput. **10**(4), 2079–2085 (2022). https://doi.org/10.1109/TETC.2021.3109127
23. Murillo, R., Mallasén, D., Del Barrio, A.A., Botella, G.: Energy-efficient MAC units for fused posit arithmetic. In: 2021 IEEE 39th International Conference on Computer Design (ICCD), pp. 138–145 (2021). https://doi.org/10.1109/ICCD53106.2021.00032
24. Murillo, R., Mallasén, D., Del Barrio, A.A., Botella, G.: Comparing Different Decodings for Posit Arithmetic. In: Conference on Next Generation Arithmetic (CoNGA). pp. 84–99 (2022). https://doi.org/10.1007/978-3-031-09779-9_6
25. Norris, C.J., Kim, S.: An approximate and iterative posit multiplier architecture for FPGAs. In: 2021 IEEE International Symposium on Circuits and Systems (ISCAS), vol. 2021-May, pp. 1–5. IEEE (2021). https://doi.org/10.1109/ISCAS51556.2021.9401158

26. NVIDIA Corporation: NVIDIA A100 Tensor Core GPU Architecture. Tech. rep., NVIDIA Corporation (2020). https://www.nvidia.com/content/dam/en-zz/Solutions/Data-Center/nvidia-ampere-architecture-whitepaper.pdf

27. Omtzigt, E.T.L., Quinlan, J.: Universal: reliable, reproducible, and energy-efficient numerics. In: Conference on Next Generation Arithmetic (CoNGA), pp. 100–116 (2022). https://doi.org/10.1007/978-3-031-09779-9_7

28. Pilipovic, R., Bulic, P.: On the design of logarithmic multiplier using radix-4 booth encoding. IEEE Access **8**, 64578–64590 (2020). https://doi.org/10.1109/ACCESS.2020.2985345

29. Rao, D.N., Charan, G.S., Sairam, D.V.V., Kamatchi, S.: Posit number division using Newton-Raphson method. In: Proceedings of the 2021 1st International Conference on Advances in Electrical, Computing, Communications and Sustainable Technologies (ICAECT 2021), pp. 17–22 (2021). https://doi.org/10.1109/ICAECT49130.2021.9392582

30. Raveendran, A., Jean, S., Mervin, J., Vivian, D., Selvakumar, D.: A novel parametrized fused division and square-root POSIT arithmetic architecture. In: 2020 33rd International Conference on VLSI Design and 2020 19th International Conference on Embedded Systems (VLSID), pp. 207–212. IEEE (2020). https://doi.org/10.1109/VLSID49098.2020.00053

31. Rouhani, B.D., et al.: Pushing the limits of narrow precision inferencing at cloud scale with microsoft floating point. In: Advances in Neural Information Processing Systems (NIPS), pp. 10271–10281 (2020)

32. Saxena, V., et al.: Brightening the optical flow through posit arithmetic. In: 2021 22nd International Symposium on Quality Electronic Design (ISQED), pp. 463–468 (2021). https://doi.org/10.1109/ISQED51717.2021.9424360

33. Swartzlander, E.E., Alexopoulos, A.G,: The sign/logarithm number system. IEEE Trans. Comput. **C-24**(12), 1238–1242 (1975). https://doi.org/10.1109/T-C.1975.224172

34. Venkataramani, S., et al.: Efficient AI system design with cross-layer approximate computing. Proc. IEEE **108**(12), 2232–2250 (2020). https://doi.org/10.1109/JPROC.2020.3029453

35. Xiao, F., Liang, F., Wu, B., Liang, J., Cheng, S., Zhang, G.: Posit arithmetic hardware implementations with the minimum cost divider and squareroot. Electronics **9**, 1622 (2020). https://doi.org/10.3390/electronics9101622

Author Index

J. Gustafson et al. (Eds.): CoNGA 2023, LNCS 13851, p. 189, 2023.
https://doi.org/10.1007/978-3-031-32180-1

Printed in the United States
by Baker & Taylor Publisher Services

Printed in the United States
by Baker & Taylor Publisher Services